# Quantitative Indicators
# in World Politics

# List of Contributors

*Richard C. Eichenberg,* Department of Political Science, Florida State University.

*Daniel S. Geller,* Department of Political Science, University of Mississippi.

*Charles W. Kegley, Jr.,* Department of Government, University of South Carolina.

*Zeev Maoz,* University of Haifa.

*Gregory A. Raymond,* Department of Political Science, Boise State University.

*J. David Singer,* Department of Political Science, University of Michigan.

*Richard J. Stoll,* Department of Political Science, Rice University.

*Frank Whelon Wayman,* Department of Political Science, University of Michigan at Dearborn.

*Brigitta Widmaier,* International Institute for Comparative Social Research, Science Center Berlin.

*I. William Zartman,* School for Advanced International Studies, Johns Hopkins University.

# QUANTITATIVE INDICATORS IN WORLD POLITICS

## Timely Assurance and Early Warning

Edited by

# J. David Singer
# and Richard J. Stoll

PRAEGER

PRAEGER SPECIAL STUDIES • PRAEGER SCIENTIFIC

New York • Philadelphia • Eastbourne, UK
Toronto • Hong Kong • Tokyo • Sydney

**Library of Congress Cataloging in Publication Data**
Main entry under title:

Quantitative Indicators in World Politics.

1. International relations—forecasting. 2. Inter-
national relations—research. I. Singer, J. David
(Joel David), 1925—      . II. Stoll, Richard J.
JX1291.Q35   1984        327′.072        83—17792
ISBN 0—03—068901—5 (alk. paper)

Published in 1984 by Praeger Publishers
CBS Educational and Professional Publishing
a Division of CBS Inc.
521 Fifth Avenue, New York, New York 10175 USA
©1984 by Praeger Publishers

456789   052   987654321

Printed in the United States of America
on acid-free paper

# Contents

# List of Tables

# List of Figures

# Quantitative Indicators
# in World Politics

# Introduction

# Basic Research:
# The Policy Relevant Spin-off

## J. David Singer and Richard J. Stoll

Among the many assignments given to the Secretary-General by the United Nations Charter is that of bringing to the attention of the Security Council "any matter which, in his opinion, may threaten the maintenance of international peace and security. . . ." The premise, of course, is that timely warning will provide the opportunity for the Secretariat, regional organizations, and national governments to ameliorate or head off the conflict before it goes to, or over, the brink of war. That assignment has been carried out on no more than a dozen occasions since 1945, and in almost every case only after the situation had reached crisis proportions.

The reasons for so low a frequency of action are many, but the one that concerns us here is the inability of the Secretariat staff—and national officials for that matter—to recognize a problem before it gets out of control. On the basis of which principles can such recognition occur? Are valid indicators available, or capable of being developed? How can false alarms be avoided? And worse yet, given the propensity of national governments to withhold and distort information in a crisis, how can we reduce the likelihood that these highly dangerous situations will be ignored for too long? Or, shifting from the problem of early warning, what evidence might be used to assure on-lookers that a government is abiding by a United Nations (UN) resolution or a treaty commitment? How might the Secretariat reassure anxious governments that a potential

1

adversary is indeed phasing out a weapons system, refraining from certain acts, preparing its citizens for diplomatic concessions, and so forth? When we consider the frequency with which governments—working as they typically do from worst case assumptions—behave in ways that escalate disputes because they are not sufficiently confident that a rival will act in good faith, it is apparent that we need better methods of prediction.

The most solid basis for prediction, be it in the physical, biological, or social sphere, is a coherent, data-based theory. Defining theory as a body of codified knowledge (rather than a set of plausible generalizations, no matter how formally and precisely articulated), we find that it has several advantages over prediction based on mere correlation. One is that the statistical relationships between and among variables in social systems are not necessarily constant across time; rather, they may be in a state of continual evolution. When characteristics of the international system change, for example, the co-variation among those characteristics is also likely to change. With a coherent theory, such change is not only likely to be expected, but also understood, as distinct from an indicator approach that rests on little more than observed and recurrent co-variation. Other virtues of working from a solid theoretical base are noted in the introduction to the earlier volume in this series (Singer and Wallace 1979) and need not be reiterated here.

In the absence of that desirable but relatively distant state of affairs, are we to follow the "counsel of perfection," and continue to leave the field to the more traditional modes of prediction, unreliable as they have been, or might we seek ways to improve our abilities, even though they still leave us short of our goal? We believe that even a modest step forward would be advantageous, and thus bring our second volume of indicators of warning and assurance to the world politics community. Our purpose here is to exploit what might be called the "spin-off" from a number of basic research projects, in order to move ahead on the policy relevant front while waiting for major advances toward more coherent, data-based theory to emerge in the world politics field. This is not, of course, the first attempt to bring together such research; in addition to the prior volume in this series, there have been several other promising efforts, notably O'Leary and Coplin (1975), and Choucri and Robinson (1978).

A glance at the chapter headings in this volume will show that, although all the authors are firmly committed to the use of the scientific method, there is a great diversity in subject matter and theoretical approach. This is as it should be. Use of the scientific method does not commit one to any particular subject matter or research technique, but to a research style. The key to this method—which sets it apart from other approaches to the study of international relations—is the emphasis on documentation and reproducibility. At every step along the way, the scientific researcher must leave a clear trail, rather than a few bread crumbs, of her or his procedures. The acid test is whether another researcher can successfully retrace the steps, and either arrive at the same findings or readily ascertain wherein the differences can be found.

This leads us to comment on what must be the greatest fallacy we encounter when discussing the scientific approach and its advantages. We have often heard that the scientific approach makes it easier for a researcher to hide his or her mistakes beneath a smokescreen of elaborate jargon and sophisticated methodology. Nothing could be further from the truth. Clearly, a reader without a background in scientific method may have difficulty following the chain of evidence, but in a well-written report, the gaps should be no greater than for any other subject matter with which the reader is unfamiliar. A good scientific report will provide an explicit description and justification of each step in the research process, and will, therefore, make it easier to evaluate. The more traditional alternative is to rely heavily on the observer's "intimate knowledge" of the situation. All too often, the justification for conclusions is "because I know it to be true," or "my many years of experience give me a 'sixth sense' about these things." The conclusions reached in this manner may be absolutely correct, but the lack of an explicit procedure renders any attempt to follow or extend the line of reasoning hopelessly problematic.


WHAT IS "POLICY RELEVANCE"?

If the above represents a crude explanation of the scientific approach and its virtues (for a more extensive essay on this subject, see Singer 1972), what attributes make a particular scientific study of use to policy makers and policy watchers? We believe that such studies have several characteristics:

• The subject of the scientific investigation must be one that is (or should be) of interest to the policy community.

Given the many problems faced by decision makers, this does not represent much of a limitation.

• The "look ahead" time frame of the study should be that of the short or middle run. Perhaps policy makers and their critics should pay more attention to the long run, but even a casual observer of the policy-making process is struck by the degree to which "today" or "tomorrow" represent their focus of attention. If our work is to aid policy makers and their critics, it must provide them with information that they can use, and at the appropriate moment in the problem solving process.

• Although it is too much to ask that a piece of research be theory based, it is not too much to ask that it point the way (albeit with a dim light) toward a coherent body of knowledge. That is to say, these efforts should advance scholarly, as well as policy, concerns.

A final desirable characteristic for this type of research would be the use of policy manipulables as predictor variables; it would be desirable to furnish the policy maker not only with a set of accurate predictions, but also to indicate what might be necessary to alter or enhance the expected outcome. But at this time, in choosing between manipulability and predictive accuracy, we believe the latter merits the higher priority.

In sum, these requirements pose no need for a radical reorientation of research priorities; rather, they merely call for a more explicit focus on policy relevance. In many cases, the only change required is to redirect the discussion and conclusion of the results of a research effort.

## INDICATORS OF EARLY WARNING AND ASSURANCE

This set of criteria leads us to emphasize the creation and validation of indicators of early warning and timely assurance. That is, the studies in this volume are directed toward the construction and validation of what might be called "leading indicators of international behavior." While they reflect a variety of approaches and range of outcome variables, most focus on the prediction of serious conflict, international and domestic. Given our emphasis on the short and medium range, this bias is understandable, inasmuch as violent conflict produces immediate and direct effects on individuals, groups, societies, and the global system. Its control and prevention is an important priority on any global agenda, although we should not overlook other issues of contention between nations and peoples. Let us now turn to a brief description of the contents of the seven papers that comprise this volume.

## PART I.  PREDICTING SUBNATIONAL CONFLICT

The first paper, by Eichenberg and Widmaier, is a report on a small portion of a larger project on global security problems in the coming decades. The object of this report is first, to describe trends in domestic conflict at the global, regional, and national levels; second, to estimate cross-sectional models of domestic conflict using readily available economic, social, and political indicators as predictors; and third, to project domestic conflict into the medium term future using the results from the first two parts. Using data from the *World Handbook of Political and Social Indicators,* the authors predict collective protest (relatively nonviolent, if unconventional, forms of political conflict) and internal violence. They begin by post-dicting past levels of these two variables from measures of total population and energy per capita. After assessing the fit and stability of this model for half-decade cross-sections from 1948 to 1977, they use projections of their two pre-dictor variables to forecast domestic conflict levels for the 1980–2000 time interval. Projections are shown for the global system and regional subsystems, and the most con-flict prone nations are identified.

The second paper, by Geller, is concerned with the same general outcome variable as the first, but with several differences. First, Geller confines himself to a more re-stricted spatial domain: the 20 major states of Latin America. Second, Geller is technically involved only in post-diction; his time period is 1965–78. Finally, he engages in a much more elaborate form of model con-struction. His work is very much in the tradition of Gurr's research into the link between relative deprivation and civil strife. Geller's model has two exogenous variables (histor-ical instability and persisting deprivation) and six en-dogenous variables (coercive force potential, political legitimacy, short term deprivation, institutionalization, social/structural facilitation, and political conflict). He uses multiple indicators to tap each concept (for the most part employing factor analysis), and simultaneous equation

estimation to predict civil strife in each year. He then
goes on to examine the residuals from his predictions, and
compares these predictions to those generated by a naive
statistical model.


## PART II. PREDICTING FOREIGN EVENTS
## AND FOREIGN INVOLVEMENTS

Part II contains two very different papers that focus on
foreign policy. The first, by Maoz, is explicitly designed
to be of aid to intelligence analysts. He begins by noting
that in a number of cases, intelligence failures have occurred not so much because of a lack of information, but
because of defective processing and misinterpretation of
available evidence. To shed further light on this problem,
he uses an experimental design to assess the ability of
three heuristics to aid intelligence analysts revising their
estimates of the probability of surprise attack in the face of
new information. Subjects were given background information on a scenario that was a fictionalized account of an
actual situation, and then given new information on it. At
various points, the subjects were asked to give their
estimates of the probability of war. The subjects were
divided into three groups, and each group was given a
different type of training in heuristics to revise intelligence
estimates: "common sense" (no specific instructions were
given about how to revise estimates), Bayesian estimation
(specific instructions were given about the use of Bayes'
theorem), and "diagnosis" (the logic underlying Bayes'
theorem was given, but not the specifics of the calculations).

The second paper in this section, by Stoll, examines
historical patterns in the use of force by the United States,
and forecasts the likelihood of high level U.S. involvement
in various regions of the world. Military forces have often
been used for political purposes in the post—World War II
era by U.S. decision makers. Using a data set of such
uses collected by Blechman and Kaplan for the time period
1946—75, the chances of a high level use of force (one that
is likely to involve some sort of combat), given that military
units are used to begin with, are estimated. The model for
the estimation uses a variety of internal and external indicators as well as specific variables for region and the
type of situation that led to U.S. involvement. After

estimating this model, forecasts for future high level U.S. involvement in the major regions of the world are made.

## PART III.  PREDICTING SERIOUS DISPUTES AND CONFLICT RESOLUTION

The two papers in Part III deal with conflictual interactions.  The first, by Wayman, constructs two different early warning indicators of conflict in the Middle East, ascertains the covariation of the indicators, and then uses them to forecast conflict.  The first indicator is based on a survey of U.S. specialists in the Middle East done in 1975, and updated for part of the sample in 1981.  These specialists were asked to rate the relative friendliness or hostility of various dyads from 1970 to 1974.  These ratings were then validated by asking members of the Arab and Israeli UN delegations to examine them.  The second indicator was taken from the World Event Interaction Survey (WEIS) data from 1970–74.  These measures of conflict and cooperation were then compared to the expert ratings.  A combination of the events data indicators and the expert judgments are used to forecast conflict in the Middle East for the 1976–78 time period.

The second paper in this section is by Zartman.  It emerged from his research into recent African crises. He is interested in identifying the "ripe moment" for conflict resolution; that time in which intervention would achieve its maximum effect.  His paper examines the utility of using events data to identify and predict this ripe moment.

## PART IV.  PREDICTING CONFLICT IN THE INTERNATIONAL SYSTEM

The final chapter in the book, by Kegley and Raymond, deals with the prediction of European major power conflict at the level of the international system.  Like several of the other authors, Kegley and Raymond are actually engaged in a post-dictive effort; they attempt to predict the frequency, scope, and intensity of serious major power disputes in the 1820–1914 time period.  They use two variables to predict these measures of conflict. The first is a measure of flexibility in alliances, based on rate of change in alliance formation.  The second variable measures the degree to which alliance commitments are regarded as binding on the signatories. This measure is based on an analysis of international law treatises during this time period. These were coded to determine the extent to which an alliance treaty was regarded absolutely binding on its signatories, or whether unilateral termination of an alliance was viewed as justified under certain conditions.

## CONCLUSION

This volume provides an eclectic survey of early warning indicators. We find the wide variety of techniques, data, and applications contained herein to be encouraging; there are many routes to the discovery and validation of early warning and timely assurance indicators. And although we have a long road to travel before we can be satisfied with the quality of our efforts and make them credible to the policy making community, we feel that this current crop of papers is more than a little encouraging. Perhaps we are justified in hoping that the future will see these efforts becoming more and more commonplace, as the gap between the scientist and the policy maker grows smaller and smaller.

## REFERENCES

Choucri, Nazli, and Thomas W. Robinson. 1978. *Forecasting in International Relations: Theory, Methods, Problems, Prospects.* San Francisco: W. H. Freeman.

O'Leary, Michael, and William Coplin. 1975. *Quantitative Techniques in Foreign Policy Analysis and Forecasting.* New York: Praeger.

Singer, J. David. 1972. *The Scientific Study of Politics: An Approach to Foreign Policy Analysis.* Morristown: General Learning Press.

Singer, J. David, and Michael Wallace. 1979. *To Augur Well: Early Warning Indicators in World Politics.* Beverly Hills: Sage.

# Part I

## Predicting
## Subnational Conflict

# 1

# Projecting Domestic Conflict Using Cross-Section Data: A Project Report

*Richard C. Eichenberg, Brigitta Widmaier, and Ulrich Widmaier*

## INTRODUCTION

This chapter reports results of a research project carried out during 1977–79 at the Science Center Berlin. The project, "Global Security Problems in the Coming Decades," prepared analyses and projections in five problem areas: domestic conflict, military spending, armed forces size, military force confrontations, and escalations processes from disputes to war. The full report of the project is available (in German) from the Science Center.[1]

Three research tasks were pursued in the domestic conflict portions of the research:

- Description of trends in domestic conflict at the global, regional, and national levels;
- Estimation of cross-section models of domestic conflict using readily available economic, social and political indicators as predictors;
- Projection of domestic conflict into the medium term future using the results of the first two steps of the analysis.

This chapter is concerned solely with the domestic conflict segments of the research, but the larger context of the work can be illustrated by the conceptual model of the overall project (Figure 1-1). By examining the linkage among domestic instability, arms accumulation, and international conflict, we hoped to provide an empirical basis not

11

Figure 1-1. Conceptual Model: Linkages Among Global Security Problems

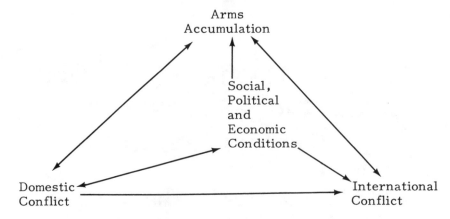

*Source:* Compiled by the authors.

just for projecting domestic conflict, but also for identifying future levels of international conflict and military resource burdens.[2]

Although the design of the research originally called for projections drawn from time-series analysis, in practice the projections were undertaken only on the basis of cross-section models of past conflict behavior because inspection of time trends revealed highly unstable patterns that provided little basis for simple time projections.[3]

Of course, the utility of projections based on past cross-sections depends on the historical stability of cross-national patterns as well as the quality of the model used to specify past behavior. We turn to these issues after describing the theoretical context of the research andthe data sources used to construct a projection model of domestic violence.

## THEORY AND DATA

Scholarly work on domestic violence is now so extensive that it has become almost a distinct subfield of macroquantitative research. Weede (1975) has identified three intellectual schools of conflict research that provide a useful guide to theorizing on the questions of how and why populations rebel against the status quo.

A first intellectual grouping works from the assumption that domestic conflict is a result of dissatisfaction, and the concept of relative deprivation forms the basis for a general hypothesis of "frustration-rebellion." The distinguishing feature of this first intellectual school is the application to collective behavior of theories developed to explain individual behavior (Muller 1980, 71–72). The work of Ted Robert Gurr is perhaps the best example of this stream of theory and research (1970).

A second body of research emphasizes the more general strains and tensions experienced by social systems (Gurr and Duval 1973). Whether the focus is on "social mobilization" (Deutsch 1961), the level or rate of change in economic growth (Olson 1963; Muller 1982), or the balance between social mobilization and political institutionalization (Huntington 1968), this second group emphasizes hypotheses relating aggregate social conditions to the level or severity of domestic conflict.

A third intellectual school of conflict research departs from the macro focus. As illustrated in the work of Hibbs (1973), this group of researchers breaks new ground in that domestic conflict is postulated as an interaction process in which conflict events are dependent upon one another in a sequence of action-reaction. Attention is thus focused on the *interdependence* of events and on the escalation processes that condition the severity of conflicts once they are underway.

In general, more recent work has tended toward the third approach noted above—domestic conflict is increasingly viewed as a continuous process rather than as a discrete series of events dependent on macro conditions. In addition, recent research places increasing emphasis on the characteristics of the parties to conflict (including the state) and attempts to explain conflict on the basis of "actor characteristics" such as differential power bases (Korpi 1974) or organizational capabilities (Widmaier 1978) of societal groups.[4]

However, these latter research approaches remain for the most part at the conceptual level (exceptions are Hibbs 1973; Gurr and Duval 1973; Gurr and Lichbach 1979; and Widmaier 1978). The reason is that, in contrast to the older approaches that rely on well-documented sources of macro social, political, and economic indicators, models employing "intraconflict" dynamics or "actor characteristics" require data that are not yet available over long periods of time or for large samples of nations.

Lack of data is also a major constraint on the present research. To undertake fully specified "post-dictive" projections reflecting the newer research approaches would have required data that are simply not available over sufficient time periods to establish the stability of relationships for different historical cross-sections. Further, even were indicators available for past periods, projection of conflict would require a plausible method for projecting predictors in the model: thus we would have faced the difficult task of projecting escalation processes or the power bases of domestic actors.

In the face of these difficulties, we chose to base our research on the older, macro theoretical tradition of domestic conflict research. Our design was to specify and estimate cross-sectional models for as many historical cross-sections as possible, providing an evaluation of the over time stability of cross-national relationships. In addition, we required that predictors used in the cross-section models be amenable to plausible projection.

The result is a simple "black box" model of domestic conflict. The model is simple because it includes only two predictors of conflict: total population and level of economic development. The black-box nature of the model results from the fact that we include only macro characteristics, to the exclusion of variables describing the dynamics of the conflict itself or the characteristics of parties to the conflict.

Data for past cross sections were drawn entirely from the forthcoming third edition of the *World Handbook of Political and Social Indicators* (Taylor and Jodice forthcoming). As noted below, the operationalization of total population is straightforward. Level of economic development is measured by energy consumption per capita (in coal units) rather than by the standard GNP measures because the energy variable was available for cross sections as far back as 1950, while GNP was available only for more recent periods.

Two summary measures of domestic conflict were constructed from the *World Handbook*'s series of domestic events indicators for the period 1948 to 1977. *Internal War* is the sum of armed attacks, assassinations, and deaths from collective group violence. *Collective Protest* is the sum of protest demonstrations and political strikes.[5] Brief definitions of the component indicators are provided in Table 1–1; for more detailed documentation, see Taylor and Hudson (1972, 59–70).

Conceptually, we conceive of the summary indicators as two different dimensions of conflict: *Collective Protest* a relatively nonviolent, if unconventional, form of political conflict, and *Internal War* a violent dimension similar to

TABLE 1-1.  Short Definition of World Handbook Variables
Used in Summary Indicators

---

## Protest Demonstrations

A protest demonstration is a nonviolent gathering of people organized for
the announced purpose of protesting against a regime, government, or one or
more of its leaders or against its ideology, policy, intended policy, or
lack of policy or against its previous action or intended action . . .
includes demonstrations for or against a foreign government, its leaders,
or its visiting representatives . . . when [it] is reported to indicate
opposition to the demonstrators' own government. . . .

## Political Strikes

Work stoppages by a body of industrial or service workers or a stoppage of
normal academic life by students to protest against a regime, a government,
government leaders, a government policy or action.  Strikes of an economic
nature are not included unless they are judged to have assumed a primary
political significance.

## Armed Attacks

Acts of violent political conflict carried out by (or on behalf of) an
organized group with the object of weakening or destroying the power
exercised by another group.  It is characterized by bloodshed, physical
struggle, or the destruction of property.

## Assassinations

Are the politically motivated murder of a high governmental official or
politician . . . Nationally prominent politicians who are not necessarily
holding office are also included, as are newspaper editors.

## Deaths from Domestic Group Violence

The number of deaths from political violence is not an event variable [as
the above variables are] but a body count.  The deaths reported occur
mainly in conjunction with armed attacks, but also with riots and to a
lesser extent with demonstrations . . . not including assassination victims
and foreigners.

---

Source: Charles L. Taylor, and Michael C. Hudson, World Handbook of
Political and Social Indicators II.  (New Haven: Yale University Press,
1972), 59-70.

common notions of civil war. In fact, much research on domestic conflict has been devoted to attempts to uncover the dimensional structure of domestic conflict, and most efforts have produced a distinction not unlike the twofold categorization used here (Zimmermann 1980, 171–72 reviews these studies exhaustively). Our own examination of the individual component indicators reinforced the bi-dimensional structure found in previous studies. The components of *Collective Protest* and *Internal War* move in much the same pattern, but the two indicators themselves reveal much different time trends (largely because internal war is highly discontinuous, while domestic protest is a much smoother series).

In summary, our strategy is to construct cross-section models of *Internal War* and *Collective Protest* to estimate parameters for the effects of population size and level of economic development and to project future values of these two summary indicators using projected values of the predictor variables.

## MODELING THE PAST

As noted above, one prerequisite of our research is the ability to produce plausible projections of predictor variables. This task, in turn, required that predictors be measured with a minimum of error over a period of time sufficient to allow calculation of trend lines and thus to extrapolate future values.

Without a doubt, the most manageable data in this regard are from the field of demography. World-model simulations and more specialized demographic studies have produced disaggregated, national level population projections to and beyond the year 2000 (more on these sources below). Of course, the exactitude of these projections tends to decrease with the duration of the projection because long term demographic development is conditioned by fertility rates that are difficult to predict. Nonetheless, they are relatively exact in the short to medium term (20 to 30 years).

Yet the availability of data begs the question of whether the relationship between total population and domestic conflict is theoretically meaningful. The literature tends to treat population size largely as a control variable: the argument is that large populations naturally contain more people available for domestic conflict. In general, this population effect is explicitly controlled in empirical research either by measuring conflict variables on a per capita basis or by entering population size in equations predicting conflict. In the latter case, the statistical impact of population is usually significant (Weede 1980; Eberwein et al. 1978).

Theoretically, the impact of population size may be due to its role as a diffuse indicator of system strain. Other things being equal, we might expect problems of integration, consensus, and communication (and perhaps also of economic development and distribution) to be more severe in larger societies than in small ones. This would explain the heavy impact of population in empirical studies. In any event, the strength of the variable in existing findings suggests that it should be taken into account in our own model and projections.[6]

There is little ambiguity in specifying level of economic development as a predictor of domestic conflict. Both theory and research findings are dominated by the relationship between conflict and national economic development (see the studies reviewed by Zimmermann 1980, 175–85). In general, hypotheses have treated conflict as a *negative* function of development, for reasons similar to Gurr's notion of "demand satisfaction"—developed societies are better able to meet material demands and thus to quiet conflict or prevent it from arising in the first place. As we will see below, however, there may also be reason to expect a positive association between economic development and *Collective Protest* (as opposed to *Internal War*).

We chose to operationalize level of economic development as energy consumption (in coal units) per capita rather than in a standard GNP measure. This indicator is available for a number of periods for a large number of nations, thus easing the task of evaluating the historical stability of cross-national variation and facilitating the extrapolation of future values of the indicator.

The dependent variables, *Collective Protest* and *Internal War*, are aggregated for each of six half-decades beginning in 1948 and ending in 1977. The aggregation is necessary to reduce the considerable year to year fluctuations in the dependent variables, and it serves to "align" the dependent variables on the cross sections for the predictor variables (that is, predictors for the year 1950 are used in the analysis of the 1948–52 half-decade, and so on).

Tables 1-2 and 1-3 report the results of regression analyses of *Collective Protest* and *Internal War* on total population size and energy consumption per capita for each of six cross sections. For our purposes, these estimates must satisfy two criteria: adequacy of specification and stability over time.

Our review of theories of domestic conflict makes it clear

TABLE 1-2.  Regression Analysis of Collective Protest

| Half Decade | Intercept | Log POP | Log ENERGY | $R^2$ | SER | F | N |
|---|---|---|---|---|---|---|---|
| 1948-52 | -4.26 | .478* (5.69) | .269* (3.87) | .38 | 1.13 | 25.49 | 86 |
| 1953-57 | -2.47 | .321* (4.00) | .212* (2.86) | .20 | 1.30 | 13.26 | 110 |
| 1958-62 | -3.26 | .447* (5.37 | .173* (2.54) | .26 | 1.36 | 20.89 | 125 |
| 1963-67 | -3.55 | .468* (5.81) | .194* (2.96) | .28 | 1.33 | 24.18 | 129 |
| 1968-72 | -5.66 | .605* (9.96) | .347* (6.86) | .56 | 1.01 | 82.40 | 131 |
| 1973-77 | -5.45 | .621* (8.76) | .253* (4.24) | .44 | 1.20 | 50.08 | 130 |

Log POP = Log (Total Population)
Log ENERGY = Log (Energy Consumption per capita)
SER = Standard Error of the Regression
Note: Figures in parentheses are t-statistics. Coefficients marked with a "*" are at least twice as large as their standard errors, i.e., they are significant (5% and less).
Source: Charles L. Taylor and David Jodice, World Handbook of Political and Social Indicators, Third Edition. (New Haven: Yale University Press, forthcoming).

that the first criterion is not fully met, as our equations do exclude potentially important determinants of domestic conflict. Yet for our purposes the critical question is not whether additional predictors should be added on theoretical grounds, but rather how much better estimates would be if additional predictors were added to the equations. To evaluate this question, we conducted a number of regression experiments with the most recent half-decade model (1972-77), for which more extensive economic and political indicators are available. The results indicated that not a great deal would be gained by using a more extensive model, for the structure of the parameter estimates and the

TABLE 1-3.  Regression Analysis of Internal War

| Half Decade | Intercept | Log POP | Log ENERGY | $R^2$ | SER | F | N |
|---|---|---|---|---|---|---|---|
| 1948-52 | -2.84 | .821* (4.65) | -.249 (-1.71) | .22 | 2.28 | 11.48 | 83 |
| 1953-57 | -.864 | .561* (3.43) | -.245 (-1.62) | .11 | 2.57 | 6.58 | 106 |
| 1958-62 | -1.51 | .732* (4.68) | -.261* (-2.08) | .16 | 2.45 | 11.51 | 121 |
| 1963-67 | .302 | .618* (4.25) | -.393* (-3.34) | .17 | 2.34 | 12.72 | 125 |
| 1968-72 | -1.07 | .726* (4.82) | -.359* (-2.93) | .18 | 2.41 | 14.04 | 127 |
| 1973-77 | -2.00 | .781* (5.17) | -.313* (-2.52) | .20 | 2.46 | 15.51 | 126 |

Log POP = Log (Total Population)
Log ENERGY = Log (Energy Consumption per capita)
SER = Standard Error of the Regression
Note: Figures in parentheses are t-statistics. Coefficients marked with a "*" are at least twice as large as their standard errors, i.e., they are significant (5% and less). Excluding nations with extreme values on the dependent variable (Nigeria, Indonesia, South Vietnam, Pakistan).
Source: Charles L. Taylor and David Jodice, World Handbook of Political and Social Indicators, Third Edition. (New Haven: Yale University Press, forthcoming).

overall explanatory power of the model were largely unaffected by the inclusion of selected additional variables (the variables tested were three different measures of GNP growth from 1960 to 1975; an index of political repression [political rights index]; and an index of ethnic-linguistic fractionalization).

This is not to argue that a better model of domestic conflict is not achievable using more intensive data collections or sophisticated modeling techniques than the single, additive equations necessarily used here. Rather, it suggests that, given the data and modeling constraints imposed by our goal of conducting projections, the sacrifice of the model's simplicity and the ability to evaluate its stability over many cross sections may not be worth the marginal addition in "post-dictive" power.

Of course, the model and subsequent projections remain *ceteris paribus*. Other predictors could improve postdiction and presumably the projections as well. Further, even the "best" of our equations accounts for only half the statistical variation in conflict, a level that is respectable by social science standards (and previous research on conflict), but that leaves considerable "unexplained" or error variance unaccounted for. Thus the post-dictive models and the projections based on them describe an "as if" world that could be disturbed by factors not specified here.

The second criterion, stability of results over many cross sections, is nicely met: the sign, significance, and magnitude of parameter estimates show a stability over time that is remarkable for social scientists accustomed to a rapidly changing global system. In every half-decade since 1948, *Collective Protest* has been positively related to population size and to level of economic development (the latter coefficient perhaps reflecting the more open institutions of the economically developed democracies). *Internal War* is also positively related to population size, but it is negatively related to economic development—it is the (younger) less-developed societies that experience more violent domestic conflict. Given these results, the question for our projections is this: assuming that the past relationships between population size, level of economic development, and domestic conflict hold in the future, what will be the future level of conflict given estimates of change in these predictor variables?


PROJECTING THE FUTURE

Our projections of domestic violence employ the parameter estimates reported above together with existing population projections and our own projections of energy consumption. The population projections are from the United Nations (UN), which has produced projections for all countries of the world to the year 2000. Of three alternatives available, the "medium" or middle version is used here, although alternative projections could obviously be produced using other versions. We used the UN's projection for the years 1985, 1990, and 2000, as published by the International Labor Organization (ILO 1977). The value for 1990 was interpolated.

The projection of energy consumption figures required a slightly more complicated procedure. The data (in coal units) were drawn from two sources. For 1950, 1955, 1960, 1965, 1970, and 1975, they were taken from the *World Handbook,* cited above. To the extent available, intervening years were drawn from the series of the Correlates of War Project at the University of Michigan. From these data, we calculated average energy consumption for half-decades from 1946 to 1975 to smooth out year-to-year fluctuations.

The next step was to calculate growth rates per half-decade and from these to calculate the overall average growth rate for the entire period. On the basis of these rates, we projected energy consumption per capita using the total population data described above. However, examination of these projections revealed problematic results. Using a linear extrapolating procedure with no upper bound, states with high growth rates in the past would, under our projections, pass the United States by the year 2000.

For this reason, we made the assumption that future energy consumption would follow a nonlinear growth path, reaching an upper limit during the 20-year time period of our projections. Thus, we assume that energy consumption will grow, but that, depending on the level of previous growth, it will level off to zero on a per capita basis (that is, it will grow only at the rate of population growth).

The following formula was used to project energy consumption per capita:[7]

$$\frac{EC_{n+1}}{TP_{n+1}} = \frac{EC_n}{TP_n} \, Z^{2^{n+1}} \quad \text{(that is, } Z \text{ to the } 2^{\frac{1}{n+1}} \text{ power)}$$

Where:
EC= Energy Consumption; TP= Total Population
n= Period; O= 1971–75, 1=1976–80...5=1996–2000
$\bar{Z}$ = average growth rate of energy consumption per capita

The effect of this formula is that past growth rates in energy consumption that are high or extremely low rapidly approach a growth rate of 1.0. Table 1-4 illustrates the progression of growth rates used to project energy consumption. We think the calculated values (not shown here) are satisfactory. Conceptually, the nonlinear projection seems more valid than a linear projection with no upper

TABLE 1-4. Development of Selected Values of $\bar{Z}$

| $\bar{Z} =$ | $Z^{\frac{1}{K}}$ (that is, Z to the 1/K power) | | | | |
|---|---|---|---|---|---|
|  | K = 1 | K = 2 | K = 3 | K = 4 | K = 5 |
| 0.5 | 0.707 | 0.841 | 0.917 | 0.958 | 0.979 |
| 0.8 | 0.894 | 0.946 | 0.972 | 0.986 | 0.993 |
| 0.9 | 0.949 | 0.974 | 0.987 | 0.993 | 0.936 |
| 1.0 | 1 | 1 | 1 | 1 | 1 |
| 1.1 | 1.049 | 1.024 | 1.012 | 1.006 | 1.003 |
| 1.2 | 1.095 | 1.047 | 1.023 | 1.011 | 1.006 |
| 1.3 | 1.140 | 1.068 | 1.033 | 1.017 | 1.008 |
| 1.6 | 1.265 | 1.125 | 1.061 | 1.030 | 1.015 |
| 2.0 | 1.414 | 1.189 | 1.091 | 1.044 | 1.022 |
| 3.0 | 1.732 | 1.316 | 1.147 | 1.071 | 1.035 |
| 3.7 | 1.924 | 1.387 | 1.178 | 1.085 | 1.042 |
| 4.0 | 2.000 | 1.414 | 1.189 | 1.091 | 1.044 |
| 4.7 | 2.168 | 1.472 | 1.213 | 1.102 | 1.050 |

$\bar{Z}$ = Average Growth Rate
K = Period (1 = 1976-80, ..., 5 = 1996-2000)
Source: Compiled by the authors.

bound. Empirically, the nonlinear projection produces values that appear realistic and that produce a good degree of mobility in the global system—as one would expect with differential growth rates.

We turn now to the actual projection of domestic conflict. Our method was simple: we weighted the projected value of the predictor variables using the parameters from the last half-decade model reported above. We used the most recent half-decade on the assumption that it best represents current patterns of cross-national variation. However, as we have seen, the choice of cross-sections is not crucial since the parameters for each of the six estimated are similar.

The results of the projections are reported in Table 1-5 (*Internal War*) and Table 1-6 (*Collective Protest*). The left-hand side of each table contains projected values of domestic conflict and the right-hand side the resulting global rank orders for the top 25 nations.

Independent of the indicator projected, rank orders remain relatively stable. In particular, the ranks of the

TABLE 1-5.  Projected Value and Rank Order for Top 25 Nations on
Internal War

| Country | Projected Values | | | | | Rank Order | | | | |
|---|---|---|---|---|---|---|---|---|---|---|
| | 1980 | 1985 | 1990 | 1995 | 2000 | 1980 | 1985 | 1990 | 1995 | 2000 |
| IND | 785 | 850 | 920 | 988 | 1057 | 1 | 1 | 1 | 1 | 1 |
| PRC | 623 | 624 | 636 | 654 | 676 | 2 | 2 | 2 | 2 | 2 |
| INS | 259 | 280 | 302 | 324 | 346 | 3 | 3 | 3 | 3 | 3 |
| NIG | 186 | 206 | 229 | 260 | 289 | 4 | 4 | 4 | 4 | 4 |
| PAK | 153 | 165 | 181 | 199 | 217 | 5 | 5 | 5 | 5 | 5 |
| BRA | 150 | 163 | 178 | 195 | 213 | 6 | 6 | 6 | 6 | 6 |
| USR | 144 | 147 | 150 | 154 | 157 | 7 | 7 | 8 | 9 | 9 |
| ETH | 133 | 142 | 154 | 171 | 188 | 8 | 8 | 7 | 7 | 7 |
| BUR | 131 | 139 | 150 | 162 | 174 | 9 | 9 | 9 | 8 | 8 |
| USA | 102 | 106 | 109 | 112 | 115 | 10 | 12 | 12 | 15 | 15 |
| CON | 102 | 113 | 126 | 142 | 157 | 11 | 10 | 10 | 10 | 10 |
| PHI | 98 | 108 | 119 | 130 | 142 | 12 | 11 | 11 | 11 | 11 |
| NEP | 87 | 104 | 103 | 118 | 132 | 13 | 13 | 15 | 12 | 12 |
| THI | 91 | 98 | 107 | 116 | 126 | 14 | 14 | 13 | 13 | 14 |
| AFG | 85 | 89 | 96 | 105 | 113 | 15 | 16 | 16 | 16 | 16 |
| JPN | 84 | 85 | 86 | 87 | 88 | 16 | 17 | 19 | 21 | 23 |
| MEX | 82 | 92 | 103 | 116 | 129 | 17 | 15 | 14 | 14 | 13 |
| EGY | 77 | 83 | 90 | 98 | 105 | 18 | 8 | 17 | 18 | 18 |
| TAZ | 70 | 78 | 88 | 100 | 111 | 19 | 19 | 18 | 17 | 17 |
| TUR | 70 | 76 | 83 | 90 | 96 | 20 | 20 | 20 | 19 | 19 |
| KHM | 66 | 73 | 80 | 88 | 96 | 21 | 21 | 21 | 20 | 20 |
| SUD | 62 | 68 | 76 | 85 | 93 | 22 | 22 | 22 | 22 | 21 |
| UGA | 58 | 64 | 71 | 80 | 88 | 23 | 23 | 23 | 23 | 22 |
| SRI | 54 | 58 | 62 | 65 | 68 | 24 | 25 | 27 | 28 | 28 |
| COL | 53 | 58 | 64 | 70 | 76 | 25 | 24 | 24 | 25 | 26 |

Note: See Appendix for list of abbreviations.
Source: Compiled by author.

five or six leaders remain unchanged through the half-
decade ending in the year 2000.  The stability of the
leaders is to be expected.  The heavy influence of population size in our projection parameters ensures that those
with large populations or rapid population growth rates
remain among the leaders in domestic conflict.  Nonetheless,
the *order* in which nations are ranked varies between the
projections for *Internal War* and *Collective Protest*.

TABLE 1-6.  Projected Value and Rank Order for Top 25 Nations on Collective Protest

| Country | Projected Values | | | | | Rank Order | | | | |
|---|---|---|---|---|---|---|---|---|---|---|
| | 1980 | 1985 | 1990 | 1995 | 2000 | 1980 | 1985 | 1990 | 1995 | 2000 |
| PRC | 122 | 133 | 140 | 147 | 153 | 1 | 1 | 1 | 1 | 1 |
| USA | 96 | 99 | 102 | 105 | 107 | 2 | 2 | 2 | 2 | 2 |
| USR | 90 | 94 | 98 | 100 | 102 | 3 | 3 | 3 | 3 | 3 |
| IND | 2 | 78 | 84 | 90 | 95 | 4 | 4 | 4 | 4 | 4 |
| JPN | 50 | 53 | 54 | 55 | 56 | 5 | 5 | 5 | 5 | 5 |
| FRG | 37 | 37 | 38 | 38 | 39 | 6 | 7 | 7 | 7 | 8 |
| UK | 34 | 35 | 35 | 36 | 36 | 7 | 8 | 8 | 9 | 10 |
| BRA | 34 | 38 | 41 | 45 | 49 | 8 | 6 | 6 | 6 | 6 |
| FRA | 31 | 32 | 33 | 34 | 34 | 9 | 9 | 10 | 11 | 11 |
| ITA | 31 | 32 | 32 | 33 | 33 | 10 | 10 | 12 | 12 | 12 |
| INS | 28 | 30 | 33 | 35 | 37 | 11 | 11 | 11 | 10 | 9 |
| MEX | 27 | 30 | 34 | 37 | 41 | 12 | 12 | 9 | 8 | 7 |
| CAN | 24 | 25 | 26 | 27 | 28 | 13 | 13 | 13 | 15 | 16 |
| SPA | 21 | 22 | 23 | 24 | 25 | 14 | 16 | 17 | 17 | 17 |
| IRN | 20 | 23 | 25 | 28 | 30 | 15 | 14 | 15 | 14 | 14 |
| SAF | 20 | 22 | 24 | 26 | 28 | 6 | 17 | 16 | 16 | 15 |
| PAK | 20 | 23 | 25 | 28 | 30 | 17 | 15 | 14 | 13 | 13 |
| ROK | 9 | 20 | 22 | 23 | 24 | 18 | 18 | 18 | 18 | 19 |
| ROM | 18 | 9 | 20 | 21 | 21 | 19 | 20 | 21 | 22 | 23 |
| TUR | 18 | 20 | 21 | 23 | 25 | 20 | 19 | 19 | 19 | 18 |
| GDR | 17 | 18 | 18 | 18 | 18 | 21 | 23 | 24 | 28 | 29 |
| CZE | 7 | 17 | 17 | 18 | 18 | 22 | 25 | 29 | 30 | 30 |
| ARG | 16 | 17 | 18 | 18 | 19 | 23 | 24 | 25 | 26 | 28 |
| PHI | 16 | 18 | 20 | 22 | 23 | 24 | 22 | 22 | 21 | 21 |
| THI | 16 | 18 | 20 | 22 | 24 | 25 | 21 | 20 | 20 | 20 |

Note: See Appendix for list of abbreviations.
Source: Compiled by author.

Also common to both sets of equations is that, compared to the observed values for 1975, projected values are underestimated. Tables 1-7 and 1-8 show global and regional projections for both summary indicators of the actual and projected values for 1975. The underestimation of actual values is caused by the use of the logarithmic transformation of the variables, employed to reduce the variation of the original cross-sectional series. As a

TABLE 1-7. Projected Global Totals and Half-Decade Growth Rates

|  | Collective Protest | | Internal War | |
|---|---|---|---|---|
| 1973/77 | 1305 | (3231)* | 5628 | (174239)* |
| 1978/82 | 1430<br>(9.5%**) | | 5860<br>(12%) | |
| 1983/87 | 1538<br>(7.5%) | | 6243<br>(6.5%) | |
| 1988/92 | 1636<br>(6.4%) | | 6704<br>(7.3%) | |
| 1993/97 | 1730<br>(5.7%) | | 7256<br>(8.2%) | |
| 1990/2002 | 1818<br>(5.1% | | 7804<br>(7.6%) | |

* observed values for 1973-77.
** percent change from previous half-decade.
Source: Compiled by the authors.

result, however, the transformed series are "smoothed," and the higher the value of the dependent variable, the higher the underestimate. In effect, since we use a procedure that weights extreme values less than small or medium values, we obtain *conservative* estimates of the projected values.

Nevertheless, it is still the case that we project continuing increases in both indicators of conflict. When we observe the global change rates from one half-decade to the next, we see that increases in *Collective Protest* tend to grow smaller, while *Internal War* declines in the first projected half-decade but increases thereafter until the year 2000. However, the global pattern is not repeated in every region (Table 1-8). Whereas Europe and North America show relatively modest increases, there are high growth rates in Africa, Latin America, Asia, and the Middle East, reflecting the impact of comparatively high population growth in the region.

TABLE 1-8.  Projected Regional Totals and Half-Decade Growth Rates

|  | NA (N=2) | LA (N=25) | EU (N=27) | AFR (N=36) | ME (N=18) | ASIA (N=21) |
|---|---|---|---|---|---|---|
| **Collective Protest** | | | | | | |
| 1975* | 115 | 163 | 406 | 125 | 121 | 371 |
| 1980 | 120 (4.3% | 182 (11.7%) | 428 (5.4%) | 140 (12%) | 139 (14.9%) | 418 (12.7%) |
| 1995 | 124 (3.3%) | 200 (9.9%) | 442 (3.3%) | 156 (11.4%) | 155 (11.5%) | 456 (9.1%) |
| 1990 | 128 (3.2%) | 218 (9%) | 454 (2.7%) | 171 (9.6%) | 171 (10.3%) | 488 (7.0%) |
| 1995 | 131 (2.3%) | 236 (8.2%) | 464 (2.2%) | 191 11.7%) | 187 (9.4%) | 517 (5.9%) |
| 2000 | 135 (3.0%) | 253 (7.2%) | 472 (1.7%) | 208 (8.9%) | 202 (8.0%) | 544 (5.2%) |
| **Internal War** | | | | | | |
| 1975* | 118 | 578 | 610 | 1217 | 567 | 2535 |
| 1980 | 122 (3.4%)** | 619 (7.1%) | 603 (-0.1%) | 1300 (6.8%) | 600 (5.8%) | 2613 (3.1%) |
| 1985 | 126 (3.3%) | 674 (8.9%) | 607 (0.07%) | 1420 (9.2%) | 652 (8.7%) | 2760 (5.6%) |
| 1990 | 131 (3.9%) | 737 (9.3%) | 616 (1.4%) | 1569 (10.4%) | 716 (9.8%) | 2933 (6.3%) |
| 1995 | 134 (2.3%) | 808 (9.6%) | 626 (1.6%) | 1765 (12.5%) | 787 (9.9%) | 3132 (6.8%) |
| 2000 | 138 (3.0%) | 879 (8.8%) | 637 (1.8%) | 1955 (10.8%) | 858 (9.0%) | 3334 (6.5%) |

* observed values.  ** percent change from previous decade.
Source: Compiled by the authors.

26

The regional figures provide an interesting case study in the utility (and uncertainty) of projections that are based on *past* behavioral patterns. Consistent with much current speculation, the Middle East region is projected to have the strongest growth in protests through the half-decade ending in 1987. This result is due to the rapidly growing population in the region and the strong increases in energy consumption in the recent past, and both of these variables carry positive coefficients in our projection model. But the increases slow as projected energy consumption reaches the upper limit discussed above.

Perhaps most interesting, the negative energy coefficient used to project *Internal War* results in a different regional distribution in the projection of this indicator; here the Middle East shows less violent conflict than other regions (especially Africa), due to the negative effect of level of economic development. In sum, based on past cross-national patterns, we project that population increases and economic development in the Middle East will place it among the leaders in the increase of *protest,* but this *will not* result in its being among the most violent regions of the world.

When one ponders this pattern, it raises questions beyond the specific regions and ranks projected here. The result is clearly due to the fact that in the past the most economically developed systems have had the least domestic conflict—thus the negative coefficients in the models estimated for past cross sections. But has this stability rested on economic advantage (an ability to satisfy most demands at a fairly high level) or on the democratic institutions that also characterize these states, or are these two characteristics intertwined (Muller 1982)?

If the latter, then obviously political developments are one of the additional factors that must be kept in mind in weighing these "as if" projections. If not, the projections suggest what at present is probably a minority view: that the Middle East, although it will experience increasing domestic mobilization of populations in domestic protest, will not necessarily have a similar rate of increase in violent forms of domestic protest.

Switching the focus to specific nations, there are interesting patterns both in terms of which states will lead on the two summary indicators and which states will experience the most change over the next 20 years. For *Collective Protest,* the top group consists of China, the United States, the Soviet Union, India, and Japan. For *Internal War*, the leaders are India, China, Indonesia, Nigeria, and Pakistan. Obviously, the positive effects of population influences both these lists, with the differentiation occurring because of the different effect of economic development on the two forms of conflict. Not surprisingly, the countries with the largest jump in global ranks over the projection period are those with large populations and low economic growth rates (relative to other states).

## DISCUSSION

The projection of behavior is beset with many of the same difficulties of post-dictive modeling. Before evaluating the larger significance of our effort, therefore, it is useful to examine problems that could throw our findings into doubt.

Of course, one potentially serious problem is measurement error in the dependent variable, a well-known difficulty for events data researchers (Azar et al. 1972). In the case of domestic conflict research, measurement error can result from underreporting in nations with less than modern newsgathering facilities. Conversely, distortion could occur because media attention is focused on the more violent, dramatic events relative to less violent forms of protest. Thus, we might actually overstate (and thus overproject) future violence if the news sources that are the source of data are skewed systematically.

Of course, measurement error is not unique to future oriented research. And the solution, thorough evaluation of sources and evaluation of the pattern of errors, should at least reduce the amount of *systematic* error in the data. We are confident that the procedures followed by Taylor and Jodice in the collection of the *World Handbook* data satisfy this requirement, and our confidence in the data is increased by the fact that, compared to the cross sections from the previous editions of the *World Handbook,* the data in the third edition produce very similar correlations, despite the fact that the number of news sources has been increased to expand coverage.

Measurement error in the predictor variables also presents a potential threat to the validity of our findings, and the problem could be compounded if the techniques used to *project* predictors is seriously flawed. As described above, we have gone to some trouble to produce a realistic series of projections for the two predictor variables, but in a sense this problem of measurement is judgmental as well. That is, there may be those who feel that population or energy consumption will develop in ways quite different from that specified here. In this case, we can only rely on normal scientific practice: having made our sources and procedures explicit, we provide the basis for others to construct alternative future measurements—projections—of the predictors to test their effect on projected outcomes.

Finally, projections are subject to the error of model misspecification. As noted above, our model is more *underspecified* than *mis*specified, as it is clear that additional predictors could be included were additional data available. But has the parsimony of our models done injustice to the state of theory and research by reducing the problem to a simple, two-variable equation?

Certainly we have, but we think this cost must be compared to the alternative of not thinking about the future at all, since data are not available to construct a historically based set of parameters to project more complex models.

Furthermore, we do not think our simple model should be sold short. In one case (*Collective Protest*), the post-dictive model accounted for over half the statistical variance, a level that is certainly "competitive" by social science standards. Further, the sign and magnitude of the parameters proved extremely robust over six different cross sections since 1948, and the theoretical interpretation of these results is consistent with research in the field. Thus, while we would hardly claim to have tested and projected the perfect model of domestic conflict, we feel that the results provide a good first cut at thinking systematically about future levels of domestic conflict in the global system.

One might legitimately ask if our projections could not have been made intuitively—after all, is it not fairly obvious that less-developed social systems experience more violent conflict and are likely to do so in the future? In a general sense, the answer is yes. But common sense or intuition do not provide specific expectations. To raise a question that can be answered from Table 1-5, would common sense tell us whether Mexico, Brazil, or Egypt will have the most unstable medium term future?

Although we do feel that projection exercises such as this provide a more concrete way of thinking of the future, we would warn against interpreting the results and resulting ranks as discrete, "point" predictions. Our models and predictions are explicitly "as if" models, and even more complicated models leave considerable amounts of unexplained variance. Our projections are therefore best thought of as a range of values and possible future ranks based on a limited understanding of the past. We think the utility of both post-dictive models and projected futures should be seen precisely in the task of enforcing a con-

crete, explicit method for thinking about the future. To
the extent that factors are omitted from the design of such
projects, they can at least be entertained in terms of future
unknowns. Will political developments intervene to change
variation in domestic conflict such that economic change will
have less of an impact? If so, what is the likely regional
distribution, given our own projections? Will expanding
military burdens allow governments to exercise more or less
control over domestic opposition?

Our argument is that questions such as these are framed
more concretely if they start from even the most simple
projections of how the world will look *ceteris paribus*. One
might argue, for example, that much of the impact of
so-called world models arises not so much from specific
forecasts but from "consciousness raising" that results from
consideration of how the world could look unless other
variables intervene to change outcomes. Given the human
toll of domestic conflict, we would be satisfied if our projections met this need for forward-looking critical thinking.

NOTES

1. This chapter is a much condensed version of
Eichenberg, Widmaier and Widmaier (1981). This longer
report contains more discussion of time trends in the domestic conflict series and includes a considerable amount of
descriptive material on the global, regional, and national
distribution of the data used here.

We are grateful to Stuart Bremer and Volker Reuss for
help with the design and implementation of the project and
to Charles Taylor and David Jodice for providing access to
the pre-release version of the new *World Handbook* data
used in this study.

2. For empirical analyses of some of these links, see:
Ward and Widmaier (1981); Cusack and Eberwein (1981);
and Eberwein (1981).

3. Trend analyses are described in detail in
Eichenberg, Widmaier and Widmaier (1981, 29–49).

Research for this chapter was sponsored and financed by
the Science Center Berlin, under a grant from the German
Society for Peace and Conflict Research (DGFK).

4. This focus owes much to the work of Charles Tilly
(1978).

5. Unlike some previous research, we do not include
riots in our aggregate *Protest* variable because preliminary
analysis revealed some errors in this variable. These will
be corrected in the final release of the *World Handbook*
data.

6. For studies of the effect of the size of social systems, see East (1973).
7. This formula was developed by Volker Reuss.


APPENDIX: Abbreviations

| | | | |
|---|---|---|---|
| AFG | Afghanistan | MEX | Mexico |
| ARG | Argentina | NEP | Nepal |
| BRA | Brazil | NIG | Nigeria |
| BUR | Burma | PAK | Pakistan |
| CAN | Canada | PHI | Philippines |
| COL | Columbia | PRC | Peoples Republic |
| CON | Congo | | of China |
| CZE | Czechoslovakia | PRK | North-Korea |
| EGY | Egypt | ROK | South Korea |
| ETH | Ethiopia | ROM | Romania |
| FRA | France | SAF | South Africa |
| FRG | Federal Republic | SAP | Spain |
| | of Germany | SRI | Sri Lanka |
| GDR | German Democratic | UD | Sudan |
| | Republic | TAZ | Tanzania |
| IND | India | THI | Thailand |
| INS | Indonesia | TUR | Turkey |
| IRN | Iran | UGA | Uganda |
| ITA | Italy | UK | United Kingdom |
| JPN | Japan | USA | USA |
| KHM | Cambodia | USR | Soviet Union |


REFERENCES

Azar, Edward A., et al. 1972. *International Events Interaction Analysis*. Beverly Hills: Sage Publications.
Cusack, Thomas, and Wolf-Dieter Eberwein. 1981. "A Descriptive Analysis of Serious International Disputes During the Twentieth Century." *International Interactions* (October 1981).
Deutsch, Karl W. 1961. "Social Mobilization and Political Development." *American Political Science Review* 55:493–514.
East, Maurice. 1973. "Size and Foreign Policy Behavior." *World Politics* 25:556–76.
Eberwein, Wolf-Dieter. 1981. "Militaerische Konfrontationen und die Eskalation zum Krieg: 1900–2000." Publication Series of the International Institute for Comparative Social Research, Science Center Berlin, IIVG/dp-81–112.

Eberwein, W.-D., et al. 1978. "Internes und externes Konfliktverhalten von Nationen, 1966–67." *Zeitschrit fuer Soziologie.* vol. 7, no. 1.

Eichenberg, Richard C., Brigitta Widmaier, and Ulrich Widmaier. 1981. *Innerstaatliche Konflikte: Hypothesen, Trends und Prognosen.* Publication Series of the International Institute for Comparative Social Research, Science Center Berlin, IIVG/dp-81–114.

Gurr, Ted Robert. 1968. "A Causal Model of Civil Strife." *American Political Science Review* 62(4):1104–24.

—————. 1970. *Why Men Rebel.* Princeton: Princeton University Press.

—————. 1972. "The Calculus of Civil Conflict." *Journal of Social Issues* 28(1):27–47.

Gurr, Ted Robert, and Raymond Duval. 1973. "Civil Conflict in the 1960's: A Reciprocal Theoretical System with Parameter Estimates." *Comparative Political Studies* 6(2):135–69.

Gurr, Ted Robert, and Mark J. Lichbach. 1979. "A Forecasting Model for Political Conflict." In J. D. Singer and Michael Wallace, eds., *To Augur Well.* Beverly Hills: Sage Publications.

Hibbs, Douglas A. 1973. *Mass Political Violence.* New York: John Wiley & Sons.

Huntington, Samuel. 1968. *Political Order in Changing Societies.* New Haven: Yale University Press.

ILO [International Labor Organization]. 1977. *Labour Force Estimates and Projections, 1950–2000.* volumes I-V, Geneva, 2nd edition.

Korpi, Walter. 1974. "Conflict, Power and Relative Deprivation." *American Political Science Review* 68(4):1569–78.

Muller, Edward. 1980. "The Psychology of Political Protest and Violence." In Ted Robert Gurr, ed., *Handbook of Political Conflict.* New York: Free Press.

—————. 1982. "Economic Development and Democracy Revisited." Paper delivered to the Annual Meeting of the Midwest Political Science Association, Milwaukee, Wisconsin.

Olson, Mancur. 1963. "Economic Growth as a Destabilizing Force." *Journal of Economic History* 23:529–52.

Taylor, Charles L., and David Jodice. Forthcoming. *World Handbook of Political and Social Indicators, Third Edition.* New Haven: Yale University Press.

Taylor, Charles L., and Michael C. Hudson. 1972. *World Handbook of Political and Social Indicators II.* New Haven: Yale University Press.

Tilly, Charles. 1978. *From Mobilization to Revolution.*

New York: John Wiley & Sons.

Ward, Michael D., and Ulrich Widmaier. 1981. "The Domestic International Conflict Nexus: New Evidence and Old Hypotheses." *International Interactions* (October). vol. 8, no. 4.

Weede, Erich. 1980. "Inequality, Wealth and Violence . . . or Are Cross-National Data on Violence Good Enough?" Unpublished manuscript, University of Cologne.

————. 1975. "Unzufriedenheit, Protest und Gewalt: Kritik an einem makropolitischen Forshungsprogramm." *Politische Vierteljarhresschrift* 1(3):409–28.

Widmaier, Ulrich. 1978. *Politische Gewaltanwendung als Problem der Organisation von Interessen.* Meisenheim/Glan:Hain.

Zimmermann, Ekkhart. 1980. "Macro-Comparative Research on Political Protest." In Ted Robert Gurr, ed., *Handbook of Political Conflict.* New York: Free Press.

# 2

# Modeling
# the Conflict Patterns of Nations

## Daniel S. Geller

INTRODUCTION

Recent events in Nicaragua and El Salvador are merely the
most conspicuous current manifestations of civil strife in
Latin America. Indeed, within the last 15 years, revolution, guerrilla warfare, coups d'état, and mass political
violence have resulted in regime changes (or irregular
executive transfers) in Argentina, Peru, Guatemala,
Ecuador, Bolivia, Honduras, Panama, Chile, and Uruguay,
in addition to the examples first cited. Although the
structural sources of these various forms of violent political
behavior can be traced to institutional weaknesses inherent
in developing states and their resultant inability to moderate group conflict, the proximate factors of internal political
violence are somewhat more complex. These include rapid
economic modernization, social mobilization, and severe
economic crises (characterized by soaring inflation rates and
service or commodity discontinuities).

Contemporary theoretical models employed to explain civil
strife have tended to coalesce around two general focuses
regarding the principal factors and dynamics that are
presumed to trigger violent political behavior. One theoretical school emphasizes expectation-achievement discrepancies (or levels of relative deprivation),[1] while the
other centers on organizational political processes (or
resource mobilization).[2] However, the distinction between
the two schools may be more apparent than real, since most

relative deprivation models incorporate organizational factors within their frameworks.

Concurrent with the development of these theories, research was being conducted to determine "types" or "dimensions" of violent subnational political behavior. In some cases the work was directly related to the test of the above theories (for example, Feierabend and Feierabend 1966; Bwy 1968; Hibbs 1973; Gurr and Duvall 1973; Gurr and Bishop 1976; Lichbach and Gurr 1979), whereas in others the delineation of conflict dimensions was simply a component of broader studies of national/international violence (for example, Eckstein 1962; Rummel 1963; Tanter 1965; Morrison and Stevenson 1971; Banks 1972; Wilkenfeld 1973). However, with only a few exceptions (Rummel 1963; Banks 1972; Gurr and Bishop 1976) these multivariate studies of conflict dimensions attempted no explicit comparison of national violence "profiles" derived from the analyses, and in those cases where this was ventured, data from multiple time-points for each nation were collapsed into summary measures thereby obscuring yearly variations. Only Sorokin (1937) and Tilly et al. (1975) tried to determine empirically cross-national longitudinal patterns of internal political conflict. Unfortunately, Sorokin's work is marred by excessively subjective and impressionistic operational definitions, while Tilly's suffers from a small number of cases (three) and from "variation in sources and sampling procedures" (Tilly et al. 1975, 245).

In sum, there appears to be a lacuna with respect to the comparative study of longitudinal conflict patterns and, perforce, an absence of information regarding the ability of forecasting models to predict variations among patterns. Hence, this chapter will describe the attempt to: (1) develop a multi-stage model of violent internal conflict for 20 Latin American nations; (2) identify cross-national longitudinal conflict patterns; and (3) test the forecasting instrument against an alternative model so as to determine its relative accuracy in predicting different patterns of violence. Indeed, it is reasonable to assume (a priori) that nations will exhibit different longitudinal conflict profiles and that specific forecasting models may tend to predict certain patterns more efficiently than others.


## A SOCIOPOLITICAL MODEL OF CONFLICT

Theoretical models for the explanation, analysis, and prediction of civil strife abound in contemporary social scientific literature. One of the most interesting of these was

developed by Ted Robert Gurr in 1968 and subsequently
clarified, expanded, and modified in later works (Gurr
1970; Gurr and Duvall 1973, 1976; Gurr and Lichbach
1979). This basic formulation has generated the greatest
amount of empirical research on domestic political violence.
Although the theory is not without its critics (for example,
Nardin 1971; Snyder 1978; Goldstone 1980), it has nevertheless accumulated a substantial body of supporting
evidence.[3]

The theory is founded on the assumption that "a psychological variable, relative deprivation, is the basic precondition for civil strife . . . and that the more widespread
and intense deprivation is among members of a population,
the greater is the magnitude of strife in one or another
form" (Gurr 1968, 1104). The relative deprivation concept
is defined as constituting "actors' perceptions of dis-
crepancy between their value expectations (the goods and
conditions of the life to which they believe they are jus-
tifiably entitled), and their value capabilities (the amounts
of those goods and conditions that they think they are able
to get and keep)" (Gurr 1968, 1104).

However, deprivation alone is not a "sufficient" cause of
violent political conflict. Gurr's initial formulation incorporated a set of additional elements presumably related
to the deprivation-conflict nexus. These factors derive
from the structural and procedural attributes of sociopolitical systems and include: historial traditions of violent
political behavior, the coercive potential of regimes, the
degrees of legitimacy and institutionalization of political
systems, and the availability of an organizational infrastructure that might facilitate mass political violence (Gurr
1968, 1104–06).

Indeed, the model explicitly describes conflict in terms
of macro social dynamics and not simply as an individual
level psychological process. It specifies the necessary
precondition for large scale violent political activity and
suggests a series of sociopolitical attributes that are likely
to mitigate or escalate the conflict levels of nations (Gurr
and Duvall 1976, 148).

Causal Structure

In his initial study, Gurr partitioned the relative deprivation concept into two components: one reflecting "short
term" and the other denoting "persisting" conditions (Gurr
1968, 1109–12). Although Gurr assumed no basic difference
with regard to their influence on political violence, other

theorists (for example, Hoffer 1951; Brinton 1952; Wolf 1959; Davies 1962, 1969; Feierabend and Feierabend 1966; Blasier 1967) have argued that the two types of privation may produce contrary effects on conflict tendencies. For example, it has been noted that long term deprivation may create a fatalistic, quiescent population (Hoffer 1951, 27–28). As Davies (1962, 7) has argued: "Far from making people into revolutionaries, enduring poverty makes for concern with one's solitary self or solitary family at best and resignation or mute despair at worst." Conversely, Davies suggests that "when a long period of rising expectations and gratifications is followed by a short period during which expectations continue to rise while gratifications fall off sharply, the probability of civil violence against the government rises rapidly" (1978, 1357).

The next factor—historical traditions of civil violence—has particular relevance in this study. It has been argued that violence breeds violence; that past or current strife contributes to the development of political orientations or attitudes that are conducive to future strife (Eckstein 1965, 158). In short, the conflict traditions of states may influence the tendency toward future violence. Indeed, Latin America has been designated as a region with a particularly strong tradition of violence in politics (Gurr 1970, 176; Payne 1965, 363).

The theoretical framework also incorporates the coercive power of regimes as an intervening factor in the conflict model. Gurr maintained that the coercive capabilities of governments (based on the size of their internal security forces plus the political inclination and ability to use those forces) is a salient determinant of both the form and extent of civil violence (Gurr 1970, 14). In other words, politicized discontent is a precondition for civil strife, but its violent manifestation is at least partially dependent upon the coercive capabilities of the regime.

Political legitimacy is another intervening factor in the model. If a regime is perceived to be "legitimate"—holding power on the basis of established (and accepted) legal procedure (and thereby deserving of at least tacit support) —then this is likely to inhibit the tendency toward violent opposition (Gurr 1968, 1106). In other words, if people view their government as lawful, only strong countervailing pressures will impel them to attempt to remove the regime through violence.

The sixth factor presumed to influence levels of strife is institutionalization (Gurr 1970, 274). Discontent leads to civil violence only when focused on political objects and when weakly established institutional frameworks provide minimal support for peaceful methods of conflict resolution. In other words, the degree to which political structures have acquired value and stability should mitigate the pressures that lead to political conflict. As Huntington (1968) has noted, the presence of strong institutions that direct discontent through nonviolent channels are elements that contribute to political stability.

The last factor in the model focuses upon organizational and environmental elements that might prove conducive to mass violence. Gurr terms this factor "social/structural facilitation" (1968, 1106). For example, it has been argued that manifest political conflict depends, at least in part, upon the presence of an organizational infrastructure— intermediate political, social, and occupational groups—to focus and direct mass discontent (Korpi 1974, 1576).

As is evident in the preceding theoretical discussion, Gurr's basic framework (1968) describes the associations expected to hold between the causal elements of the model and political conflict. However, the theoretical model is incomplete because the internal linkages among the predictors have not been specified, nor have their appropriate temporal positions been assigned. Nevertheless, certain fundamental relationships among the predictors can be rather easily designated.

For example, nations with long standing traditions of violent political conflict are not likely to evolve regimes that exercise power on the basis of established legal procedures, nor are they likely to possess governments that wield considerable physical power over their populations. Clearly, the presence of legitimate regimes is at least in part determined by the existence of preestablished patterns of peaceful political succession. In short, recent histories of violent political upheaval presage weak governments of questionable lawfulness.

Similarly, the relationship between the two types of economic deprivation ("persistent" and "short term") should be negative, since they are indicative of different systemic development levels. Persisting deprivation is generally a characteristic of economic underdevelopment, whereas short term deprivation is generally a syndrome found in more highly modernized economies. Moreover, since severe, widespread poverty is likely to be associated with underdevelopment, intermediate organizational structures will probably be weak or nonexistent in nations evidencing this form of deprivation. On the other hand, countries manifesting short term economic reversals (characterized by the combination of sagging growth rates and high inflation rates) are likely to be at a more advanced stage of industrial development and hence possess at least the rudiments of a complex organizational infrastructure. Persisting deprivation might also be expected to show a positive association to the coercive force potential of regimes, insofar as the limited resources of a poverty-stricken population might enhance the relative physical power of the central government.

Additional negative linkages may be hypothesized to exist between the force potential of regimes and both legitimacy and institutionalization since coercive regimes might be expected to rule primarily through fear rather than allegiance, which also obviates the need to create intricate processes for the settlement of political disputes.

Lastly, a positive linkage between legitimacy and institutionalization might be anticipated, since political systems that transfer power according to established legal procedure are likely to endure long enough for stable and valued political structures to evolve. (A formal statement of these hypotheses and an explanation for the temporal location of each factor is provided in Appendix A.)

This sociopolitical model of conflict includes two exogenous and six endogenous elements and can be described by the system of eight hierarchical equations depicted in Table 2-1. The factor designations are as follows:

*Exogenous Factors*

$X_1$ = Historical Instability

$X_{2,t-1}$ = Persisting Deprivation

*Endogenous Factors*

$Y_{1,t-1}$ = Coercive Force Potential

$Y_{2,t}$ = Political Legitimacy

$Y_{3,t}$ = Short Term Deprivation

$Y_{4,t}$ = Institutionalization

$Y_{5,t}$ = Social/Structural Facilitation

$Y_{6,t}$ = Political Conflict

This pretest model incorporates the set of factors presumed to affect levels of civil violence. The model utilizes

TABLE 2-1. Pretest Structural Equations for the Conflict Model

---

(1)  $X_1$ (Historical Instability) = $\mu_1$

(2)  $X_{2,t-1}$ (Persisting Deprivation) = $\mu_2$

(3)  $Y_{1,t-1}$ (Coercive Force Potential) = $\alpha_1$ - $\beta_1 X_1$ (Historical Instability)
+ $\beta_2 X_{2,t-1}$ (Persisting Deprivation) + $\mu_3$

(4)  $Y_{2,t}$ (Political Legitimacy) = $\alpha_2$ - $\beta_3 X_1$ (Historical Instability) -
$\beta_4 Y_{1,t-1}$ (Coercive Force Potential) + $\mu_4$

(5)  $Y_{3,t}$ (Short Term Deprivation) = $\alpha_3$ - $\beta_5 X_{2,t-1}$ (Persisting
Deprivation) + $\mu_5$

(6)  $Y_{4,t}$ (Institutionalization) = $\alpha_4$ - $\beta_6 Y_{1,t-1}$ (Coercive Force
Potential) + $\beta_7 Y_{2,t}$ (Political Legitimacy) + $\mu_6$

(7)  $Y_{5,t}$ (Social/Structural Facilitation) = $\alpha_5$ - $\beta_8 X_{2,t-1}$) (Persisting
Deprivation) + $\beta_9 Y_{3,t}$ (Short Term Deprivation) + $\mu_7$

(8)  $Y_{6,t}$ (Political Conflict) = $\alpha_6$ + $\beta_{10} X_1$ (Historical Instability) -
$\beta_{11} X_{2,t-1}$ (Persisting Deprivation) - $\beta_{12} Y_{1,t-1}$ (Coercive Force
Potential) - $\beta_{13} Y_{2,t}$ (Political Legitimacy) + $\beta_{14} Y_{3,t}$ (Short Term
Deprivation) - $\beta_{15} Y_{4,t}$ (Institutionalization) + $\beta_{16} Y_{5,t}$
(Social/Structural Facilitation) + $\mu_8$

---

$\beta_1$ . . . $\beta_{16}$ = Slope

$\alpha_1$ . . . $\alpha_6$ = Intercept

$\mu_1$ . . . $\mu_8$ = Disturbance Term

t . . . t-1 = Temporal Position

Source: Compiled by the authors.

time lags and specifies the anticipated associations between each of the predictors and conflict, as well as the hierarchical arrangements among them. However, before the model can be tested, adjusted (if necessary), and applied as a forecasting instrument, empirical indicators of the eight principal elements had to be developed.

Development of Indicators

Creating indicators for the constructs in this model presents certain problems. Foremost is the fact that all of the elements in this model (with the exceptions of the historical instability and political conflict factors) cannot be directly measured but rather must be inferred from the presence or absence of other phenomena (Gurr 1968, 1106). Since these constructs are high order abstractions, it was deemed preferable to use multiple measures in the development of each indicator. Given this strategy, factor analysis provides the most efficient technique for the construction of scales reflecting each of the basic theoretical elements. Hence, sets of candidate measures for each construct were factored separately, and composite factor scales were computed for seven of the eight basic elements in the model.

Since the factoring procedure was utilized here for the purposes of scaling rather than for exploration or classification (Rummel 1970, 29–32) no matrices are reproduced. Each set of candidate measures was comprised of variables deemed a priori to represent some aspect of the underlying construct. Several hundred oblique terminal solutions were then examined in an effort to produce single solutions that best reflected each construct. Weights were derived for each variable in the rotated terminal solutions for their integration into the factor. The weights themselves are based upon the variation that the element has in common with the given factor. When variables are combined in terms of these weights, factor scores are produced (Rummel 1970, 30). Table 2-2 shows the composition of the indicators with the weights of their components.

The only element in the model constructed in a different fashion was historical instability. Since this indicator should not reflect year-to-year changes, historical tradition of political violence was measured by an additive index composed of the numbers of strikes, riots, demonstrations, assassinations, incidents of guerrilla warfare, government crises, and coups d'état. Data was collected for the 19-year span (1946–64) immediately prior to the temporal period analyzed in this study (1965–78). Values on each of the component measures for each state were summed, combined in a single index, and then treated as national "constants" in the subsequent analysis.

A few words are also in order regarding the measurement of political conflict. Studies of civil violence have employed various methods for categorizing and measuring this general phenomenon. For example, the "magnitude" of political conflict may be treated in terms of its "extent" (for example, number of events, man-days of participation) or its "intensity" (for example, deaths due to civil violence).[4] In addition, many studies have attempted to distinguish among "types" of conflict (for example, protest, rebellion, subversion, turmoil, internal war).[5] However, there is no general consensus as to what constitutes the most appropriate means for measuring civil violence or as to the typologizing of its various manifestations. Indeed, many analyses note the empirical blurring of conflict "classes" (Fenmore and Volgy 1978, 554; Gurr 1968, 1117; Gurr and Duvall 1976, 144; Lichbach and Gurr 1979, 12–14) and thus cast doubt on the utility of such typologies. As a result, numerous empirical studies of civil violence employ simple "summary measures" of conflict magnitude.

A similar research strategy was followed in this project, where a set of "conflict events" variables were factor analyzed and combined to form a summary indicator on the basis of the weighted factor-score coefficients. The variables that loaded positively at .50 or above in the terminal solution were: antigovernment strikes (.74), riots (.61), political demonstrations (.57), assassinations (.65), guerrilla warfare (.73), and government crises (.71). (The rotated factor loadings of these variables are indicated in the parentheses.) These individual measures basically cover the spectrum of political conflict, and therefore a composite indicator based upon their weighted empirical patterning was deemed an appropriate summary measure of their general phenomenon.

Twenty major Latin American nations were chosen as the project sample. A time-series data base composed of approximately sixteen thousand entries on more than 60 ratio and interval-level measures was compiled for the analysis. Information on each variable was collected for the 14-year period of 1965–78, with each nation-year constituting a discrete data point.[6] However, as a result of the lagging of some indicators, the maximum N was 260. Random missing data further reduced the N to 214. All findings are based on at least this minimum number of cases.

## PRELIMINARY RESULTS

An intercorrelation matrix of the composite indicators with their designated time lags was computed with the following results: Propositions 1 through 7 (see Appendix A) were supported by the zero-order correlations, all of which were statistically significant at the .001 level. The coefficients

TABLE 2-2. Composition of Indicators (1965-78)

Composite factor-score variables were computed for each of the following seven constructs based upon rotated oblique factor solutions. The complete estimation method was utilized in this operation, employing a weighted coefficient for each variable in the factor matrix. Weak-loading variables were used as suppression measures to obtain the best estimate for each factor. The most heavily weighted (central) components are reported here.

| | Scaling | Source* | N | Factor-Score Coefficient |
|---|---|---|---|---|
| Construct 1: Political Conflict | | | | |
| (a) Number of strikes | 0 | A,G | 280 | .22124 |
| (b) Number of riots | 0 | A,G | 280 | .18448 |
| (c) Number of anitgovernment demonstrations | 0 | A,G | 280 | .16142 |
| (d) Number of assassinations | 0 | A,G | 280 | .19166 |
| (e) Incidents of guerrilla warfare | 0 | A,G | 280 | .21128 |
| (f) Government crises | 0 | A,G | 280 | .22002 |
| Construct 2: Persistent Deprivation | | | | |
| (a) Gini income distribution | .0001 | A,N,Q,R,U | 250 | .25533 |
| (b) Energy consumption in kilograms per capita | 0 | A,Q | 251 | -.22539 |
| (c) GNP per capita in constant U.S. dollars | 0 | H,S | 253 | -.22192 |
| (d) Telephones per capita | .00001 | A,Q | 271 | -.24520 |
| (e) Percentage of population literate | .1 | A | 280 | -.25818 |
| Construct 3: Short Term Deprivation | | | | |
| (a) Consumer prices--general indices | 0 | H,Q | 274 | .33528 |
| (b) Wholesale prices--general indices | 0 | H,Q | 274 | .30606 |
| (c) Percent annual change in inflation rate | .1 | H,N,Q | 271 | .24223 |

44

| | | | | |
|---|---|---|---|---|
| (d) Percent annual change in currency in circulation per capita | .01 | A,H | 280 | .28785 |
| **Construct 4: Coercive Force Potential** | | | | |
| (a) Armed forces per 1,000 population | .1 | F,L,S | 280 | .28330 |
| (b) Military influence in government | 0 | D,E,T,U | 280 | .36321 |
| (c) Regime centrality | 0 | D | 280 | .49321 |
| **Construct 5: Political Legitimacy** | | | | |
| (a) Media freedom index | 0 | D,N,O,T,U | 280 | .26279 |
| (b) Party legitimacy | 0 | A,D | 280 | .26062 |
| (c) Mode of executive selection | 0 | A | 280 | .23090 |
| (d) Independence of labor organizations | 0 | C,D,M,T,U | 280 | .22389 |
| **Construct 6: Institutionalization** | | | | |
| (a) Degree of parliamentary effectiveness | 0 | A | 280 | .48236 |
| (b) Degree of parliamentary responsibility | 0 | A | 280 | .46042 |
| (c) National government expenditures per capita | .01 | A,H,M,Q,R | 279 | .24181 |
| **Construct 7: Social/Structure Faciliation** | | | | |
| (a) Registered voters as a percentage of population | .001 | A,B,J,U | 276 | .35472 |
| (b) Votes cast in most recent election as a percentage of population | .001 | A,B,J,U | 276 | .36266 |
| (c) Unionization as a percentage of total labor force | .001 | I,M,U | 280 | .22066 |
| (d) Primary and secondary school enrollment per capita | .0001 | A,K | 271 | .20882 |

*Source Code: See Appendix B.
<u>Source</u>: Compiled by the author.

45

ranged from a high of .527 (Proposition 1) to a low of -.230 (Proposition 3). All sub-propositions with the exception of S-P 6 ($Y_{1,t-1} \gtrless Y_{2,t}$) similarly found support in the data. The coefficient for S-P 6 indicated the expected directionality, but lacked statistical significance.

An estimate of the combined predictive power of all the causal elements in the system was then computed using a simple multiple regression model. The basic equation is:

$$PC_t = \alpha + \sum_{i=1}^{n} \beta_i Y_t + \sum_{j=1}^{m} \beta_j X_{t-1} + \beta HI + \mu$$

where $PC_t$ is political conflict at time t, $y_t$ is the set i predictors at time t, $x_{t-1}$ is the set j predictors at time t-1, HI is the historical instability value, $\beta$ is the slope, $\alpha$ is the intercept, and $\mu$ is the disturbance term. The multiple R for the simple regression model was .705, providing an $R_2$ of .498.[7]

By utilizing causal modeling technique (Asher 1976), path estimates were obtained for each of the equations in Table 2-1. Of the six equations involving effects on endogenous factors (Equations 3 through 8), three were supported (Equations 3, 4, and 7) and three required revision (Equations 5, 6, and 8). Equation 5 (Short Term Deprivation) failed to include an estimated value for political legitimacy. Apparently the level of short term deprivation is a function both of persisting deprivation and the legitimacy of the regime. These latter two factors are negatively associated with brief economic downturns and produce statistically significant path estimates. Actually, the strong negative path between legitimacy and short term deprivation is not altogether surprising since legitimate regimes, whose tenure largely depends upon the continuation of public support, are not likely to promote economic policies that create hardship for major portions of the population. Equation 6 (Institutionalization) failed to include an estimate for persisting deprivation, which reveals a significant negative path value to institutionalization. In other words, nations suffering from long term poverty are not likely to evolve highly institutionalized political systems. Equation 8 (Political Conflict) required the most revision. Due to interdependencies among the predictors, the direct effects of persisting deprivation, coercive force potential, and legitimacy on political conflict assume negligible proportions. These factors remain important to the sociopolitical model, but are clearly less salient as proximate predictors of conflict.

Figure 2-1 depicts the data-corrected model of conflict linkages. This adjusted model can be described by the following system of eight hierarchical equations (which may be compared with the pretest equations in Table 2-1):

(1.1) $X_1 = \mu_1$

(2.1) $X_{2,t-1} = \mu_2$

(3.1) $Y_{1,t-1} = \alpha_1 - \beta_1 X_1 + \beta_2 X_{2,t-1} + \mu_3$

(4.1) $Y_{2,t} = \alpha_2 - \beta_3 X_1 - \beta_4 Y_{1,t-1} + \mu_4$

(5.1) $Y_{3,t} = \alpha_3 - \beta_5 X_{2,t-1} - \beta_6 Y_{2,t} + \mu_5$

(6.1) $Y_{4,t} = \alpha_4 - \beta_7 X_{2,t-1} - \beta_8 Y_{1,t-1} + \beta_9 Y_{2,t} + \mu_6$

(7.1) $Y_{5,t} = \alpha_5 - \beta_{10} X_{2,t-1} + \beta_{11} Y_{3,t} + \mu_7$

(8.1) $Y_{6,t} = \alpha_6 + \beta_{12} X_1 + \beta_{13} Y_{3,t} - \beta_{14} Y_{4,t} + \beta_{15} Y_{5,t} + \mu_8$

The final equation in this model, using only four predictors, provides a multiple R for political conflict of .695 and an $R_2$ of .483. When this is compared with the $R_2$ for the simple regression model (.498), it is evident that there is a loss of only 1.5 percent of explained variance while at the same time three predictors have been trimmed from the final equation. In short, the adjusted model accounts for almost 50 percent of the variance in political conflict in Latin America.

## FORECASTING POLITICAL CONFLICT

At this stage the model may be used to generate forecasts of conflict levels for specific nations as well as general predictions for the entire Latin American region. By employing Equation 8.1 (which specifies only the factors with direct effects on civil violence) a "predicted" conflict score can be computed for any nation in any given year. If this predicted score is subtracted from the actual (or "observed") conflict score for the same nation in the same year then a residual value (either positive or negative) remains—indicating the error of prediction (Cutright 1963, 577–78). Table 2-3 shows the results of this process for the mean values for 1965 through 1977, and for 1977 alone.[8] One method of determining the accuracy of the predictions based on Equation 8.1 is to calculate the "root mean square error" of the forecasts:

Figure 2-1. Model of Conflict Linkage

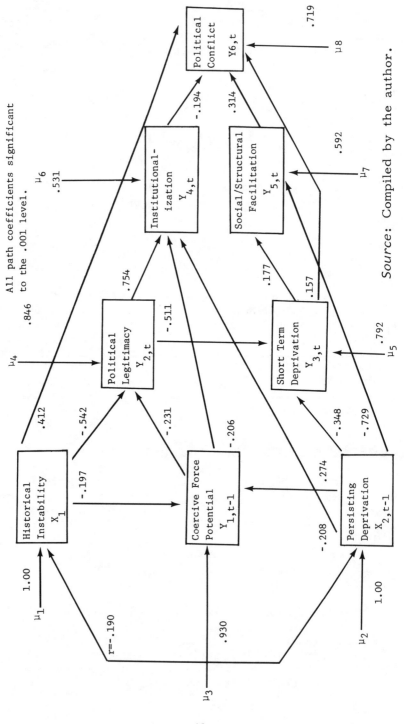

All path coefficients significant to the .001 level.

*Source:* Compiled by the author.

48

TABLE 2-3. Analysis of Residuals

| | Political Conflict 1965-77 | | | Political Conflict 1977 | | |
|---|---|---|---|---|---|---|
| Countries | Mean Observed Conflict | Mean Predicted Conflict | Mean Residual | Observed Conflict | Predicted Conflict | Residual |
| Argentina | 2.6537 | 2.3340 | .3197 | .6845 | 2.8356 | -2.1511 |
| Bolivia | .1153 | .2701 | -.1548 | -.6307 | .3668 | -.9975 |
| Brazil | 1.0591 | 1.2369 | -.1778 | 1.3930 | 1.7095 | -.3165 |
| Chile | .6049 | .4556 | .1493 | -.3396 | 1.7004 | -2.0400 |
| Colombia | .1533 | .1668 | -.0135 | .4020 | .4870 | -.0850 |
| Costa Rica | -.6147 | -.5024 | -.1123 | -.6215 | -.5614 | -.0601 |
| Dominican Republic | -.1950 | -.0434 | -.1516 | -.6076 | -.1205 | -.4871 |
| Ecuador | -.2865 | -.3200 | .0335 | -.4338 | -.2473 | -.1865 |
| El Salvador | -.5384 | -.8178 | .2344 | -.6395 | -.8093 | .1698 |
| Guatemala | -.0287 | -.2723 | .2436 | -.0547 | -.0642 | -.1189 |
| Guyana | -.5797 | -.6003 | .0206 | -.6516 | -.6336 | -.0180 |
| Haiti | -.5257 | -.5877 | .0620 | -.6548 | -.4711 | -.1837 |
| Honduras | -.5734 | -.7036 | .1302 | -.4670 | -.7836 | .3166 |
| Mexico | .6750 | .5695 | .1055 | .6180 | .9588 | -.3408 |
| Nicaragua | -.5702 | -.4646 | -.1056 | -.4989 | -.4225 | -.0764 |
| Panama | -.4595 | -.1490 | -.3105 | -.6310 | .0146 | -.6456 |
| Paraguay | -.5747 | -.3300 | -.2447 | -.6429 | -.3147 | -.3282 |
| Peru | -.1046 | -.2517 | .1471 | .7604 | -.0615 | .8219 |
| Uruguay | .1491 | -.0798 | .2289 | -.5755 | .1446 | -.7201 |
| Venezuela | -.2495 | .2808 | -.5303 | -.2799 | .3391 | -.6190 |
| Root Mean Square Error | | .2103 | | | .7926 | |

Prediction Equation: Political Conflict, $Y_{6,t} = -.6335$ (constant) $+ .0172$ (Historical Instability, $X_1$) $+ .2074$ (Short Term Deprivation, $Y_{3,t}$) $- .2124$ (Institutionalization, $Y_{4,t}$) $+ .3641$ (Social/Structural Facilitation, $Y_{5,t}$)

Source: Compiled by the author.

$$RMSE_f = [T^{-1} \Sigma (O_t - P_t)^2]^{1/2}$$

where RMSE$_f$ is the root mean square error of the forecasts, O is the observed conflict score, P is the predicted conflict score, and T is the number of forecasts. The value of the RMSE$_f$ indicates the degree of dispersion around the line of perfect forecasts; the closer the value is to zero, the less the overall error of prediction (Klein 1974, 442–44).

The nations in Table 2-3 that show positive residual values evidenced more conflict than was predicted by Equation 8.1; those countries with negative residuals experienced less conflict than was predicted by their four-factor profile. Cutright (1963, 580–81) has argued that the magnitude and direction of these residual values may be interpreted as an indicator of systemic tension. Since states that evidence negative residuals are exhibiting less conflict than was forecast on the basis of their other attributes, it may be reasonable to assume that they are experiencing system wide stress and have a high potential for civil violence in the near future. The states with the largest negative residuals for 1977 are Argentina (-2.1511), Chile (-2.0400), Bolivia (-.9975), Uruguay (-.7201), and Panama (-.6456). A "regional" forecasts can also be derived from Equation 8.1. Given that only nine states show negative mean residuals for the period of 1965 through 1977, whereas seventeen show negative residuals for 1977 alone, this may be interpreted as an indication that the violence potential in the Latin American region is increasing.

Up to this point, the only measure of forecast accuracy for the conflict model is the RMSE$_f$. As might be expected (see Table 2-3), there is less overall prediction error when the entire temporal period for the region is examined (.2103) than when only a single year is considered (.7926). However, since the RMSE$_f$ is a nonparametric measure, it provides no means of assessing a *single* model's forecast accuracy. In other words, judgments regarding the RMSE$_f$ can only be made comparatively—by juxtaposing the RMSE$_f$ of two or more contending or alternative theoretical models. If alternative theoretical models are unavailable (or are impractical to employ due to data constraints), a determination of model forecast accuracy can still be made by comparing the accuracy of the model's predictions against that of a mechanistic atheoretical alternative (Ostrom 1978, 66). The most widely used of such alternatives is the naive model test, whereby the prediction errors of one model are compared with those of a mechanistic "naive" model. If the substantive forecasting model can produce smaller prediction errors than the naive alternative, then its forecasts can be considered at least minimally adequate (Christ 1966, 572).

In essence, the naive model rests on a "no-change" assumption—"same today as yesterday." Formally, this model establishes the value at time t equal to the value at time t-1 "plus a random normal disturbance term with a zero mean and a constant but unknown variance" (Ostrom 1978, 67). The equation takes this form:

$$Y_t = Y_{t-1} + \mu_t$$

If the disturbance term is eliminated the naive model forecast is

$$Y_t = Y_{t-1}$$

Obviously the naive model does not constitute a scientific theory or explanation of anything, and therefore cannot be seriously considered as an adequate predictive instrument, but it does provide an objective criterion of comparison for determining the adequacy of a theoretical model's forecasts. Indeed, the goal of scientific inquiry is to understand the uniformities underlying given classes of phenomena. Theories attempt to explain such patterns and to provide a more fundamental understanding of the processes and entities in the physical world (Hempel 1966, 70). One means of testing theoretical models is to determine how well they predict occurrences that they purport to explain. No real confidence can be placed in theories or models (that is, explanations) that fail the test of prediction. All theoretical models presume to have identified the fundamental forces that account for change in the physical world. The question is whether a given model is at least minimally better than a formulation that says there are no forces underlying change. The naive model, which states that "the value of each variable next year will be identical with its value this year, is precisely such a [formulation]; it denies . . . the existence of any forces making for change from one year to the next" (Friedman 1951, 109). If a theoretical model can produce predictions of no greater accuracy than such a formulation, then by implication it fails to incorporate the fundamental forces underlying change, and it is of no utility as a scientific theory.

Once forecasts have been produced and their accuracies determined by computing the $RMSE_f$, the adequacy of the substantive theoretical model relative to that of the naive model can be assessed by calculating an accuracy ratio:

$$\frac{RMSE \text{ theory}}{RMSE \text{ naive}}$$

An accuracy ratio of less than 1.00 indicates that the prediction error of the theoretical model is smaller than that of the naive model. In other words, if the accuracy ratio is less than 1.00, the theoretical model is more accurate than its naive counterpart; if the accuracy ratio is equal to or greater than 1.00, the theoretical model is less adequate than the naive formulation. As Ostrom (1978, 68) notes, if the forecasts of a theoretical model have been shown to be more accurate than its naive alternative, then the substantive model can be tentatively accepted as an efficient forecasting instrument.

Table 2-4 depicts a comparison of the forecast accuracies of the theoretical (that is, hierarchical) and naive models of political conflict broken down by countries. Of the 20 Latin American nations in the sample, the accuracy ratios of the hierarchical model are superior to those of the naive model in 14 cases. Of the six cases where the naive model produced more efficient forecasts, two (El Salvador and Honduras) had seven or less complete observations due to missing data and were therefore underweighted in the calculation of the prediction equation. (Nicaragua had only eight complete observations, but produced a marginally superior accuracy score for the hierarchical model.)

Although the overall accuracy ratio of the hierarchical model indicates that it is an acceptable forecasting instrument, the country-by-country variation in its success raises some interesting questions. For example, are there different longitudinal "conflict patterns" that affect the forecasting accuracy of the model? Similarly, if multiple conflict patterns exist, are these longitudinal patterns associated with particular national attributes? If so, then it is possible that different forecasting models may be more aptly suited to predicting specific conflict patterns likely to be associated with particular types of states.

Table 2-5 indicates country classifications on the basis of system-type, variance of observed conflict, longitudinal conflict pattern, and most efficient predictor. Regarding the first column, contemporary Latin American political systems may be classified with minimal distortion through a four-fold typology: democratic, traditional-authoritarian,

TABLE 2-4. Two-Model Comparison of Forecast Accuracy (1965-77)

| Countries | $RMSE_f$ Naive Model | $RMSE_f$ Hierarchical Model | Accuracy Ratio | Number of Observations |
|---|---|---|---|---|
| Argentina | 2.7172 | 2.4255 | .8926 | 12 |
| Bolivia | 1.1866 | .8524 | .7183 | 13 |
| Brazil | .8250 | .6943 | .8415 | 13 |
| Chile | .9722 | .9404 | .9672 | 12 |
| Colombia | .5513 | .4680 | .8489 | 13 |
| Costa Rica | .0798 | .2483 | 3.1115 | 13 |
| Dominican Republic | .5114 | .4710 | .9210 | 13 |
| Ecuador | .5627 | .3801 | .6754 | 13 |
| El Salvador | .1352 | .2697 | 1.9948 | 7 |
| Guatemala | 1.0961 | .8451 | .7710 | 13 |
| Guyana | .1866 | .1430 | .7663 | 11 |
| Haiti | .2143 | .3027 | 1.4125 | 13 |
| Honduras | .1274 | .2947 | 2.3131 | 6 |
| Mexico | 1.1450 | .7945 | .6938 | 12 |
| Nicaragua | .1521 | .1492 | .9809 | 8 |
| Panama | .5658 | .5168 | .9133 | 10 |
| Paraguay | .1220 | .2849 | 2.3352 | 13 |
| Peru | .5190 | .4621 | .8903 | 13 |
| Uruguay | .7775 | .6654 | .8558 | 13 |
| Venezuela | .2682 | .5651 | 2.1070 | 13 |
| Overall Accuracy Ratio | | | .9259 | |

$$RMSE_f = [T^{-1} \Sigma(O_t - P_t)^2]^{1/2}$$

$$\text{Accuracy Ration} = \frac{RMSE_{hm}}{RMSE_{nm}}$$

Source: Compiled by the author.

53

military populist, and bureaucratic-authoritarian.[9]  These categories highlight variations among systems principally in terms of levels of mass political activation and regime orientation toward political participation.  Of major importance is whether the regime is "incorporating" (one that intentionally seeks to broaden the scope of political participation), or "exclusionary" (one that seeks to severely limit the scope of participation in the political processes). Similarly, the typology differentiates among system-types with politically "mobilized" populations and those with "inert" or politically uninvolved populations (O'Donnell 1973, 53–55).  In essence, the typology—with sub-categories—is as follows:

| System Type | Participation | Activation |
|---|---|---|
| • Democratic: | incorporating | mobilized |
| • Traditional-Authoritarian: | exclusionary | inert |
| • Military Populist: | incorporating | inert |
| • Bureaucratic-Authoritarian: | exclusionary | mobilized |

The second column in Table 2-5—variance of observed conflict—is based on each nation's factor-score values for 1965 through 1977.  The variance figures have been divided into three clusters (large, moderate, and small) to facilitate comparison.  The third column—conflict pattern—is based upon a comparative examination of the longitudinal patterns created by the yearly conflict values for each nation. Three general longitudinal patterns were in evidence: Class I (explosive, short burst conflict of high magnitude); Class II (semistable conflict levels of moderate magnitude); and Class III (stable conflict levels of low magnitude).  The last column—predictor—indicates the most efficient forecasting model.

A number of interesting observations may be derived from Table 2-5.  Seven countries exhibit Class I longitudinal conflict patterns and all of these manifest high levels of conflict variance.  In terms of system-type, this group includes all five bureaucratic-authoritarian regimes and two unstable traditional-authoritarian systems. Bureaucratic-authoritarian regimes tend to appear at a rather advanced stage of socioeconomic development (O'Donnell 1973; Geller 1982a) where high levels of social mobilization are also present; the regimes are "exclusionary" but must deal with politically active populations.  These systems have been described as "pressure cookers" since

TABLE 2-5. Country Classifications (1965-77)

| Countries | System-Type* | Variance of Observed Conflict† | Longitudinal Conflict Pattern▽ | Most Efficient Predictor |
|---|---|---|---|---|
| Argentina | DEM/B-A√ | Large | Class I | Hierarchical |
| Bolivia | TRAD | Large | Class I | Hierarchical |
| Brazil | B-A | Large | Class I | Hierarchical |
| Chile | DEM/B-A√ | Large | Class I | Hierarchical |
| Colombia | DEM | Moderate | Class II | Hierarchical |
| Costa Rica | DEM | Small | Class III | Naïve |
| Dominican Republic | DEM | Moderate | Class II | Hierarchical |
| Ecuador | TRAD | Moderate | Class II | Hierarchical |
| El Salvador | TRAD | Small | Class III | Naïve° |
| Guatemala | DEM | Large | Class I | Hierarchical |
| Guyana | TRAD | Small | Class III | Hierarchical |
| Haiti | TRAD | Small | Class III | Naïve° |
| Honduras | TRAD | Small | Class III | Naïve° |
| Mexico | B-A | Large | Class I | Hierarchical |
| Nicaragua | TRAD | Small | Class III | Hierarchical° |
| Panama | TRAD | Moderate | Class II | Hierarchical |
| Paraguay | TRAD | Small | Class III | Naïve |
| Peru | MP | Moderate | Class II | Hierarchical |
| Uruguay | DEM/B-A√ | Large | Class I | Hierarchical |
| Venezuela | DEM | Small | Class III | Naïve |

*System-Type:  B-A = Bureaucratic-Authoritarian; DEM = Democratic; MP = Military Populist;
 TRAD = Traditional-Authoritarian

†Variance: Large = maximum - .2800; Moderate = .2799 - .1400; Small = .1399 - 0.0000

▽Conflict Pattern:   Class I    --explosive, short-burst conflict, high magnitude
 Class II   --semistable conflict levels, moderate magnitude
 Class III -- stable conflict levels, low magnitude

√System-type changed during period

°Missing data

Source: Compiled by author.

55

they attempt to deactivate or encapsulate large social co-
alitions that are demanding greater influence in the
decision making structures of the system (O'Donnell 1973,
1977; Kaufman 1975, 1979; Collier 1978). Hence these
states are subject to sporadic outbursts of large scale
political violence. The hierarchical model is the most
efficient predictor of Class I conflict patterns (see Figures
2-2 and 2-3).

Five countries exhibit Class II longitudinal conflict
patterns and all of these indicate moderate levels of conflict
variance. With regard to system-type, this is a rather
diversified group: two shaky democracies, one military
populist system, and two traditional-authoritarian systems.
These nations all exhibit semistable conflict patterns of
moderate magnitude. In terms of socioeconomic development, these states generally cluster in the middle range of
the Latin American spectrum for 1965 through 1977 (Banks
1981, 402) and their regimes must deal with populations that
are becoming increasingly mobilized. Those systems that
are "incorporating" (Colombia, Dominican Republic, and
Peru) may prove capable of modulating this pressure,
whereas the "exclusionary" systems (Ecuador and Panama)
are perhaps more likely to move to a Class I pattern. The
hierarchical model is the most efficient predictor of Class II
conflict patterns as well (see Figures 2-4 and 2-5).

Eight countries exhibit Class III longitudinal conflict
patterns and all of these indicate low levels of conflict
variance for 1965 through 1977. Unfortunately, three of
these nations (Nicaragua, Honduras, and El Salvador) were
missing large amounts of data (eight or less valid observations on each) and were therefore underweighted in the
calculation of the prediction equation. Of the remaining
five nations, three are stable democracies and two are
stable traditional-authoritarian systems. Conflict magnitude
is uniformly low in these countries and the yearly values
are steady. As a result the naive model is the most efficient predictor in four out of these five cases (see Figures
2-6 and 2-7).


CONCLUSION

This chapter has described the attempt to develop a multi-
stage sociopolitical model of civil strife and to apply the
model as a forecasting instrument for 20 Latin American
nations. The pretest equations for the model were adjusted
on the basis of a path analysis of conflict linkages for 1965
through 1978, a new data-corrected model of linkages was

developed, and a prediction equation computed. This hierarchical model was then tested against a mechanistic atheoretical alternative—a "naive model"—in an effort to determine its effectiveness as a predictor of political violence. Although the hierarchical model was superior to its "naive" counterpart in most instances, its variability as an efficient forecasting instrument led to an analysis of longitudinal conflict patterns among the states in the sample. Three temporal patterns of violent political conflict were discovered. Class I conflict patterns were explosive, short burst manifestations of high magnitude violence. These patterns were generally associated with highly modernized states possessing exclusionary political systems. The hierarchical model was clearly the best predictor of this pattern.

Class II conflict patterns were semistable manifestations of violence at moderate magnitude levels. Countries that exhibited this pattern generally had shaky democratic regimes or traditional-authoritarian governments. Moreover, these states were in the middle range of the socioeconomic spectrum and their regimes were beginning to confront pressure from previously politically inert populations. The future conflict levels in these countries may well depend upon whether the systems adapt to include these new social forces within their political processes or attempt to exclude them from participation. The hierarchical model was also the most efficient predictor of this pattern.

Class III conflict patterns were composed of highly uniform yearly values of low magnitude. Three of five Latin American democracies and two stable traditional-authoritarian regimes fell within this group. Four of the five countries in this set (for which uninterrupted data was available) tended toward the lower end of the socioeconomic spectrum. The exception (Venezuela) has avoided severe short term economic disruption through its control of vast petroleum resources. Since these nations exhibited stable year-to-year conflict scores, the naive model was the most efficient predictor in the majority of these cases.

In sum, the conflict potential of the Latin American region appears to be increasing primarily as a result of the pressures created by socioeconomic development.[10] General longitudinal patterns of conflict do exist, and forecasting models tend to predict certain patterns more efficiently than others. This finding suggests the possibility of designing forecasting models that are highly sensitive to particular conflict patterns. For policy-making purposes, since it is easier to predict the occurrence of violent political behavior than to forecast its outcome (for example, suppression;

Figure 2-2. Class I Conflict Pattern (Brazil 1965-77): Observed Versus Predicted Scores

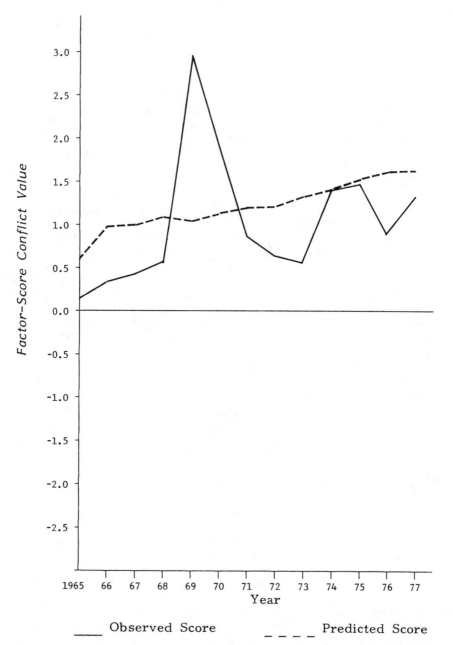

_Source_: Compiled by author.

Figure 2-3.   Class I Conflict Pattern (Bolivia 1965-77): Observed Versus Predicted Scores

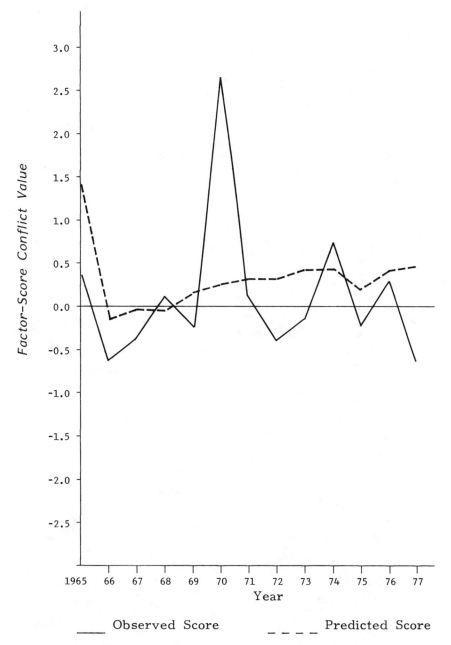

_____ Observed Score          _ _ _ _ Predicted Score

*Source*: Compiled by author.

Figure 2-4.  Class II Conflict Pattern (Peru 1965-77): Observed Versus Predicted Scores

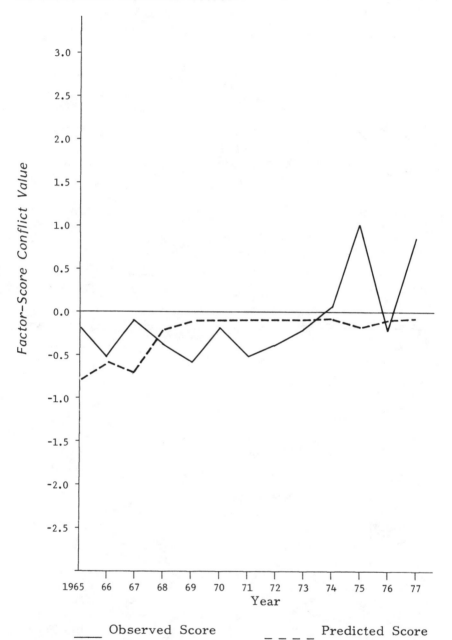

_Source_: Compiled by author.

Figure 2-5.   Class II Conflict Pattern (Colombia 1965-77): Observed Versus Predicted Scores

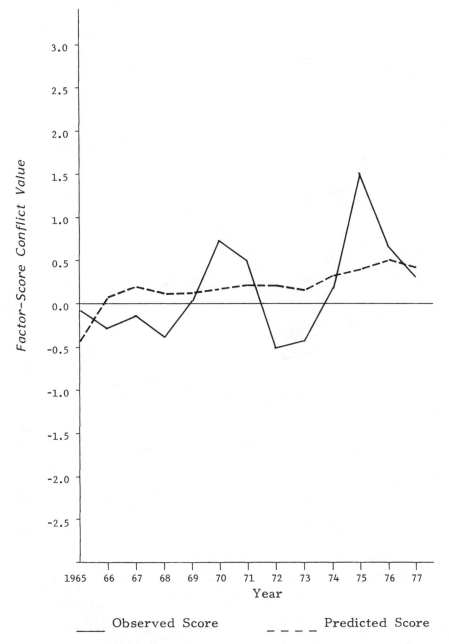

_____ Observed Score          _ _ _ _ Predicted Score

*Source*: Compiled by author.

Figure 2-6. Class III Conflict Pattern (Costa Rica 1965-77): Observed Versus Predicted Scores

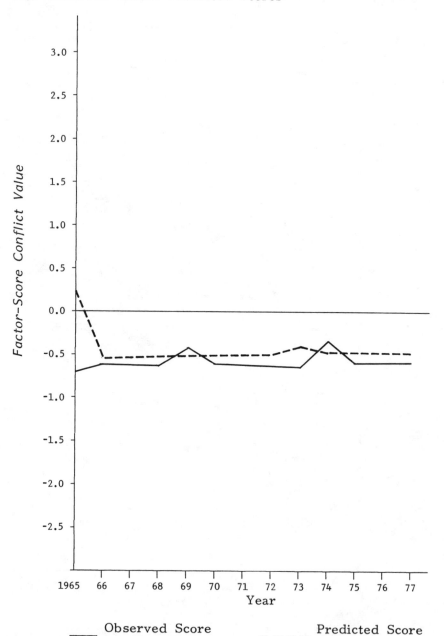

_____ Observed Score      _ _ _ _ Predicted Score

*Source*: Compiled by author.

Figure 2-7. Class III Conflict Pattern (Haiti 1965-77): Observed Versus Predicted Scores

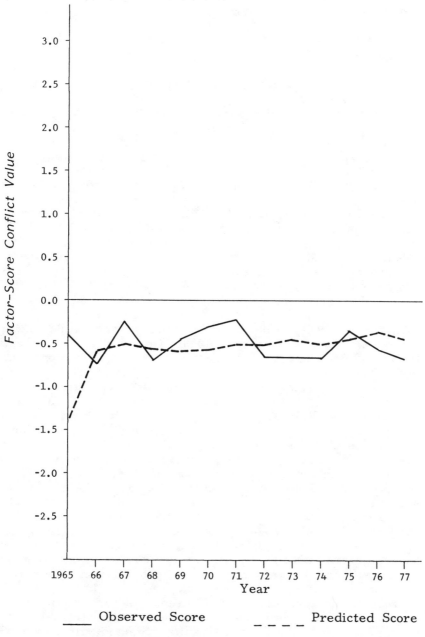

Source: Compiled by author.

relaxation of social, economic, or political restrictions; new elections; or successful revolution), it appears advisable to develop specialized predictive models susceptive to each of the longitudinal patterns of civil strife.

NOTES

1. Studies characteristic of this general orientation include Davies 1962, 1969; Feierabend and Feierabend 1966, 1972; Gurr 1968, 1970; Gurr and Duvall 1973, 1976; Gurr and Lichbach 1979; Geschwender 1968; Bowen et al. 1968; Crawford and Naditch 1970; Morrison 1971; and Schwartz 1972.

2. For example, see Tilly 1975, 1978; Snyder and Tilly 1972; Oberschall 1973; Gamson 1975; Wilson and Orum 1976; McCarthy and Zald 1977.

3. To be sure, not all tests of the theory have produced supportive findings (that is, Snyder and Tilly 1972; Hibbs 1973). Nevertheless, this basic formulation does constitute a major paradigm in the study of civil strife, especially since evidence in support of alternative formulations is also less than conclusive (Snyder 1978, 507).

4. For examples of the ways in which conflict "magnitude" has been operationalized, see Sorokin 1937; Richardson 1960; Russett 1964; Tilly and Rule 1965; Feierabend and Feierabend 1966; Gurr 1968; Gurr and Duvall 1973; Gurr and Lichbach 1979; and Fenmore and Volgy 1978.

5. A few examples of these analyses are Rummel 1963; Tanter 1965; Wilkenfeld 1973; Bwy 1968; Gurr 1968; and Gurr and Duvall 1973.

6. This analysis utilizes a pooled cross-sectional time-series design (Zuk and Thompson 1982). In its present form it permits the study of conflict processes and patterns both within and across nations, and therefore combines the benefits of time-series as well as cross-sectional analysis. However, the design has been criticized as violating a basic assumption of regression analysis, that is, the independence of sequential observations for single nations over time (Lijphart 1975; Klingman 1980). Ordinary least squares (OLS) regression (which is appropriate in cross-sectional designs) may be inappropriate in time-series analysis if serial correlation is present. Indeed, autoregressive disturbances have been discovered in many time-series studies. If the assumption of uncorrelated error terms does not hold, then results obtained through OLS regression may be flawed (Ostrom 1978). A solution can be

found by transforming autocorrelated data and then applying OLS (an approach called generalized least squares or GLS regression) whereby the assumption of random error terms is no longer violated. GLS has been used extensively in time-series analyses.

However, it is inappropriate to simply assume the presence of serial correlation, since there are tests designed to detect it. Whether or not autocorrelation is present in time-series data is an empirical question. If autocorrelation is evident in sequential observations, then steps can be taken to remove its influence. Otherwise (if no serial correlation is present), multiple observations over time can be treated as independent cases and OLS estimates may be accepted as efficient and without bias (Ostrom 1978, 34).

Another issue involves the possibility of spatial diffusion in cross-sectional analyses. Sometimes referred to as "Galton's Problem," the issue revolves around the attribution of a causal association between specific societal traits on the basis of cross-sectional correlation when in fact the relationship may be the result of the "diffusion" of traits among societies. A considerable literature has developed on this subject (see Klingman 1980) but there is no agreement yet regarding either the importance of the issue or its tractability to statistical solution. Three studies (Putnam 1967; Midlarsky 1970; Li and Thompson 1975) examined this problem as it pertains to military coups. Li and Thompson suggest that the results of diffusion analyses seem to depend upon the time period under scrutiny and the statistical model used to test for the presence of such processes. However, for Latin America at least, Putnam found no evidence of "coup contagion" and Midlarsky's findings were mixed, as were those of Li and Thompson.

7. If either positive or negative serial correlation within sets of nation-year observations were contaminating the results, a characteristic "trail" would remain in the residual values not accounted for by the equation (Ostrom 1978, 12–17). To check for the presence of autoregressive disturbances, a Geary test was conducted for each set of 13 nation-year residuals generated by the equation. The results indicated no serial correlation problem at the .01 level and thus produced no evidence for the rejection of the hypothesis of independence within each nation-year set.

8. The greatest amount of missing data occurred for 1978. Although this year was included in the analysis, the following tables were compiled for the 13-year period of 1965 through 1977 so as to maximize uniformity of comparison.

9. These categories are suggested by O'Donnell (1973). Also see Malloy (1977, passim) and Collier (1979, passim) for descriptions of Latin American system-types.

10. For a theoretical discussion of the socioeconomic development/political conflict nexus, see O'Donnell (1973). Additional empirical evidence tending to support this hypothesis may be found in Geller (1982a, 1982b).

## APPENDIX A: ELEMENTS OF THE PRETEST CONFLICT MODEL

Time Lags

The model incorporates specified temporal positions for each factor. With the exception of the historical instability measure (which is a constant for each nation), all factors are related to time t conflict at either t or t-1. Persisting deprivation—a measure of protracted economic hardship—is lagged one year. Coercive force potential is similarly lagged, since dissidents' evaluation of the efficacy of time t violence must take place at an earlier date. The other predictors are all measured at the same temporal period as civil violence, since these factors would appear to have a contiguous relation to conflict behavior.

Formal Statement of Hypotheses

*Propositions (Predictor → Political Conflict Relationships)*

- PROPOSITION 1 ($X_1 \overset{+}{\to} Y_{6,1}$): Historical traditions of civil strife should evidence a positive relationship to current political conflict.

- PROPOSITION 2 ($X_{2,t-1} \overset{-}{\to} Y_{6,t}$): Persisting deprivation should evidence a negative relationship to political conflict.

- PROPOSITION 3 ($Y_{1,t-1} \overset{-}{\to} Y_{6,t}$): The coercive force potential of regimes should evidence a negative relationship to political conflict.

- PROPOSITION 4 ($Y_{2,t} \overset{-}{\to} Y_{6,t}$): Regime legitimacy should evidence a negative relationship to political conflict.

- PROPOSITION 5 ($Y_{3,t} \overset{+}{\to} Y_{6,t}$): Short term deprivation should evidence a positive relationship to political conflict.

- PROPOSITION 6 ($Y_{4,t} \overset{-}{\to} Y_{6,t}$): Institutionalization should evidence a negative relationship to political conflict.

- PROPOSITION 7 ($Y_{5,t} \overset{+}{\to} Y_{6,t}$): Social/structural facilitation should evidence a positive relationship to political conflict.

## Subpropositions (Internal Linkages among Predictors)

- SUBPROPOSITION 1 ($X_1 \overset{-}{\to} Y_{2,t}$): Historical instability should evidence a negative relationship to legitimacy.

- SUBPROPOSITION 2 ($X_1 \overset{-}{\to} Y_{1,\ t-1}$): Historical insta-bility should evidence a negative relationship to co-ercive force potential.

- SUBPROPOSITION 3 ($X_{2,t-1} \overset{+}{\to} Y_{1,t-1}$): Persisting deprivation should evidence a positive relationship to coercive force potential.

- SUBPROPOSITION 4 ($X_{2,t-1} \overset{-}{\to} Y_{3,t}$): Persisting depriva-tion should evidence a negative relationship to short term deprivation.

- SUBPROPOSITION 5 ($X_{2,t-1} \overset{-}{\to} Y_{5,t}$): Persisting depriva-tion should evidence a negative relationship to social/structural facilitation.

- SUBPROPOSITION 6 ($Y_{1,t-1} \overset{-}{\to} Y_{2,t}$): Coercive force potential should evidence a negative relationship to legitimacy.

- SUBPROPOSITION 7 ($Y_{1,t-1} \overset{-}{\to} Y_{4,t}$): Coercive force potential should evidence a negative relationship to institutionalization.

- SUBPROPOSITION 8 ($Y_{2,t} \overset{+}{\rightarrow} Y_{4,t}$): Legitimacy should evidence a positive relationship to institutionalization.
- SUBPROPOSITION 9 ($Y_{3,t} \overset{+}{\rightarrow} Y_{5,t}$): Short term deprivation should evidence a positive relationship to social/structural facilitation.

## APPENDIX B: SOURCE CODE

(A) Banks, Arthur S. *Cross-Polity Time-Series Data.* Cambridge, Mass.: M.I.T. Press, 1971.
————. "Cross-National Time-Series Data Archive." Center for Comparative Political Research, State University of New York at Binghamton, 1980 (unpublished).

(B) Bernard, Jean-Pierre, Silas Cerqueira, Hugo Neira, Hélène Graillot, Leslie F. Manigat, and Pierre Gilhodès. *Guide to the Political Parties of South America.* Translated by Michael Perl. Harmondsworth, England: Penguin Books, 1973.

(C) Collier, Ruth B., and David Collier. "Inducements Versus Constraints: Disaggregating 'Corporatism.'" *American Political Science Review* 73:967–86.

(D) *Political Handbook and Atlas of the World.* 1964–80 editions.

(E) Denton, Charles F., and Preston L. Lawrence. *Latin American Politics: A Functional Approach.* San Francisco: Chandler, 1972.

(F) Dupuy, Trevor N. *Almanac of World Military Power.* Dunn Loring, Virginia: T. N. Dupuy Associates, 1970.

(G) *Facts on File.* New York: Facts on File Inc., 1973–77.

(H) International Monetary Fund. *International Financial Statistics Yearbook.* 1967–79.

(I) Kantor, Harry. *Patterns of Politics and Political Systems in Latin America.* Chicago: Rand McNally, 1969.

(J) McDonald, Ronald H. *Party Systems and Elections in Latin America.* Chicago: Markham Publishing, 1971.

(K) Organization for Economic Cooperation and Development. *Educational Statistics Yearbook.* Vol. I, 1974.

(L) Sellers, Robert C., ed. *Armed Forces of the World.* 3rd edition. New York: Praeger Publishers, 1971.

(M) *Statesman's Yearbook.* 1964–79.

(N) *Statistical Abstract of Latin America.* 1977.

(O) Taylor, Charles L., and Michael C. Hudson. *World Handbook of Political and Social Indicators.* 2nd edition. New Haven: Yale University Press, 1972.
(P) *United Nations Demographic Yearbook.* New York: Statistical Office of the United Nations, Department of Economic and Social Affairs, 1965–79.
(Q) *United Nations Statistical Yearbook.* 1965–79.
(R) *United Nations Yearbook of National Account Statistics.* 1965–78.
(S) United States Arms Control and Disarmament Agency. *World Military Expenditures and Arms Trade, 1963–1973.* Washington, D.C.
————. *World Military Expenditures, 1970.*
————. *World Military Expenditures, 1971.*
————. *World Military Expenditures and Arms Transfers, 1966–1975; 1967–1976; 1968–1977.*
(T) Wiarda, Howard J., and Harvey F. Kline, eds. *Latin American Politics and Development.* Boston: Houghton Mifflin, 1979.
(U) Case studies.

REFERENCES

Asher, Herbert B. 1976. *Causal Modeling.* Beverly Hills: Sage University Paper on Quantitative Applications in the Social Sciences, Series No. 07-003.
Banks, Arthur S. 1981. "An Index of Socio-Economic Development 1869–1975." *Journal of Politics* 43:390–411.
————. 1972. "Patterns of Domestic Conflict: 1919–39 and 1946–66." *Journal of Conflict Resolution* 16:41–50.
Blasier, Cole. 1967. "Studies of Social Revolution: Origins in Mexico, Bolivia, and Cuba." *Latin American Research Review* 2:28–64.
Bowen, Don R., Elinor Bowen, Sheldon Gawiser, and Louis H. Masotti. 1968. "Deprivation, Mobility, and Orientation Toward Protest of the Urban Poor." In Louis H. Masotti and Don R. Bowen (eds.), *Riots and Rebellion: Civil Violence in the Urban Community.* Beverly Hills: Sage.
Brinton, Crane. 1952. *The Anatomy of Revolution.* New York: Vintage Books.
Bwy, Douglas. 1968. "Dimensions of Social Conflict in Latin America." In Louis H. Masotti and Don R. Bowen (eds.), *Riots and Rebellion: Civil Violence in the Urban Community.* Beverly Hills: Sage.
Christ, Carl F. 1966. *Econometric Models and Methods.* New York: John Wiley.

Collier, David. 1979. *The New Authoritarianism in Latin America* (edited). Princeton: Princeton University Press.
──────. 1978. "Industrial Modernization and Political Change: A Latin American Perspective." *World Politics* 30:593–614.
Crawford, Thomas J., and Murray Naditch. 1970. "Relative Deprivation, Powerlessness, and Militancy: The Psychology of Social Protest." *Psychiatry* 33:208–23.
Cutright, Phillips. 1963. "National Political Development: Its Measurement and Social Correlates." *American Sociological Review* 27:253–64.
Davies, James C. 1978. "Communication: The J–Curve Theory." *American Political Science Review* 72:1357–58.
──────. 1969. "The J–Curve of Rising and Declining Satisfactions as a Cause of Some Great Revolutions and a Contained Rebellion." In Hugh Davis Graham and Ted Robert Gurr (eds.), *Violence in America: Historical and Comparative Perspectives*. New York: Signet Books.
──────. 1962. "Toward a Theory of Revolution." *American Sociological Review* 27:5–19.
Eckstein, Harry. 1965. "The Etiology of Internal War." *History and Theory* 4:133–63.
──────. 1962. "Internal War: The Problem of Anticipation." *Social Science Research and National Security.* Washington, D.C.: Smithsonian Institution Research Group in Psychology and the Social Sciences.
Feierabend, Ivo K., and Rosalind L. Feierabend. 1972. "Systematic Conditions of Political Aggression: An Application of Frustration–Aggression Theory." In Ivo K. Feierabend, Rosalind L. Feierabend, and Ted Robert Gurr (eds.), *Anger, Violence, and Politics: Theories and Research*. Englewood Cliffs, N.J.: Prentice-Hall.
──────. 1966. "Aggressive Behavior Within Polities, 1948–1962: A Cross-National Study." *Journal of Conflict Resolution* 10:249–71.
Fenmore, Barton, and Thomas J. Volgy. 1978. "Short-Term Economic Change and Political Instability in Latin America." *Western Political Quarterly* 31:548–64.
Friedman, Milton. 1951. "Comments." In National Bureau of Economic Research (ed.), *Conference on Business Cycles*. New York: National Bureau of Economic Research.
Gamson, William A. 1975. *The Strategy of Social Protest.* Homewood, Ill.: Dorsey.
Geller, Daniel S. 1982a. "Economic Modernization and Political Instability in Latin America: A Causal Analysis of Bureaucratic-Authoritarianism." *Western Political*

*Quarterly* 35:33–49.

————. 1982b. "Expectation-Achievement Discrepancies and Political Conflict in Latin America: A Sociopolitical Model." Paper presented at the XII World Congress of the International Political Science Association, Rio de Janeiro, Brazil, August 9–14.

Geschwender, James A. 1968. "Explorations in the Theory of Social Movements and Revolution." *Social Forces* 47:127–35.

Goldstone, Jack A. 1980. "Theories of Revolution: The Third Generation." *World Politics* 32:425–53.

Gurr, Ted Robert. 1970. *Why Men Rebel*. Princeton: Princeton University Press.

————. 1968. "A Causal Model of Civil Strife: A Comparative Analysis Using New Indices." *American Political Science Review* 62:1104–24.

Gurr, Ted Robert, and Vaughn F. Bishop. 1976. "Violent Nations, and Others." *Journal of Conflict Resolution* 20:79–110.

Gurr, Ted Robert, and Raymond D. Duvall. 1976. "Introduction to a Formal Theory of Political Conflict." In Lewis A. Coser and Otto N. Larsen (eds.), *The Uses of Controversy in Sociology*. New York: Free Press.

————. 1973. "Civil Conflict in the 1960's: A Reciprocal Theoretical System with Parameter Estimates." *Comparative Political Studies* 6:135–69.

Gurr, Ted Robert, and Mark Irving Lichbach. 1979. "Forecasting Domestic Political Conflict." In J. David Singer and Michael D. Wallace (eds.), *To Augur Well: Early Warning Indicators in World Politics*. Beverly Hills and London: Sage.

Hempel, Carl G. 1966. *Philosophy of Natural Science*. Englewood Cliffs, N.J.: Prentice-Hall.

Hibbs, Douglas A. 1973. *Mass Political Violence: A Cross-National Causal Analysis*. New York: Wiley.

Hoffer, Eric. 1951. *The True Believer*. New York: Harper.

Huntington, Samuel P. 1968. *Political Order in Changing Societies*. New Haven: Yale University Press.

Kaufman, Robert R. 1979. "Industrial Change and Authoritarian Rule in South America: A Concrete Review of the Bureaucratic-Authoritarian Model." In David Collier (ed.), *The New Authoritarianism in Latin America*. Princeton: Princeton University Press.

————. 1975. "Notes on the Definition, Genesis, and Consolidation of Bureaucratic-Authoritarian Regimes." Manuscript. Department of Political Science, Rutgers University, New Brunswick, N.J.

Klein, Lawrence R. 1974. *A Textbook of Econometrics*. Englewood Cliffs, N.J.: Prentice-Hall.

Klingman, David. 1980. "Temporal and Spatial Diffusion in the Comparative Analysis of Social Change." *American Political Science Review* 74:123–37.

Korpi, Walter. 1974. "Conflict, Power, and Relative Deprivation." *American Political Science Review* 68:1569–78.

Li, P. Y., and William R. Thompson. 1975. "The 'Coup Contagion' Hypothesis." *Journal of Conflict Resolution* 19:63–88.

Lichbach, Mark I., and Ted Robert Gurr. 1979. "The Conflict Process: A Self-Generative Model." Manuscript to appear in *Journal of Conflict Resolution*.

Lijphart, Arend. 1975. "The Comparable Cases Strategy in Comparative Research." *Comparative Political Studies* 8:158–77.

Malloy, James M. 1977. *Authoritarianism and Corporatism in Latin America* (edited). Pittsburgh: University of Pittsburgh Press.

McCarthy, John D., and Mayer N. Zald. 1977. "Resource Mobilization and Social Movements: A Partial Theory." *American Journal of Sociology* 82:1212–41.

Midlarsky, Manus. 1970. "Mathematical Models of Instability and a Theory of Diffusion." *International Studies Quarterly* 14:60–84.

Morrison, Denton E. 1971. "Some Notes Towards a Theory on Relative Deprivation, Social Movements, and Social Change." *American Behavioral Scientist* 14:675–90.

Morrison, Donald G., and Hugh M. Stevenson. 1971. "Political Instability in Independent Black Africa: More Dimensions of Conflict Behavior Within Nations." *Journal of Conflict Resolution* 15:347–68.

Nardin, Terry. 1971. *Violence and the State: A Critique of Empirical Political Theory*. Sage Professional Papers, Comparative Politics Series, vol. 2. Beverly Hills: Sage.

Oberschall, Anthony. 1973. *Social Conflict and Social Movements*. Englewood Cliffs, N.J.: Prentice-Hall.

O'Donnell, Guillermo. 1977. "Corporatism and the Question of the State." In James M. Malloy (ed.), *Authoritarianism and Corporatism in Latin America*. Pittsburgh: University of Pittsburgh Press.

————. 1973. *Modernization and Bureaucratic-Authoritarianism: Studies in South American Politics*. Politics of Modernization Series, no. 9. Berkeley: University of California, Berkeley.

Ostrom, Charles W. 1978. *Time Series Analysis: Regression Techniques*. Beverly Hills: Sage University

Paper on Quantitative Applications in the Social Sciences, Series No. 07-009.

Payne, James. 1965. "Peru: The Politics of Structured Violence." *Journal of Politics* 27:362–74.

Putnam, Robert D. 1967. "Toward Explaining Military Intervention in Latin America." *World Politics* 20:83–110.

Richardson, Lewis F. 1960. *Statistics of Deadly Quarrels.* Pittsburgh: Boxwood.

Rummel, Rudolph J. 1970. *Applied Factor Analysis.* Evanston: Northwestern University Press.

—————. 1963. "Dimensions of Conflict Behavior Within and Between Nations." *General Systems Yearbook* 8:1–50.

Russett, Bruce M. 1964. "Inequality and Instability: The Relation of Land Tenure to Politics." *World Politics* 16:442–54.

Schwartz, David C. 1972. "Political Alienation: The Psychology of Revolution's First Stage." In Ivo K. Feierabend, Rosalind L. Feierabend, and Ted Robert Gurr (eds.), *Anger, Violence, and Politics: Theories and Research.* Englewood Cliffs, N.J.: Prentice-Hall.

Snyder, David. 1978. "Collective Violence: A Research Agenda and Some Strategic Considerations." *Journal of Conflict Resolution* 22:499–534.

Snyder, David, and Charles Tilly. 1972. "Hardship and Collective Violence in France, 1930–1960." *American Sociological Review* 37:520–32.

Sorokin, Pitirim A. 1937. *Social and Cultural Dynamics: Fluctuation of Social Relationships, War, and Revolution,* vol. III. New York: American Book.

Tanter, Raymond. 1965. "Dimensions of Conflict Behavior Within Nations, 1955–1960: Turmoil and Internal War." *Peace Research Society Papers* 3:159–83.

Tilly, Charles. 1978. *From Mobilization to Revolution.* Reading, Mass.: Addison-Wesley.

—————. 1975. "Revolutions and Collective Violence." In Fred I. Greenstein and Nelson W. Polsby (eds.), *Handbook of Political Science,* vol. III. Reading, Mass.: Addison-Wesley.

Tilly, Charles, and James Rules. 1965. *Measuring Political Upheaval.* Princeton: Center of International Studies, Princeton University.

Tilly, Charles, Louise Tilly, and Richard Tilly. 1975. *The Rebellious Century.* Cambridge, Mass.: Harvard University Press.

Wilkenfeld, Jonathan. 1973. "Domestic and Foreign Conflict." In Jonathan Wilkenfeld (ed.), *Conflict Behavior and Linkage Politics.* New York: David McKay.

Wilson, Kenneth L., and Anthony M. Orum. 1976. "Mobilizing People for Collective Political Action." *Journal of Political and Military Sociology* 4:187–202.
Wolf, Eric R. 1959. *Sons of the Shaking Earth*. Chicago: University of Chicago Press.
Zuk, Gary, and William R. Thompson. 1982. "The Post-Coup Military Spending Question: A Pooled Cross-Sectional Time Series Analysis." *American Political Science Review* 76:60–74.

# *Part II*

## Predicting
## Foreign Events and Foreign Involvements

# 3

# Scientific Logic and Intuition in Intelligence Forecasts

## Zeev Moaz

## INTRODUCTION

We live in a complex world, a world of numerous uncertainties, trying constantly to make sense of our sur-
rounding environment and impose some meaning upon it.
We know quite a few things about our past, something
about the present, but very little about our future. Thus,
uncertainty regarding ourselves and our environment
increases as we move from interpretations of the past
toward projections of the future, and the tools for descriptive or casual understanding of reality become
increasingly unreliable as we move from post-diction to
prediction.

We are engaged in forecasting tasks at almost any instance of our life because forecasts are an integral part of
the decisions we make. When we open the front door in the
morning, we estimate the probability of rain so we can

This chapter has benefited from the perceptive comments
of Robert Axelrod, Richard Nisbett, J. David Singer, and
Raymond Tanter on earlier drafts. Needless to say, I bear
sole responsibility for the weaknesses that still remain. An
earlier version was presented at the 22nd Annual Convention of the International Studies Association,
Philadelphia, March 18–21, 1981.

decide whether to take an umbrella to work; when we play tennis, we estimate the direction and the speed of the ball coming at us so we can decide to which corner of the field to run and how fast; and when we hear a statement of a political leader from an opponent state, we try to figure out his underlying intentions so we can decide on counter-measures.

Failures to correctly estimate which future events will take place vary in terms of their price. If we under-estimate the probability of rain and thus do not carry an umbrella to work, we might end up spending the next few days in bed. If we fail to predict the direction and speed of a coming ball in a tennis game, we might, at worse, lose a game. However, if we underestimate the probability of an imminent attack by our enemy, we might end up suffering an enormous amount of casualties, if not lose the war due to our unpreparedness. On the other hand, if we over-estimate the probability of war, we might end up missing opportunities or lead to self-fulfillment of our gloomy predictions by unnecessarily escalating "dormant conflicts."

Available psychological evidence suggests that there are a number of heuristics used by laypersons in estimation and judgmental tasks. These heuristics might lead to consistent misestimation of the likelihood of future events. Among these heuristics, the following are of particular importance:

- Availability: People tend to estimate future events according to the ease with which they are able to recall similar events. If events similar to those that they are required to estimate are easily accessible in their memory, people are likely to overestimate the future events. Conversely, events that are not readily available in one's memory are likely to be underestimated (Nisbett and Ross 1980, 18–23; Tversky and Kahneman 1973). Since accessibility of events in processes of memory, perception, and construction from imagination does not necessarily correlate with their relative frequency, the use of the availability heuristic is likely to result in biased estimates.
- Representativeness: When people try to relate a certain piece of evidence to an event or an hypothesis, they compare the evidence on a number of salient attributes to some familiar class of events. To the extent that the attributes of the evidence seem to fit the class of recalled events, and to the extent that the class of recalled events is perceived as similar to the event people are required to estimate, overestimation is likely

to occur. This is so because the fit between the evidence and the class of recalled events may have very little to do with the relative frequency of this particular class in the entire population. In other words, people are likely to ignore base rate information in favor of current representative indicators (Bar Hillel 1977; Kahneman and Tversky 1973; Nisbett and Ross 1980, 24–28).

- Causal Schemas: People tend to estimate the probability of future events according to some prior premises or beliefs they have concerning such events. Consequently, they would be selective with respect to the processing and interpretation of evidence related to such events. That is, people would tend to discount or ignore information that does not fit their causal schemas, and upgrade evidence supporting those schemas (Axelrod 1973; Jervis 1968, 1976, 143–71). Moreover, people fail to acknowledge that evidence consistent with their prior premises may be also consistent with a competing set of premises (Jervis 1976, 181–87). To the extent that the prior premises stand on poor grounds, estimates are likely to be consistently biased (Nisbett and Ross 1980, 28–41, 175–87).[1]

There is ample experimental evidence suggesting that the application of these heuristics results in consistent misestimation or misjudgment of probabilities of events and frequency distribution of classes. Tversky and Kahneman (1973) have presented subjects with two lists of names of celebrities, each list consisting of an equal proportion of male/female celebrities. When required to estimate the male/female proportion for each list, subjects consistently overestimated the frequency of male celebrities in the list that consisted of very famous male celebrities, and not-so-famous female celebrities. Similarly, subjects consistently overestimated the frequency of female celebrities in the list consisting of very famous females and not-so-famous males. In another study (Kahneman and Tversky 1973), subjects were presented with a frequency distribution of students in two fields, 80 percent liberal sciences and 20 percent computer sciences (or 80 percent lawyers and 20 percent engineers) and then were required to estimate the probability that a person with a number of traits (for example, need for order and clarity, technical writing) will belong to any of the classes. Subjects consistently overestimated the probability that a person having such traits will be a computer scientist or an engineer, rather than a liberal sciences student or a lawyer. Similarly, Bar Hillel (1977) reports that subjects in a number of problem-solving experiments considerably deviated from statistical probability theory since they tended to ignore population base rates. Her explanation of this tendency, however, is that both base rates and current indicators compete for relevance in one's mind, and that recency, rather than representativeness, accounts for the overwhelming dominance of current indicators over base rates.

Phillips and Edwards (1966) have shown that while Bayesian rules demand logarithmic revision of opinion in light of highly diagnostic information, peoples' revision process is linear in nature. That is, people are unduly conservative in revising their opinions in light of strongly diagnostic discrepant evidence. But is this conservatism a function of the complexity and importance of the forecasting task? Alker and Hermann (1971) argue that it is. By varying the complexity and significance of the task presented to the subjects, these researchers have shown that conservatism increases as both complexity and importance of predictions increase. Related to that point is evidence presented by Brown, Kahr, and Peterson (1974, 430–34), which shows that weather forecasters are significantly better calibrated (that is, more accurate probabilisticly) than military analysts. Ascher in a fascinating evaluation-study of the accuracy of trend and point forecasts in a variety of policy relevant areas, argues that failure to revise erroneous core assumptions leads to highly inaccurate forecasts (1979, 202).

When one moves to the realm of specialized politico-military forecasting, several additional points have to be noted. First, military analysts do not have statistically established base rates that cover the enormous variety of events to be predicted. Second, the modal case of prediction is one for which there are few or no empirically validated indicators. Third, the costs of under or over-estimation are considerably high, especially when the events to be predicted are war or peace. Fourth—and this is the point that concerns the researchers of intelligence analysis rather than the intelligence analyst—politic-military forecasts are often presented in forms that preclude evaluation (Ascher 1979, 204).

However, there is one common finding in most, if not all, of the studies of intelligence failures. This is the theme suggesting that it is not the lack of information that accounts for intelligence failures, but rather the defective processing and misinterpretation of available evidence (Betts 1978, 63; Wohlstetter 1962). Even the most efficient and competent intelligence agencies may produce estimates that are unduly influenced by flawed prior premises and strategic assumptions, and hence, overly conservative. When strategic assumptions regarding the adversary's capabilities and intentions are deeply rooted in the analyst's mind, contradictory evidence is likely to be ignored or downgraded as unreliable or random (Axelrod 1973; Ben Zvi 1976; Handel 1976; Jervis 1976; Shlaim 1976).[2]

## SOME INFERENTIAL
## AND POLICY PRESCRIPTIONS

Although there exists considerable agreement among students of intelligence regarding the nature of the cognitive mechanisms that produce biased and inaccurate estimates, there is an acute debate regarding the underlying causal interpretations of such biases. Consequently, there also exists a diversity of prescriptions with respect to the correctional strategies that ought to be pursued in order to reduce the rate and frequency of misestimation. Four notable schools of thought can be mentioned in this regard: the systematically derived knowledge school, the institutional reform school, the muddling-through school, and the scientific logic school.

The systematically derived knowledge school contends that intelligence failures are due to the fact that analysts fail to use available objective knowledge regarding the preconditions for, and the indicators of, such events as war and peace. The prescription of this school is simple. Replace intuitive prediction by systematic prediction based on empirically tested and validated theories (Andriole and Young 1977; McClelland 1977; Singer 1971, 25–30; Singer 1973, 6–10; Singer and Small 1974, 294–95; Singer 1978, 9; Singer and Wallace 1979, 7–12). This prescription is a long range shot, however. Proponents of the systematically derived knowledge school acknowledge the fact that much research needs to be done before highly diagnostic indicators are established. Students belonging to this school are also aware of the adverse effects of premature utilization of tentative evidence in intelligence forecasts. Moreover, indicators that were proven to be empirically diagnostic, in terms of their potency to predict war or crisis eruption, have led to an alarming rate of false alarms. Background indicators such as changes in military preparedness, alliances, and contiguity, as well as interactional indicators such as frequency and intensity of conflict/cooperation, have led to predictions of crisis or war in many historical instances where crisis or war did not, in fact, occur (Daly and Davies 1978; Stoll and Champion 1980). Although many seem to agree with the prescriptions of this school, only few disagree that the application of these prescriptions is of limited value in this short range.

The organizational reform school contends that the cause of intelligence failures lies in peoples' disposition to reject information contradicting their beliefs, premises, or strategic assumptions. More important, this school contends that intelligence failures are inevitable given the complexity of international politics and the ambivalence of data existing in this realm (Betts 1978; Handel 1976). The prescription advocated by this school is that foreign policy makers should create a system of "multiple advocacy" (George 1972), or at least to allow for a personal or organizational "devil's advocate" to voice its opinion (Ben Zvi 1976; Handel 1976; Janis and Mann 1977, 397–400; Jervis 1976, 415–17).

Although appealing in theory, such a prescription is almost impossible to implement in practice. In individual choice processes it is virtually self-negating. If psychological biases are the causes underlying misperception and misestimation, and if people constantly ignore or downgrade information contradicting their beliefs and causal schemas, how can we expect a person to be his or her own "devil's advocate"? Moreover, even in group or organizational settings, one can institutionalize multiple advocacy and assure that a "devil's advocate" would be heard, but it is impossible to assure that a "devil's advocate" would actually be listened to. In other words, it is one thing to institutionalize multiple advocacy, but it is quite another thing to make sure that such advocacies will receive due consideration in the estimation and decision process.

The muddling-through school agrees with the diagnoses of the other two schools regarding the underlying causes of misestimation, but generally disagrees with their prescriptions. Proponents of the muddling-through school contend that decision and estimation processes in the political realm, although far from optimal, are by and large satisfactory. Intelligence failures are the exception rather than the rule. Disastrous decisions, however costly, are very rare, and people or organizations manage to survive and do it fairly well. The costs of changing existing systems of intelligence estimation are much too high, and the marginal benefits of the prescribed changes are much too uncertain, if not nil. There is no replacement to general knowledge and good intuition (Gazit 1980).

This kind of argument is hard to confront because there is no record of performance for alternative forecasting systems in the field of political intelligence. We can only evaluate the performance of existing intelligence estimation methods and systems, but not the performance of the systems and methods we prescribe.

Finally, the scientific logic school contends that people constantly err in inferential and judgmental tasks because their inferential heuristics sharply deviate from, and often violate, formal scientific logic. Consequently, the prescription of this school is that even intuitive estimates and judgments can be improved by basing the process of prediction and judgment on formal scientific logic and laws (Kahneman and Tversky 1977; Nisbett and Ross 1980). There is some empirical evidence to support this prescription. Dawes (1980) reports the findings of a study where psychology professors were required to estimate the school performance of graduate psychology students. Estimators were considerably off target when compared to regression analysis that uses undergraduate grade point average, graduate record exam scores, and undergraduate school ratings as predictors of graduate performance. However, a model based on intuitive weights assigned to the predictor variables did significantly better than the professors who based their estimates on an impressionistic evaluation of the students. Ascher (1979, 199–200) argues that variations in forecasting methodologies do not make much of a difference when core assumptions are erroneous. He acknowledges, however, the existence of rare exceptions where different methodologies differ in their predictive potency if core assumptions are correct, and where methodologies can compensate for erroneous core assumptions.

The prescriptions of the scientific logic school have not escaped normative criticism, however. Schweitzer (1976, 1978), who has applied Bayesian analysis to intelligence estimation tasks at the Central Intelligence Agency (CIA), contends that Bayesian methods lead to overly rapid revision of estimates the more current indicators enter the system. But this criticism holds only to the extent that current informational items all point to the same direction, not when different pieces of information point to different directions, or when current evidence varies in terms of diagnosticity (that is, indicative validity). Another critical point is that scientific estimation methods are far from perfect. For instance, in Bayes' theorem, the same weight is assigned both to prior probability ratios based on background information or population base rates, and to likelihood ratios based on single pieces of current information. However, prior probabilities may be based on considerably more data than the single piece of evidence upon which the likelihood ratio is based. But this criticism implies that the more information is incorporated into the prior probability ratio, subsequent informational items should be assigned increasingly reduced weights regardless of their diagnosticity. This is so because in a revision process, the posterior odds of one revisional step become the prior odds of the subsequent revisional step. The outcome of such a process is precisely what the critics of Bayesian analysis would like to avoid; namely, that estimates would become increasingly conservative, the more information they have. The following mathematical presentation demonstrates the logical flaw inherent in this criticism of Bayes' theorem:

The Bayes theorem:

$$\frac{P(H_1/D_1)}{P(H_2/D_1)} = \frac{P(D_1/H_1)}{P(D_1/H_2)} \times \frac{P(H_1)}{P(H_2)}$$

The criticism of Bayes implies:

for the first revisional step

$$\frac{P(H_1/D_1)}{P(H_2/D_1)} = \left[\frac{P(H_1)}{P(H_2)} \times \frac{k}{k+1}\right] \times \left[\frac{P(D_1/H_1)}{P(D_1/H_2)} \times \frac{1}{k+1}\right]$$

for the second revisional step

$$\frac{P(H_1/D_1, D_2)}{P(H_2/D_1, D_2)} =$$

$$\left[\frac{P(H_1/D_1)}{P(H_2/D_1)} \times \frac{k+1}{k+2}\right] \times \left[\frac{P(D_2/H_1)}{P(D_2/H_2)} \times \frac{1}{k+2}\right]$$

and for the nth revisional step

$$\frac{P(H_1/D_1, D_2, \ldots, D_n)}{P(H_2/D_1, D_2, \ldots, D_n)} =$$

$$\left[ \frac{P(H_1/D_1, D_2, \ldots D_n)}{P(H_2/D_1, D_2, \ldots D_n)} \times \frac{k+(n-1)}{k+n} \right] \times \left[ \frac{P(D_n/H_1)}{P(D_n/H_2)} \times \frac{1}{k+n} \right]$$

Where:

$H_1$* = Hypothesis (future state, statement, etc.) 1
$H_2$* = Hypothesis (future state, statement, etc.) 2
P = Probability
D = Datum
k = Number of informational items on which the prior probabilities are based.

## THE RESEARCH PROBLEM

The bottom line of the preceding discussion is that consensus on the nature of heuristics leading to misestimation is not a sufficient condition for consensus on the causal interpretation of these heuristics, nor is it a sufficient condition of consensus on the appropriate corrective procedures for improving accuracy of intelligence estimates.

The four approaches to improving the accuracy of intelligence estimates are not mutually exclusive. Each has its advantages, but neither is perfect from a theoretical or practical point of view. Although debate among proponents of these approaches as to the causal interpretation of intelligence failures is highly empirical, debates regarding appropriate corrective procedures turn out to be highly abstract. This is understandable given the lack of data that enables one to assess the relative utility of corrective procedures. Here is where the present study fits in. The major research questions presented by this study are the following. Assuming we know a fair amount about the inferential heuristics that lead to misestimation, and

*Both hypotheses are mutually exclusive and logically exhaustive.

assuming that we have a good sense of the cognitive causes of the application of these heuristics, what is the marginal utility of our prescriptions? Does the introduction of scientific logic and/or methods lead to a significant improvement in the quality of estimates, and if so, by how much?

In other words, this study attempts to turn a normative argument into an empirical question by examining the marginal utility of the scientific logic school's prescriptions, and by comparing the observed consequences of those prescriptions to the observed consequences of the widely used method (or nonmethod) of intuitive estimation. The reason for being interested in the prescriptions of the scientific logic school is that this school offers a fairly economical and practical strategy for improving peoples' estimates. It does not call for a change in organizational structures of forecasting systems, nor does it call for the utilization of such early warning indicators that we do not have. Rather, it calls for education of the present analysts and asks them to supplement their general substantive knowledge and experience with systematic methods of information processing.

Translating our research question into more operational language, we ask whether the incorporation of Bayesian analysis into intelligence forecasting tasks would produce better estimates, on the average, when compared to intuitive "common sense" strategies? In addition, we ask whether the incorporation of the logic underlying Bayes' theorem, without incorporation of the calculations involved in the method, will also produce better estimates than those resulting from intuitive estimation techniques.

These questions will be tested within an experimental design. The choice of an experimental design is due to the following reasons. Empirical data on the consequences of different estimation methods in the intelligence realm are difficult to acquire, simply because there is little or no variation in the type of estimation methods used by intelligence analysts for the types of problems we are interested in. Most, if not all, intelligence agencies rely almost exclusively on intuitive estimation techniques for forecasting future events. Second, an experimental design allows us to create an artificial reality whose features and outcomes are known to the experimenter, and hence, it allows us to establish a criterion of quality. That is, an experimental design allows the researcher to determine which estimates are "good" or "bad." This is not a trivial thing, since in nonexperimental designs, when analyzing past events or processes, one often struggles with the question of "what would have happened if? . . ." For instance, what would have happened if in cases of intelligence failures, analysts had been more receptive to discrepant information, or more systematic in their interpretations? Would they have produced significantly different estimates than those they actually produced?

Without overlooking the problems involved in extrapolation from experimental findings to the real world,[3] the following experiment has been devised to test the questions introduced above.

## METHOD

One hundred thirty-two undergraduate students at the University of Michigan were used as subjects in this experiment. Each of the subjects was required to estimate the probabilities of two mutually exclusive and logically exhaustive events—war and no war—for two cases. The information for each case consisted of a scenario providing the necessary background information for the generation of the prior probability ratio, and five informational items serving as current indicators. Subjects were asked to estimate the probability of the war/no war events on the basis of the scenario. Then, having read each additional datum, subjects were requested to revise their probability estimates on the basis of the additional information.

In order to allow evaluation of the quality of estimates, subjects were presented with fictitious versions of four real cases of intelligence failures. Two of these cases involved surprise attacks, that is, cases in which intelligence agencies predicted low likelihood of war, but war nevertheless occurred. The other two cases are cases of false alarm, that is, cases where intelligence analysts predicted a high likelihood of an imminent enemy attack when the enemy nation had no intention of going to war, and indeed did not go to war. The cases of surprise attack selected for this experiment were the 1973 Egyptian-Syrian attack on Israel, and the 1962 Chinese attack of India. The cases of false alarm were the 1911 Agadir crisis between Prussia and France, and the 1977 Sadat visit to Jerusalem.[4] The scenarios corresponding to these cases specify the predominant strategic assumptions that misguided intelligence analysts in the real cases in their revision processes.

The informational items consist of facts that were clearly known to the intelligence analysts in the historical cases. Two out of the five items in each of the cases included "noise" or deceptive information. ($D_2$ and $D_4$)—as they were designed to be, or happened to be in the historical cases. The other three items are strongly diagnostic, that is, highly indicative of the real historical outcome.[5] (See Appendix 2 for scenarios and data.)

A good estimate is one resulting in a high probability of war in the surprise attack cases, and a low likelihood of war in the false alarm cases. Thus, the higher the probability of war in a surprise attack case, the better the estimate; and the lower the probability of war in a false alarm case, the better the estimate.

## EXPERIMENTAL CONDITIONS

Subjects were divided at random into three groups. The first, labeled as the "Common Sense Group," received no specific instructions as to the method the subject should use for the revision process. The instructions directed them to use their common sense in assessing the likelihood of the two events (see Appendix 1.A). The second group, labeled as the "Bayesian Group," was instructed to use both the logic and the calculations of the Bayes formula. The written instructions explicated the application of this formula by way of a love affair example (see Appendix 1.B). In order to ascertain that subjects belonging to this group understand how to use the Bayes formula, the experimenter went over the example verbally and actually did the calculations for the love affair example together with the subjects. The third group, labeled as the "Diagnosis Group,"[6] was instructed to use the logic underlying the Bayes theorem. That is, subjects were instructed to generate the likelihood ratio for each datum, but were not instructed to combine prior probabilities and likelihood ratios in the process of revision. Here we wanted to examine the effects of partial use of scientific logic on quality of estimates (see Appendix 1.C).[7]

Our hypotheses are the following. To the extent that scientific logic and methods make a difference in terms of the quality of estimates, then in all four cases:

- The Bayesian Group should come up with the best estimates, on the average. That is, in the surprise cases, the Bayesian Group's mean probability of war should be significantly *higher* than the mean probability of war of any of the other two groups. Similarly, in false alarm cases, the mean probability of war of the Bayesian Group should be lower than that of any of the other two groups.

- The Common Sense Group should come up with the worst estimates, on the average. That is, the mean probability of war for this group should be lower than those of the other two groups in the surprise attack cases, and higher than the mean probability of war of the other groups in the false alarm cases.
- The Diagnosis Group should fall somewhere in the middle in terms of the quality of its predictions.

## RESULTS

In contrast to other experiments, we were not interested in the revision process per se, but rather in the *outcome* of this process. However, we wanted to make sure that our manipulation attempts were effective. First, we wanted to see whether the subjects fell for the misleading premises in generating their initial estimates, as we wanted them to. Second, we wanted to make sure that there were no significant differences among groups as far as initial estimates were concerned. Third, we wanted to make sure that the planted "noises" or deceptive informational items did mislead the subjects. The answers to these queries are presented in Figures 3-1–3-6.

These figures clearly show that, by and large, our attempts to manipulate the subjects proved effective. First, with the exception of the 1977 Sadat case, attempts to make subjects believe in a set of erroneous premises while generating initial probabilities on the basis of the scenario information proved successful. In the two cases of surprise attack, the prior probabilities of war for all groups were generally low. In the false alarm case of 1911 Agadir, the initial probability of war for all groups was better than even, that is, markedly high. Even in the 1977 Sadat case, the initial probabilities of war for all groups were slightly higher than in the two cases of surprise attack, but not significantly so. Second, between-group differences in prior probabilities were insignificant for all four cases. Moreover, the figures suggest that there is no evidence that any of the groups systematically start with either higher or lower prior estimates than the estimates of the other groups. Third, those informational items that represented noise or deceptive information indeed affected revision to the predicted direction. With the exception of $D_4$ in the 1973 case, a "noise" or deceptive datum led to a decrease in the mean probability of war for all groups. In

Figure 3-1. Mean Estimates of the Probability of War by Group: The 1973 Israeli Case (Surprise Attack)

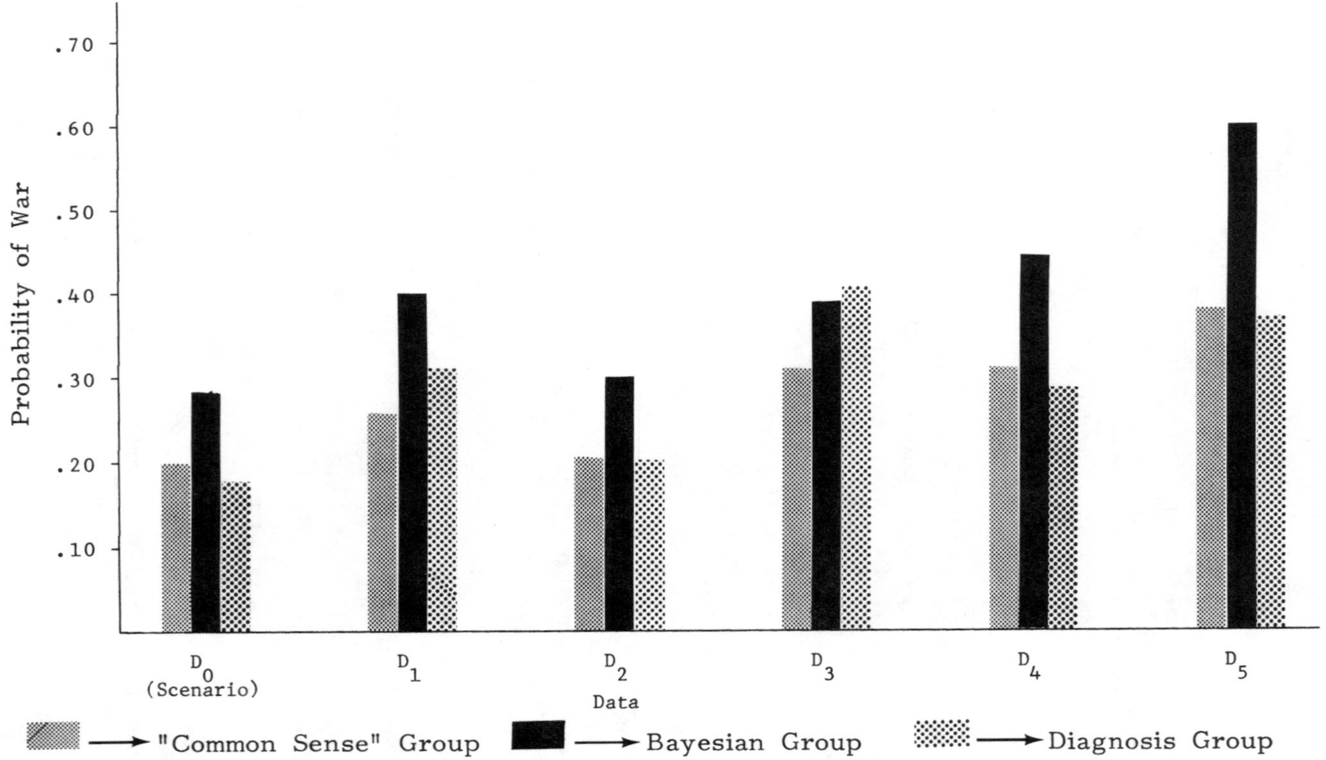

Source: Compiled by the author.

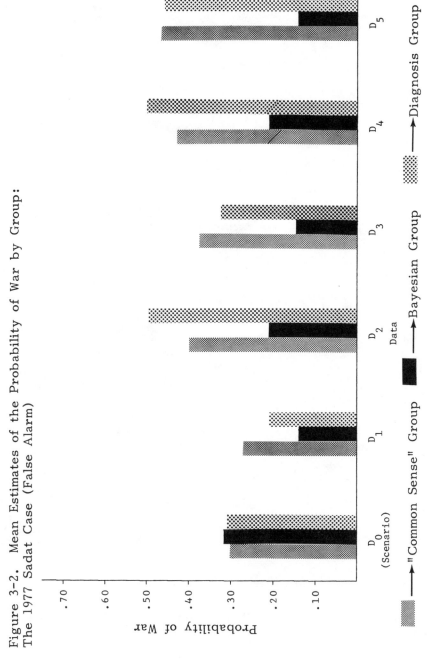

Figure 3-2. Mean Estimates of the Probability of War by Group: The 1977 Sadat Case (False Alarm)

Source: Compiled by the author.

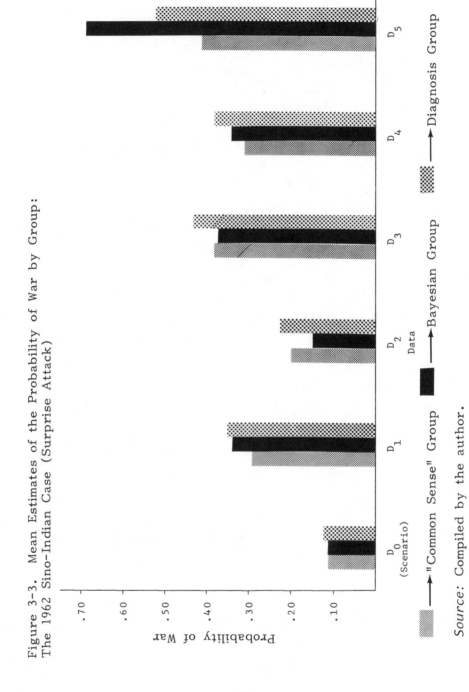

Figure 3-3. Mean Estimates of the Probability of War by Group:
The 1962 Sino-Indian Case (Surprise Attack)

*Source:* Compiled by the author.

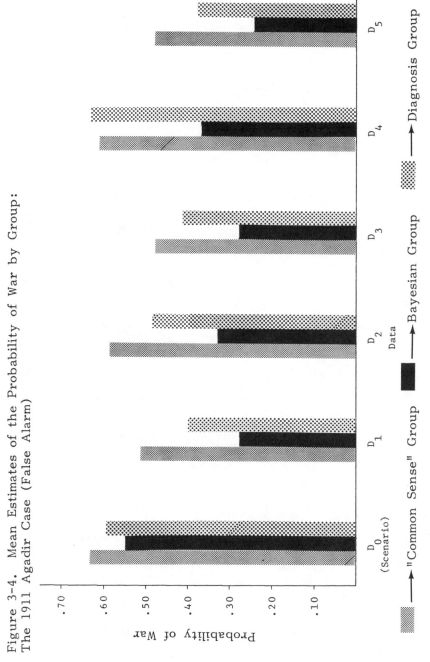

Figure 3-4. Mean Estimates of the Probability of War by Group:
The 1911 Agadir Case (False Alarm)

Probability of War

.70
.60
.50
.40
.30
.20
.10

$D_0$ (Scenario)    $D_1$    $D_2$    $D_3$    $D_4$    $D_5$

Data

→ "Common Sense" Group

→ Bayesian Group

→ Diagnosis Group

Source: Compiled by the author.

93

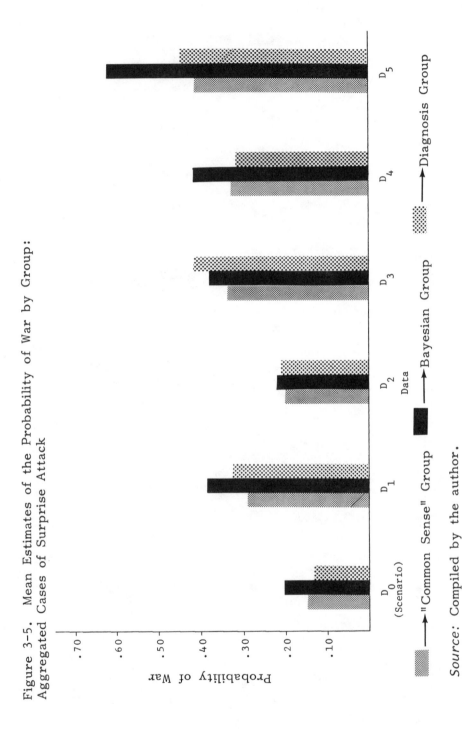

Figure 3-5. Mean Estimates of the Probability of War by Group: Aggregated Cases of Surprise Attack

Source: Compiled by the author.

94

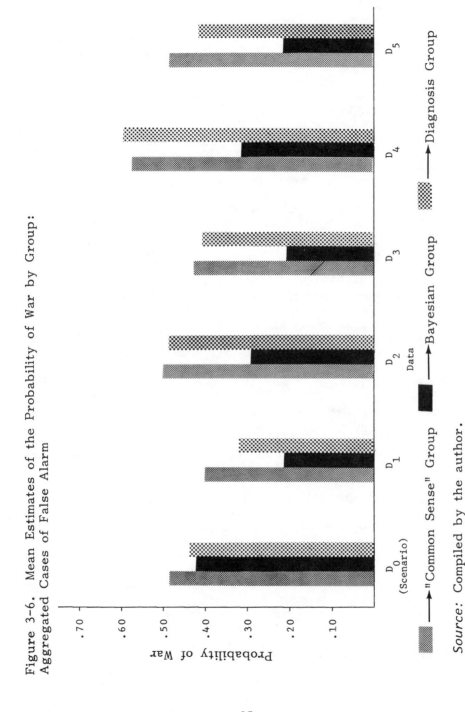

Figure 3-6. Mean Estimates of the Probability of War by Group: Aggregated Cases of False Alarm

*Source:* Compiled by the author.

the false alarm cases, a "noise" or deceptive datum led to an increase in the mean probability of war for all three groups.

In order to assess the relative quality of estimates for all groups, the final estimates for each case were taken. That is, we looked at the probability of war resulting from the final revision step in each case, that is, $P(E_1/D_5)$. Table 3-1 presents the result of this analysis.

The results in Table 3-1 suggest that our first hypothesis was strongly supported by the data. The Bayesian Group does considerably better than any of the other two groups, whether we are dealing with a case of false alarm, or with a case of surprise attack.

The second and third hypotheses have a mixed record of support. In the 1973 and 1977 cases, the Diagnosis Group did worse than the Common Sense Group in terms of its final estimates of the probability of war. However, the differences between these two groups were statistically insignificant. In the 1962 and 1911 cases, the Diagnosis Group did better than the Common Sense Group. For these two cases, the between-group differences for the Diagnosis and Common Sense Groups were statistically significant. These findings are displayed in Table 3-2.

The aggregation of the results by type of case (that is, surprise attack cases vis-à-vis false alarm cases) confirms our previous findings. The Bayesian Group did significantly better (that is, produced significantly higher estimates of war) than any of the other groups in the surprise attack cases; and in the false alarm cases, the Bayesian estimates of war were significantly lower. The Diagnosis Group produced slightly better estimates than the Common Sense Group in both types of cases. But the differences between the Diagnosis and the Common Sense Groups were statistically insignificant.

Why did subjects of the Bayesian Group come up repeatedly with significantly better final estimates, despite the fact that their initial estimates were equally bad when compared to non-Bayesian groups? Why did the quasi-Bayesian (Diagnosis) group fail to come up with significantly better estimates than those of the non-Bayesian (Common Sense) group? To answer these questions, two measures of the magnitude of revision were generated. The first measure was labeled as mean revision rate and was obtained by averaging across changes in probability estimates from one revisional step to another. The second measure was that of overall revision, and was obtained by subtracting the first estimate (Do) from the last estimate

TABLE 3-1.  Analysis of Variance for the Mean Final Estimates
of the Probability of War (by Case and Type of Case)

| Case | Type of Case | Group | N | Mean Prob. of War | F-ratio* | P≤ |
|------|------|------|------|------|------|------|
| 1973 | Surprise | Com. Sense | 23 | 0.38 | 5.44 | 0.01 |
|  | Attack | Bayesians | 23 | 0.60 | (2,61) |  |
|  |  | Diagnosis | 18 | 0.36 |  |  |
|  |  | Total    = | 64 | Mean = 0.45 |  |  |
| 1977 | False | Com. Sense | 23 | 0.47 | 17.55 | 0.001 |
| Sadat | Alarm | Bayesians | 23 | 0.16 | (2,61) |  |
|  |  | Diagnosis | 18 | 0.52 |  |  |
|  |  | Total    = | 64 | Mean = 0.36 |  |  |
| 1962 | Surprise | Com. Sense | 26 | 0.43 | 6.90 | 0.002 |
| Sino-Indian | Attack | Bayesians | 23 | 0.69 | (2,65) |  |
|  |  | Diagnosis | 19 | 0.55 |  |  |
|  |  | Total    = | 68 | Mean = 0.55 |  |  |
| 1911 | False | Com. Sense | 26 | 0.49 | 5.02 | 0.01 |
| Agadir | Alarm | Bayesians | 23 | 0.27 | (2,65) |  |
|  |  | Diagnosis | 19 | 0.38 |  |  |
|  |  | Total    = | 68 | Mean = 0.39 |  |  |
| 1973,1962 | Surprise | Com. Sense | 49 | 0.41 | 10.83 | 0.001 |
| (aggregated) | Attack | Bayesians | 46 | 0.65 | (2,129) |  |
|  |  | Diagnosis | 37 | 0.45 |  |  |
|  |  | Total    = | 132 | Mean = 0.50 |  |  |
| 1977,1911 | False | Com. Sense | 49 | 0.48 | 18.27 | 0.001 |
| (aggregated) | Alarm | Bayesians | 46 | 0.22 | (2,129) |  |
|  |  | Diagnosis | 37 | 0.42 |  |  |
|  |  | Total    = | 132 | Mean = 0.37 |  |  |

*The numbers in parentheses represent degrees of freedom.
Source: Compiled by the author.

($D_5$). These measures of revision rates were compared for
the three groups, and the results of this analysis are
displayed in Table 3-3.

The results reported in Table 3-3 indicate that the
quality of the Bayesian subjects' estimates was largely due

TABLE 3-2. Two Sample T-Tests of the Mean Probability of War for the Common Sense and Diagnosis Groups (by Case and Type of Case)

| Case | Type of Case | Mean Probability of War | | T | DF* | P≤ |
| | | Common Sense | Diagnosis | | | |
| --- | --- | --- | --- | --- | --- | --- |
| 1973 | SA** | 0.38 | 0.36 | 0.43 | 39 | 0.66 |
| 1977 | FA*** | 0.47 | 0.46 | 0.80 | 39 | 0.93 |
| 1962 | SA | 0.43 | 0.55 | -1.94 | 43 | 0.06 |
| 1911 | FA | 0.49 | 0.38 | 2.02 | 43 | 0.05 |
| 1973, 1962 | SA | 0.41 | 0.45 | -1.03 | 84 | 0.31 |
| 1977, 1911 | FA | 0.48 | 0.42 | 1.39 | 81 | 0.17 |

* DF = Degrees of Freedom
** SA = Surprise Attack
*** FA = False Alarm
Source: Compiled by the author.

to the significantly higher revision rate of this group, compared to the revision rates for the other two groups. Although the between-group differences in the 1911 Agadir case were insignificant, the raw mean and overall revision scores for the Agadir case tell the same story, namely, the rate and magnitude of revision is higher for Bayesians than for non-Bayesians. The Diagnosis Group, by and large, had higher revision rates than the Common Sense Group, but not significantly so. Thus, when the mean prior estimates for this group were worse than the mean priors of the Common Sense Group, the Diagnosis Group did not produce better final estimates. This finding suggests that if an analyst is strongly misled by a set of erroneous premises or strategic assumptions, and the incoming data is not uniformly discrepant, he needs a method that would allow rapid revision rates in order to come up with accurate forecasts. Partial utilization of scientific logic is not sufficient in such cases.[8]

Critics of Bayesian analysis would certainly agree with this conclusion. However, their corollary question would be: if Bayesian methods generate high revision rates, could they not become a liability when prior premises are empirically correct, but incoming data points to different directions? In other words, if the situation does not require rapid revision, a method that produces high revision rates may be a liability rather than an asset. To answer such a question authoritatively, we would have to analyze cases of intelligence success where correct strategic assumptions led to accurate forecasts despite the ambivalence of information. This is beyond the scope of the present study. However, a partial and tentative answer can be given by looking at the 1977 Sadat case.

We have noted earlier that the 1977 case was the only case where subjects were not deceived by the prior erroneous premises of the scenario. That is, they started out with low initial probabilities of war. If we look at the absolute scores for mean and overall revision for this case, and compare them to other cases, we notice two things.[9] First, the revision rate for the Bayesian Group in the 1977 Sadat case was the *lowest,* when compared to the revision rates of the Bayesian Group in other cases. Second, the difference between the Bayesian and the non-Bayesian groups, completely disappears. Thus, the tentative empirical answer is that rapid revision rates are not an inherent attribute of the Bayesian method, but rather a function of the prior probabilities and the diagnosticity of the data. If you start with a fairly accurate initial estimate, the use of Bayesian methods will not adversely affect your final estimates. Hence, both the formal analysis of the implications of the critique regarding Bayesian revision, and the experimental results for the 1977 Sadat case suggest that this critique seems to be ill founded.


## DISCUSSION

This chapter has converted a normative debate into an empirical question. The findings strongly support the prescriptions of the "scientific logic" school and cast serious doubt on the prescriptions of the muddling-through school. To the extent that the modal conditions under which intelligence analysts operate are high ambiguity, ambivalent data, and a variety of institutional constraints, a good substantive understanding of their area and substantial experience may simply not be enough. Given the high costs of intelligence failures, and given the strong association between predictional and decisional failures, the need for improvement in the accuracy of intelligence forecasts is of major importance.

TABLE 3-3.  Analysis of Variance of Mean and Absolute Revision of the
Probability of War (by Group and Case)

| Case | Type of Case | Group | N | Mean Rev. of P(War) | Overall Rev. of P(War) | F-Ratio* | P≤ |
|------|------|------|------|------|------|------|------|
| 1973 | SA** | Com. Sense | 23 | 3.4% | 17.0% | 2.7 | 0.08 |
| | | Bayesians | 23 | 6.1 | 30.6 | (2,61) | |
| | | Diagnosis | 18 | 3.4 | 17.0 | | |
| | | Grand = | 64 | 4.4 | 21.9 | | |
| 1977 | FA*** | Com. Sense | 23 | 3.3% | 16.6% | 23.4 | 0.001 |
| | | Bayesians | 23 | -3.6 | -17.9 | (2,61) | |
| | | Diagnosis | 18 | 2.8 | 14.2 | | |
| | | Grand = | 64 | 0.7 | 3.5 | | |
| 1962 | SA | Com. Sense | 23 | 6.1% | 30.7% | 6.3 | 0.01 |
| | | Bayesians | 23 | 11.4 | 56.9 | (2,65) | |
| | | Diagnosis | 19 | 8.1 | 40.7 | | |
| | | Grand = | 68 | 8.5 | 42.3 | | |
| 1911 | FA | Com. Sense | 26 | -3.3% | -16.7% | 0.9 | -- |
| | | Bayesians | 23 | -5.5 | -27.3 | (2,65) | |
| | | Diagnosis | 18 | -4.4 | -22.2 | | |
| | | Grand = | 68 | -4.4 | -21.8 | | |
| 1973, 1962 | SA | Com. Sense | 49 | 4.9% | 24.3% | 6.9 | 0.01 |
| | | Bayesians | 46 | 8.9 | 43.8 | (2,129) | |
| | | Diagnosis | 37 | 5.8 | 29.1 | | |
| | | Grand = | 132 | 6.5 | 32.4 | | |
| 1977, 1911 | FA | Com. Sense | 49 | -0.2% | - 1.0% | 8.2 | 0.001 |
| | | Bayesians | 46 | -4.5 | -22.6 | (2,129) | |
| | | Diagnosis | 37 | -0.9 | - 9.5 | | |
| | | Grand = | 132 | -1.9 | -9.5 | | |

*Obviously, the F-ratios are the same for the mean revision and the
absolute revision variables, since the sum of means is equal to the mean
of sums.  We decided to present these two variables in the table for illustration purposes.
    ** SA = Surprise Attack
    *** FA = False Alarm
    Source: Compiled by the author.

100

It is probably true that using more rigorous tools of inference in forecasting tasks is only a supplement—not a substitute—to what Lindbloom and Cohen (1979, 14–18) call ordinary knowledge. Nevertheless, as the findings in this study suggest, it is a very important one that may decide the difference between a good forecast and a bad one. Improving collection quality, as Gazit (1980, 55–56) suggests, is a very cheap prescription to make, but a very expensive and difficult one to accomplish given the increasing complexity and interdependence of international politics. The essential question remains how to improve the quality of analysis of data, not how to minimize the need for analysis.

Before discussing this question in light of the findings, some cautionary remarks regarding the generalizability of the findings of this experiment are in order. First, the criterion of quality established in this experiment to differentiate among estimates is certainly not the most rigorous one. Since the data taken for these cases is based on real events, a good estimate was considered as one that came close to the event that had actually taken place. One may argue that we have used the wisdom of hindsight to manipulate subjects in believing in an erroneous set of prior premises, when we are not certain regarding the impact of these premises on analysts in the real cases.

Second, one may question our datum selection criteria. The argument here is that analysts in the real cases were faced with a multitude of data, only a fraction of which was presented to the subjects. Moreover, we do not know definitely whether the proportion of signals to noise in the real cases was not different than the one presented to the subjects. Even if the noise/signal distribution is unbiased, the indicators themselves may not be the ones that actually influenced estimates in the real cases.

Third, even if one accepts the experimental findings as valid, one may still ask to what extent can we make inferences on real-world intelligence analysis. The subjects for this experiment have no experience in intelligence analysis, have no knowledge of the context and process of intelligence work, and do not carry the burden of responsibility for inaccurate forecasts (Gazit 1980, 38). The experiment may be internally valid, but has low external generalizability.

Let me tackle these problems step by step. First, the criterion of quality used in this study is indeed far from perfect. However, I took one additional step to that of other investigators who (implicitly or explicitly) assume that

Bayesian analysis is an optimal method of inference and evaluate inferential procedures or outcomes according to the extent to which they approximate Bayesian outcomes (for example, Alker and Hermann 1971; Kahneman and Tversky 1973).[10]

Second, the data presented to the subjects may indeed have been a biased sample of the data available to analysts in the real cases. I have attempted to rely on the insights and empirical observations of studies examining the real cases, but one can never be sure that one did not misinterpret what has actually happened in those cases. However, I do not claim that our Bayesian subjects could have done a better job than the analysts in the real cases. What I argue is that the introduction of rigorous inference methods can minimize the rate of intelligence failures, not eliminate them. Moreover, if I did provide subjects with a biased sample of the actual data, then everyone should have been misled in the same way, regardless of one's method of estimation. Since this did not happen, I believe our findings to be valid.

Third, anticipating criticism with regard to the external generalizability of the findings, several personal background variables were solicited from the subjects. Neither the year level of the subjects as an indicator of scholarly experience, nor their grade point average, as an indicator of scholarly achievement, accounted for differences in estimates. It would be extremely interesting to conduct a similar experiment with real intelligence analysts as subjects; however, we suspect the results to be the same as the ones reported here. In addition, Dawes (1980) documents evidence from a variety of expert judgment tasks that points to the same direction; namely, intuitive judgments even by the most knowledgeable experts are prone to significant error rates.

Coming back to the question of how to improve hit rates of intelligence forecasts, a few concluding comments are in order. Even if we are able to replace intuitive intelligence analyses by systematic forecasts based on a set of empirically validated early warning indicators, it would be presumptuous to expect that those early warning indicators would cover the enormous variety of issue areas and problems that intelligence analysts or decision makers face. Military surprise is not the only concern of intelligence analysts or decision makers. Handel's (1980) discussion of diplomatic surprise is an excellent illustration of another domain with which decision makers have been concerned, but in which efforts to generate such early warning indicators are virtually nonexistent. Lacking the objective and usable knowledge to replace intuition in all issue areas of foreign and domestic politics, and having some good sense as to why ordinary knowledge is insufficient for accurate forecasting, the behavioral scientist can still be of major aid to the decision maker. The behavioral scientist can teach decision makers to make their prior premises explicit, to examine the fit between data and rival hypotheses, and to combine prior background information with current indicators in a way that would minimize the risks of biased inferences. In short, if the scholar can not provide policy makers with answers to all the questions the latter may have, the scholar can at least improve the methods decision makers use in order to generate subjective answers to such questions. In so doing, the scholar can help decision makers to come up with significantly better answers than the ones the latter usually produce.

## NOTES

1. It is no way implied that the use of these heuristics always leads to misestimation. On the contrary, these heuristics are extremely economical and useful tools of intuitive inference. However, indiscriminatory utilization of these heuristics may result in consistent misestimation to the extent that it is often accompanied by neglect of complementary tools. For instance, inference based on availability that is not combined with indications of relative frequency, representativeness of evidence that neglects base rates, and prior beliefs that are not matched by null hypotheses, are all likely to lead to misestimation. See Tversky and Kahneman (1974), and Nisbett and Ross (1980).

2. A note of caution is in order. Most studies of intelligence estimates deal with the causes and circumstances of intelligence failures. The cases selected for these analyses are mostly cases where intelligence analysts failed to foresee imminent enemy attacks. Cases of intelligence success or cases of false alarm are rarely dealt with in the literature. One obvious reason for this bias in the case selection is the low availability of nonclassified data concerning intelligence successes and false alarm cases. But a more important reason is that success and false alarm cases are very difficult to verify because of the strong association between intelligence forecasts and war pre-

parations of the analyst's nation (Betts 1978, 62; Handel 1976; Shlaim 1976, 378).

3. Some of these problems that directly relate to the experiment conducted in this study will be dealt with in the discussion section.

4. Since the cases of false alarm are relatively less known, a few words on each are in order. The Agadir case involves a dispute between France and Germany over French attempts to establish a protectorate in Morocco and Germany's claims for French concessions in the Congo. Both the French and their British allies estimated the probability of war as high, although there was a firm German decision not to go to war regardless of what Germany got in the Congo. The Sadat case involves an estimate of Israel's intelligence analysts that the probability of war is high, *after* Sadat announced his intention to visit Jerusalem in November 1977.

5. The scenarios and data for the historical cases are derived from the following sources. For the 1973 case: Handel (1976); Ben Zvi (1976); Shlaim (1976); Brecher (1980); and Stein and Tanter (1980). For the 1977 case: Yediot Aharonot (1977); and Ha'aretz (1977). For the 1962 Sino-Indian war: Ram (1973); Jetly (1979); and Vertzberger (1978). For the 1911 Agadir crisis: Barlow (1940); and Williamson (1969).

6. The Diagnosis Group, which is manipulated to overemphasize current indicators, received its title from a medical analogy. Medical diagnosis usually involves inquiry about the patient's medical history as well as identification of symptoms, a process of diagnosis similar to the mental process of revision used by the third group.

7. The experimental material was presented to the subjects in the following sequence: (1) General instructions (Appendix 1.A). (2) Scenario 1 (or 3). In this step subjects were required to estimate initial probabilities for the war/no war events. (3) Scenario 2 (or 4). Again, subjects were requested to generate initial estimates. (4) Group instructions. (5) Data for case 1 (or 3). At this point, subjects were requested to revise their estimates on the basis of the data. (6) Data for case 2 (or 4). In a previous run of the experiment, where subjects were provided first with the group instructions and only later with the scenarios and the data, we found significant differences among the prior probabilities of the three groups. This should not have happened since all groups use intuition for the generation of initial probabilities. It was hypothesized that being Bayesian or quasi-Bayesian does something to

the analyst. To avoid the recurrence of these inter-group differences, we requested the subjects to generate initial estimates before they received group-specific instructions for revision.

8. One of the reasons for the mixed record of success for the second and third hypotheses may lie in the fact that three subjects who did the 1973 and 1977 cases and belonged to the Common Sense Group, identified the historical cases despite the fictitious disguise. Thus, their estimates for both cases were highly accurate. Although this fact was insufficient to distort the differences between the Bayesian and the Common Sense Group because the Bayesians did considerably better, it may have been very instrumental in erasing the differences between the Common Sense and Diagnosis Groups.

9. By looking at absolute rates, I mean ignoring the signs of the revision scores; in other words, ignoring the direction of revision. What we want to see is *by how much* an analyst changed his mind, not whether the analyst increased or decreased his estimated probability of war.

10. It is not that optimal evaluation criteria are not available as some (for example, Janis and Mann 1977, 11) may argue. One criterion or procedure appropriate to the kind of problems we have investigated is that of calibration (Brown, Kahr, and Peterson 1974, 424–37). This procedure examines the fit between subjective estimates and the observed frequency of occurrence of an event, given a probabilistic estimate. For instance, in weather forecasting, we take all the days in which a forecaster estimated the probability of rain as 0.60 and see what proportion of rain days we had among this group. We do the same for all probability estimates. Figure 3-7 shows how evaluation is done on the basis of this procedure. However, it is obvious that an enormous amount of data is required for this procedure.

APPENDIX 1.A:
GENERAL INSTRUCTIONS

You are a senior analyst in the military intelligence of nation A. Your nation has been involved in a long and bitter conflict with nation B. Your job is to provide the political leaders of your nation with probabilistic estimates regarding the following events:

Figure 3-7. Calibration of Assessments: An Example

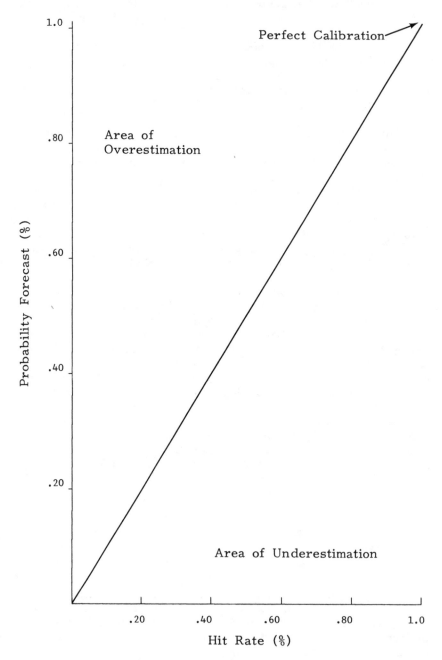

*Source:* Compiled by the author.

Event 1 ($E_1$): Nation B is going to attack us within the next month.

Event 2 ($E_2$): Nation B is *not* going to attack us within the next month.

Note that only one of these two events can occur at the same time. Thus, the probabilities that you assign to these two events *have to sum up to 1.0 (or 100%)*.

You will have to perform your analysis on two cases. For each case, the information you will be given is divided into two sections. First, you will get a short paragraph summarizing the history of the conflict and your experience in estimating each scenario. Please assign probabilistic estimates to the two events. In order to generate these estimates, rely on your common sense and intuition. Your estimates of these events based on the information provided by scenario 1 should appear in the first part of the answer sheet entitled Case 1. Your estimates based on scenario 2 should appear in the first part of the answer sheet entitled Case 2.

Having done this, you turn back and reread the first scenario. At this point you get the first group of data relating to the first case. This set of data consists of five informational items that will help you confirm or revise your initial estimates. Each informational item carries a chronological number and a date. Having read an item, you should decide whether to change your prior estimates. If you decide not to change it, please write down in the appropriate place on the answer sheet to Case 1 your previous estimate. If you choose to revise your estimate, please write down your new estimate. Do the same thing with the set of informational items relating to case 2.

Please remember: your estimates of the attack/no attack events must always sum up to 1.0 (or 100%), whether you revise them or not!

APPENDIX 1.B:
INSTRUCTIONS FOR GROUP II

In order to revise your initial estimates of the attack/no attack events, you will be using a special statistical method called Bayesian analysis. This method is very simple, but in order to make sure that you understand how to use it, I will introduce it by using a simple example.

Suppose you have been dating John for quite a while. You feel that you have become increasingly attached to him, but before you get into a serious emotional involvement with him, you want to make sure that John feels the same about you. Hence, your hypotheses are:

$$H_1 = \text{John loves me;}$$
$$H_2 = \text{John does not love me.}$$

1. In order to determine the likelihood of these hypotheses, you look into John's past dating record. This record shows that John has dated six girls in the past five years. In two of those cases, John was serious about the girls he dated. With his other four dates, he just "fooled around." On the basis of this dating record, what is the probability of:

$H_1$   John loves me---------- =   _____ %

$H_2$   John does not love me-- =   _____ %

What you have just done is to generate the prior probability ratio. This is precisely what you did when you assigned probabilities to the attack/no attack events on the basis of the information given in the scenario. That is, you generated initial estimates on the basis of background information that does not relate directly to the case at hand.

2. The next step is to revise your estimates as new information reaches you. In terms of our love affair example, you want to look into John's behavior toward you to ascertain the likelihood of your hypotheses. The first thing that you have noticed is that whenever you talk about your future aspirations, plans, and concerns, John becomes seriously interested and listen very carefully. You ask yourself: what is the probability that John will display such an interest in my future plans if he loves me?

Probability of John displaying an interest in my plans, assuming that John loves me, is:

$$\text{----} = P(D_1/H_1) = \underline{\hspace{2cm}} \%$$

Now you ask yourself another question: what is the probability that John will display an interest in my future plans if John *does not* love me?

> Probability of John displaying an interest in my plans, assuming that John *does not* love me is:

$$---- = P(D_1/H_2) = \underline{\hspace{2cm}}\%$$

Now you have the two elements needed for Bayesian analysis. You have the prior probability ratio that you obtain from your estimates in step 1, by dividing:

$$\frac{P(H_1)}{P(H_2)}$$

You also have the second element, the likelihood ratio, that is obtained by your estimates in step 2.

$$\text{Likelihood Ratio} = \frac{P(D_1/H_1)}{P(D_1/H_2)}$$

3. The next step is to combine your estimates. This is done by multiplying the prior probability ratio by the likelihood ratio in the following way:

$$\frac{P(H_1)}{P(H_2)} \times \frac{P(D_1/H_1)}{P(D_1/H_2)} = \frac{P(H_1/D_1)}{P(H_2D_1)}$$

The ratio $\dfrac{P(H_1/D_1)}{P(H_2/D_1)}$ is called: the posterior odds.

4. In the next step you want to incorporate additional data into your estimation process. You have noticed that

whenever you signaled John that you are interested in his meeting your folks, he seemed to become very reluctant. You ask the same questions as you did in the previous step.

What is the probability that John will be reluctant to meet my folks, assuming that John loves me? This gives you:

$$P(D_2/H_1) \quad = \quad \underline{\hspace{2cm}} \%$$

What is the probability that John will be reluctant to meet my folks, assuming that John *does not* me? This gives you:

$$P(D_2/H_2) \quad = \quad \underline{\hspace{2cm}} \%$$

Now, again you combine the current estimates with the previous one. This is done by taking the posterior odds (that is, the outcome of step 3) and the new likelihood ratio and multiplying them.

$$\frac{P(H_1/D_1)}{P(H_2/D_1)} \quad \times \quad \frac{P(D_2/H_1)}{P(D_2/H_2)} \quad = \quad \frac{P(H_1/D_1,D_2)}{P(H_2/D_1,D_2)}$$

The same operation is performed for each additional datum. Note that while the prior probability ratio must always equal 1.0 (or 100%), when the numerator and denominator are summed, the likelihood ratio—summed—may be greater or smaller than 1.0 (or 100%).

If you have any problems understanding the method or applying it to the intelligence cases, please feel free to ask me. I will be glad to help you.

APPENDIX 1.C:
INSTRUCTIONS FOR GROUP 3

In order to revise your estimates you do the following things:

1. On the basis of the scenario you estimate the probabilities of the two events ($E_1$ and $E_2$).

2. For each datum you ask the following questions:

a) What is the probability of observing this datum if $E_1$ were true, that is, if nation B is going to attack your nation *for sure*. This gives you $P(D/E_1)$.

b) What is the probability of observing this datum if $E_2$ were true, that is, if nation B is *not* going to attack your nation. This gives you $P(D/E_2)$.

3. Having answered the questions in (2) by assigning the appropriate probabilities, you are now in a better position to revise your estimates, given the new information. Now you can determine the new probabilities of $E_1$ and $E_2$.

APPENDIX 2.A:
SCENARIO I

This is a brief summary of major events in the conflict between your nation (A) and your enemies (nations B and C).

In the past 25 years your nation has been involved in four major wars with nations B and C. Your nation has won in each of these wars. The victory in the third war (which occurred six years ago) was largely due to the overwhelming superiority of your nation's air force. In that war your enemies lost virtually their entire aircraft fleet. Although B and C have replaced most of their losses in aircraft due to massive shipments from superpower U, your nation's aerial superiority remains unchallenged. In the fourth war, which was essentially a war of attrition, your nation's air force operated almost without interference in your enemies' territory.

This overwhelming aerial superiority has not changed over the years. You have every reason in the world to believe that as long as your enemies have not achieved sufficient aerial capability, they would not dare to attack your nation. No one would be stupid enough to initiate a war when he knows that he is going to be defeated for sure.

Several months ago, nation B declared a general state of alert and built up its troops along its border with A. The leaders of your nation were alarmed, but you argued that as long as there is no change in the balance of aerial capabilities, the likelihood of war is extremely low. You were, of course, right, and your political leaders were wrong. Since then, everything was very calm along the borders, and no significant events or changes in your enemies' capabilities have taken place.

Data for Case 1

*Datum #1 ($D_1$)*

Date: 1 January 1984

The president of nation B met with the president of nation C. The defense ministers of these two nations also attended the meeting. No information regarding the issues discussed or the outcome of the meeting has been released, except the fact that the discussion concerned issues of common interests to the two nations.

*Datum #2 ($D_2$)*

Date: 3 January 1984

The foreign minister of nation B left today for the United States. He is scheduled to meet with the United Nations (UN) secretary general and with the U.S. secretary of state. Before leaving B's national airport, the foreign minister of B stated that the purpose of his visit to the United States is to find ways in which a just and durable settlement to the dispute with A can be secured.

*Datum #3 ($D_3$)*

Date: 10 January 1984

A massive build-up of troops and equipment has been observed along areas in B and C's territories bordering your nation. Both nations have concentrated a large number of tanks and infantry in these areas. Also, a large number of antiaircraft missile batteries have been moved by B and C closer to their borders with A. The deployment of B's and C's troops is defensive in nature. It was publicly announced in B's national TV news broadcast on the opening of the annual military exercise. Your experience indicates that B's army always holds its annual maneuvers at this time of the year.


*Datum #4 (D$_4$)*

Date: 13 January 1984

The official newspaper of nation B announced today that the general staff of B's army is organizing a study-tour for some 100 senior and petty officers to a number of European countries. The officers will visit the training bases of the armies of those states and will examine new training methods. This tour will take place in mid-February. Officers interested in the tour are urged to fill in applications by the end of January.


*Datum #5 (D$_5$)*

Date: 16 January 1984

A large scale evacuation of the military advisers of superpower U stationed in B and C and their families has begun today. Recently, the relations between B and U have been somewhat strained. A year ago, B's government expelled all foreign military personnel stationed in its country. U's military advisers returned after a few months, but relations between B and U have not been too friendly. Your experience indicates, however, that in periods of high tension between B and A, the families of the foreign military (and technical) personnel have been evacuated.


APPENDIX 2.B:
SCENARIO 2

The year is 1990. Five years ago (while you were on leave abroad) nations B and C launched an all-out surprise attack and caught your nation's army totally unprepared. In the war that followed your nation won, but the price paid for the military victory was very heavy in terms of casualties. The failure of your superiors to provide the army with an early warning of the imminent attack cost them with their job. They have been fired and you have been called in to replace the chief of military intelligence.

The result of this war was an agreement between your nation and nations B and C. Demilitarized zones have been established along the borders. This agreement was conducted by the representatives of superpower K who assumed the role of mediator, since the leaders of nations B and C refused to negotiate directly with your nation's leaders.

Since then, everything has been calm along the borders. Additional efforts to move toward a comprehensive settlement of the conflict, conducted under the auspices of K's representatives, were only partially successful. This was so because the leaders of B and C continued to deny your nation's legitimate rights for security, and refused to negotiate with A's leaders directly. Although B has violated several times the agreement by moving its armed forces into the demilitarized zone, the violations were not too serious. Each time a violation was discovered, B withdrew its forces from the demilitarized zone.

Another important development in the area was that B has severed its relations with superpower U, B's former chief supplier of arms. This meant that B had serious troubles in finding spare parts for its weapons systems; and as a result, the balance of military capabilities largely favored your nation.

However, you have learned one important lesson from the surprise attack: things are not always as they seem to be at first glance. Your enemies are sneaky and do not hesitate to deceive you, because their only chance to succeed militarily in a war depends upon their capacity to surprise you and catch you unprepared. Thus, you believe that you should be very cautious in your interpretation of the intelligence data and not repeat your mistakes twice, because there might not be a third time for corrections.


Data for Case 2

*Datum #1 ($D_1$)*

Date: 15 September 1990

The president of nation B declared in a speech to his parliament that in order to prove to the world that his efforts to achieve a comprehensive peace settlement with A are sincere, he is willing to come to your nation's capital and open direct negotiations with your nation's leaders. He said that he will visit your nation as soon as he gets a formal invitation from your nation's president.

*Datum #2 (D$_2$)*

Date: 17 September 1990

A new and major violation of the demilitarization agreement has been discovered today. A large number of B's troops have moved into the demilitarized zone. Such a large scale violation of the demilitarization has never occurred before.

*Datum #3 (D$_3$)*

Date: 19 September 1990

B's president announced today that he had received a formal invitation from A's president to come to visit nation A. He said that the trip is scheduled for September 26. B's president also said that he is planning to speak to A's parliament and convince A's politicians of the sincerity of his peaceful intentions.

Foreign observers said that this move by B's president might raise widespread opposition within B itself.

*Datum #4 (D$_4$)*

Date: 19 September 1990

A general state of alert has been declared in B's army. Leaves have been canceled, and formal events in which senior military officials were supposed to participate have been postponed indefinitely. Foreign observers interpreted this move as an attempt by B's president to secure the army's support of his unexpected decision to visit A. Also, this has been seen as a precaution against any potential uprising initiated by B's militant opposition.

*Datum #5 (D$_5$)*

Date: 23 September 1990

B's president arrived at C's capital for a 24-hour visit. The reported purpose of the visit is to persuade C's president to join the peace initiative. Specific contents of the discussion between the two leaders were not released, but no joint communique was issued. This indicates basic differences between the two leaders' positions. Moreover, after B's president had left C, the president of nation C criticized in a press conference B's policy of appeasement. He argued that B's policy is counterproductive and serves A's aggressive purposes.

APPENDIX 2.C:
CASE 3: SCENARIO

Date: 7 September 1983

You are a senior analyst in the military intelligence service of nation A. Your nation has a history of good relations with nation B that resides to the northeast. However, a border region where the boundaries have never been clearly demarked has been a source of dispute between your nation and nation B during the last several years. Talks that were held between the diplomats of nations A and B failed to produce any agreement. Three years ago, a small unit of B's army entered into a territory that A claimed to belong to her by right and by history. A brief border skirmish followed, resulting in very few casualties. It seemed that nation B was very reluctant to escalate the dispute into a military confrontation.

Nations A and B share a wide variety of common interests. Both nations lead a large bloc of small nations that opposes the intervention of the superpowers in the region and calls for cooperation among the developing countries. Your nation's diplomats were often used by nation B as a channel of communication to those nations with which B has no diplomatic relations. In addition, your nation mediated negotiations between B and superpower Q that terminated a long war between B and Q.

This wide variety of common interests between A and B, as well as the fact that since both nations gained independence they never fought each other, makes you confident in the possibility of resolving the border dispute diplomatically. Common interests overshadow the differences between A and B regarding the border territory, and you believe that with good will and patience a compromise can be reached.

Data for Case 3

*Datum #1 (D$_1$)*

Date: 20 September 1983

B's forces crossed the line in which they have been previously stationed and entered A's territory in the northeast sector of the disputed border. Although the size of B's force was fairly small, A's troops stationed in a border post in this region had to withdraw. No severe casualties were reported.

*Datum #2 (D$_2$)*

Date: 23 September 1983

B's prime minister sent a letter to A's president suggesting a mutual withdrawal of A and B to a distance of 13 miles along the entire frontier. The letter also included a proposal for a meeting between A and B's delegates without any preconditions, setting the date of October 15 as a target of the beginning of negotiations.

*Datum #3 (D$_3$)*

Date: 30 September 1983

Another border skirmish erupted, this time in a different region of the disputed border. B's troops opened fire on a border post of A, and A's troops responded by firing back. An exchange of artillery fire ended after a few hours, resulting in only a few casualties on both sides.

*Datum #4 (D$_4$)*

Date: 9 October 1983

B's diplomats resumed their call for mutual withdrawal and negotiations without preconditions. Despite A's government's refusal to discuss the eastern sector the disputed territory, B's prime minister suggested that everything should be open for negotiations and that each side may bring up any issue it sees relevant.

*Datum #5 (D$_5$)*

Date: 18 October 1983

A report of B's troop movements along the entire frontier has just arrived. Though troop movements have been quite frequent in recent years, the scale of these movements is larger than previous ones.

APPENDIX 2.D:
CASE 4: SCENARIO

Date: 5 July 1998

Now you are a senior analyst in the military intelligence of major power A. The 1990s are an era of new colonialism. Many of the small countries have disintegrated domestically, and the major power (five in number) have stepped in, seizing virtual control over a large number of small states in remote areas. Your government has special interests in country M, which is undergoing a chaotic process of disintegration. Your government is determined to protect its citizens and economic interests in M, wishing to establish actual control of A over this small country. However, this desire clashes with major power B's interests in M. B's desires to secure equal opportunities for its economic activities in M.

Six years ago, a similar crisis developed over the same issues. B made a number of threats that it would go to war with A if a protectorate over M was established. The crisis went to the brink of war, but war was prevented only as a result of intervention by A's ally, major power K, on A's side. At a conference summoned to resolve this crisis, B agreed to the establishment of a police force, manned by A's troops, in country M. This meant a great diplomatic victory for your country.

However, B's behavior in that crisis indicated to you that it is willing to risk war in order to prevent full domination of A over M. Moreover, the support of your ally K regarding the protectorate business is weaker now than it was six years ago. Thus, the constraints that operated on B six years ago have been reduced, and the incentives to clash with A militarily have increased markedly.

As a result of increasing chaos in state M, your government has recently decided to send a strong military expedition to M's capital to enforce "law and order."

Data for Case 4

*Datum #1 ($D_1$)*

Date: 6 July 1998

B's reaction to the military expedition of A to M's capital was angered protest and a demand for a conference to be held between the foreign ministers of A and B. However, in the course of the conference, B's foreign minister somehow modified his position. Instead of rejecting A's claim for control over M, he recognized A's special interests in M, but required compensation for B in the form of concessions of territories and economic opportunities in another colony, J, where the two have competing interests.

*Datum #2 ($D_2$)*

Date: 12 July 1998

B's largest gunboat, *Dude,* anchored in M's major port. B claimed that this move was designed to protect B's citizens in the port city, although no B citizens were present in that city.

*Datum #3 ($D_3$)*

Date: 18 July 1998

B's major and only ally, major power U, expressed its discontent with B's latest move. U's head of state stated officially that U would not support B because the military alliance between U and B does not cover contingencies relating to hostilities in remote areas.

*Datum #4 ($D_4$)*

Date: 26 July 1998

A conference, summoned by A's ally, nation K, to resolve the crisis, ended in stalemate. When asked by K's foreign minister, what does B want, B's foreign minister replied that B wants to establish full control over country J. A's foreign minister stated that this is out of the question. At that point, B's foreign minister made a blunt statement that B would go to "extreme lengths" to get what it wants.


*Datum #5 ($D_5$)*

Date: 31 July 1998

In an additional meeting between the foreign ministers of A and B, the latter made a significant concession. He stated that B is willing to accept only a fraction of J's territory, but with access to the sea. Observers have indicated that this is much more acceptable a proposition than previous claims by B.


REFERENCES

Alker, Henry A., and Margaret C. Hermann. 1971. "Are Bayesian Decisions Artificially Intelligent? The Effect of Task and Personality on Conservatism in Processing Information." *Journal of Personality and Social Psychology* 19(1):31–41.

Andriole, Steven J., and Robert A. Young. 1977. "Toward the Development of an Early Crisis Warning System." *International Studies Quarterly* 21:107–50.

Ascher, William. 1979. *Forecasting: An Appraisal for Policy Makers and Planners.* Baltimore: Johns Hopkins University Press.

Axelrod, Robert. 1973. "Schema Theory: An Information Processing Model of Perception and Cognition." *American Political Science Review* 67(4):1248–66.

Bar Hillel, Maya. 1977. "The Base-Rate Fallacy in Probability Judgment." Advanced Research Projects Agency: Research Monograph. Eugene, Oregon: *Decisions and Designs.*

Barlow, Ima C. 1940. *The Agadir Crisis.* Chapel Hill: North Carolina University Press.

Ben Zvi, Abraham. 1976. "Hindsight and Foresight: A Conceptual Framework for the Analysis of Surprise Attacks." *World Politics* 28(3):381–95.

Betts, Richard K. 1978. "Analysis, War, and Decision: Why Intelligence Failures Are Inevitable." *World Politics* 31(1):61–89.

Brecher, Michael. 1980. *Decisions in Crisis: Israel, 1967 and 1973.* Berkeley and Los Angeles: University of California Press.

Brown, Rex V., Andrew S. Kahr, and Cameron Peterson. 1974. *Decision Analysis for the Manager.* New York: Holt, Reinhart, and Winston.

Daly, Judith A., and Thomas R. Davies. 1978. "The Early Warning and Monitoring System: A Progress Report." *Decisions and Designs, Inc.* McLean, Va.: Defense Advanced Research Projects Agency, July 1978.

Dawes, Robyn M. 1980. "The Robust Beauty of Improper Linear Models." *American Psychologist* 35(7).

Gazit, Shlomo. 1980. "Estimates and Fortune Telling in Intelligence Work." *International Security* 4(4):36–56.

George, Alexander L. 1972. "The Case for Multiple Advocacy in Making Foreign Policy." *American Political Science Review* 66(3):751–94.

Ha'aretz. 1977. (Hebrew Daily). Issues of Nov. 14–20, 1977.

Handel, Michael. 1980. "Surprise and Change in International Politics." *International Security* 4(4):57–85.

Handel, Michael I. 1976. *Perception, Deception, and Surprise: The Case of the Yom Kippur War.* Jerusalem: Jerusalem Papers on Peace Problems, No. 19.

Janis, Irving L., and Leon Mann. 1977. *Decision Making: A Psychological Analysis of Conflict, Choice and Commitment.* New York: Free Press.

Jervis, Robert. 1976. *Perception and Misperception in International Politics.* Princeton: Princeton University Press.

——————. 1968. "Hypotheses on Misperception." *World Politics* 20(4):454–79.

Jetly, Nancy. 1979. *India-China Relations, 1947–1977.* New Delhi: Radiant Publishers.

Kahneman, Daniel, and Amos Tversky. 1977. "Intuitive Prediction: Biases and Corrective Procedures." Research Monograph. Eugene, Oregon: *Decisions and Designs.*

——————. 1973. "On the Psychology of Prediction." *Psychological Review* 80(4):237–51.

Lindbloom, Charles E., and David K. Cohen. 1979. *Usable Knowledge: Social Science and Social Problem Solving.* New Haven: Yale University Press.

McClelland, Charles F. 1977. "The Anticipation of International Crisis." *International Studies Quarterly* 21:15–38.

Nisbett, Richard E., and Lee Ross. 1980. *Human Interference: Strategies and Shortcomings of Social Judgment.* Englewood Cliffs: Prentice Hall.

Phillips, L. O., and Ward Edwards. 1966. "Conservatism in a Simple Probability Inference Task." *Journal of*

*Experimental Psychology* 72:346–54.

Ram, Mohan. 1973. *Politics of Sino-Indian Confrontation.* New Delhi: Vikas Publishing House.

Schweitzer, Nicholas. 1978. "An Application of Bayesian Approaches to Intelligence Estimation." In *Quantitative Approaches to Political Intelligence: The CIA Experience.* Ed. Heuer Richards. Boulder, Colo.: Westview Press.

————. 1976. "Bayesian Analysis for Intelligence: Some Focus on the Middle East." Paper presented at the 17th Annual Convention of the International Studies Association, Toronto, February 28, 1976.

Shlaim, Avi. 1976. "Failures in National Intelligence Estimates: The Case of the Yom Kippur War." *World Politics* 28(3):348–80.

Singer, J. David. 1978. "The Correlates of War." *Michigan Alumnus,* April 1978, pp. 7–9.

————. 1973. "The Peace Researcher and Foreign Policy Prediction." *Papers of Peace Science Society (International)* 23(1):1–13.

————. 1971. *The Scientific Study of Politics: An Approach to Foreign Policy Analysis.* Morristown: General Learning Press.

Singer, J. David, and Melvin Small. 1974. "Foreign Policy Indicators: Predictors of War in History and in the State of the World Message." *Policy Sciences* 5:271–96.

Singer, J. David, and Michael D. Wallace, eds. 1979. "Introduction." In *To Augur Well: Early Warning Indicators in World Politics.* Beverly Hills: Sage, pp. 7–16.

Stein, Janice G., and Raymond Tanter. 1980. *Rational Decision-Making: Israel's Security Choices.* Columbus: Ohio State University Press.

Stoll, Richard J., and Michael Champion. 1980. "Predicting the Escalation of Serious Disputes to International War." Paper delivered at the 15th North-American Peace Science Society (International). Philadelphia, Pa., November 1977 (revised and updated February 1980).

Tversky, Amos, and Daniel Kahneman. 1974. "Judgment under Uncertainty: Heuristics and Biases." *Science* 185:1124–30.

————. 1973. "Availability: A Heuristic for Judging Frequency and Probability." *Cognitive Psychology* 5:207–32.

Vertzberger, Ya'acov. 1978. "India's Border Crisis with China." *Jerusalem Journal of International Relations* 3(2–3).

Williamson, Samuel R. 1969. *The Politics of Grand Strategy.* Cambridge, Mass.: Harvard University Press.

Wohlstetter, Roberta. 1962. *Pearl Harbor: Warning and Decision*. Stanford: Stanford University Press.

*Yediot Aharonot*. 1977. (Hebrew Daily). Issues of Nov. 14–20, 1977.

# 4

# The Use of Force by the United States: Contingent Forecasts

*Richard J. Stoll*

INTRODUCTION

The United States, like most governments, often calls upon its armed forces to serve political, as well as military, purposes. The political purpose is to influence the perceptions and behavior of foreign leaders and groups, usually in conjunction with some diplomatic communication. This instrument has utility if foreign leaders (or groups) believe that the U.S. government is serious, and may very well escalate the use of its armed forces from symbolic to combat activity. Thus, the use of military forces is an indicator of both current serious involvement by the U.S. government and possible future combat, even war. Forecasting the level of this involvement is, therefore, an important task.

This chapter is an attempt to apply the tools of the scientist to this policy-oriented forecasting problem. After ascertaining the relationship between a set of indicators and the level of U.S. involvement, a number of conditional forecasts will be made that predict the probability of a high level of U.S. involvement in a variety of geographic regions under both internal and external circumstances. The data used to generate these forecasts are taken from a recent study by Blechman and Kaplan (1978) that documents the use of U.S. armed forces as a policy instrument during the time period 1946–75.

## THE DATA SET

The definition of a political use of the armed forces used in this paper is as follows:

> A political use of the armed forces occurs when physical actions are taken by one or more components of the uniformed military services as part of a deliberate attempt by the national authorities to influence, or to be prepared to influence, specific behavior of individuals in another nation without engaging in a continuing contest of violence (Blechman and Kaplan 1978, 12).

Five elements make up a political use of armed forces:

- A physical change in the disposition of at least part of the armed forces.
- Behind this activity there had to have been a consciousness of purpose.
- The decision makers must have sought to attain their objectives by gaining influence in the target state, not by physically imposing their will.
- The decision makers must have sought to avoid a significant contest of violence.
- A specific behavior had to have been desired of another actor (Blechman and Kaplan 1978, 12–14).

Surveying three categories of sources (official records of military operations, chronologies of international events, and compilations of U.S. military activity prepared by government agencies and other researchers), 226 discrete uses of the armed forces as a political instrument by the U.S. government were uncovered from 1 January 1946 through 31 December 1976. Blechman and Kaplan believe that, though they obtained less than the universe of such incidents, they have "an adequate representation of all the instances in which the U.S. armed forces were used in a way that would fit the terms of the definition" (Blechman and Kaplan 1978, 16). An examination of their list supports this claim.

The data set collected by Blechman and Kaplan contains seven types of variables:

- Incident identification numbers and dates.
- Contextual characteristics of the incident.

- Types and sizes of U.S. armed forces used in the incident.
- Movement and readiness status of U.S. armed forces used in the incident.
- Activities of the U.S. armed forces used in the incident.
- Number and types of actors in the incident besides the U.S.
- U.S. public opinion of the president before and after the incident (Kaplan 1977, 25).

## INDICATORS FOR THE MODEL

A number of variables from the Blechman and Kaplan data set were used to create the forecasts. These variables are divided into three categories: the outcome variable; the predictor variables; and finally, the regional/situational variables that describe the likely "hot spots" to be faced by the United States in the near future.

### The Outcome Variable: Level of Action (LEVEL)

The specific outcome variable of this study is the level of activity undertaken by the U.S. military during the situations in which it is used to further U.S. foreign policy objectives. Blechman and Kaplan's data set contains coding for the presence or absence of 13 specific categories of action by the U.S. military, plus a residual category ("other activity"). For the purposes of this study, activities were crudely scaled from low to high, in terms of the propensity of the activity to lead to U.S. involvement in combat. This scaling was then collapsed to a dichotomous variable representing low and high levels of activity. Table 4-1 displays the grouping of the activities into the low and high categories.[1]

Note that in any particular situation the coding of level represents the "high water mark" of activity by the U.S. military. But given my desire to identify and forecast the most dangerous situations of U.S. involvement, I do not consider this to be a drawback. The ordering of activities shown in Table 4-1 appears to be reasonable. One could argue for a different threshold between the low and high categories, but the five activities in the high level do represent serious, substantial activities that by their very nature raise the possibility of combat.

Predictor Variables

In addition to the seven regional/situational variables used to generate the forecasts, eight predictor variables with substantive content are used to estimate the probability of a high level of action by the U.S. military.

TABLE 4-1. Categorization of Activity by the U.S. Military into Low and High Levels of Activity

| Low Levels of Activity | High Levels of Activity |
|---|---|
| 1. Forces made present in or near area. | 9. Establishment of selective or complete blockade. |
| 2. Exercise or demonstration. | 10. Interposition between two foreign actors. |
| 3. Visit to foreign nation. | 11. Emplacement of ground forces. |
| 4. Exercise of right to transit. | 12. Patrol, reconnaissance. |
| 5. Transport equipment to a foreign actor. | 13. Firepower used or other violent action. |
| 6. Escort foreign actor forces, equipment, or operatives. | |
| 7. Transport foreign actor forces, equipment, or operatives. | |
| 8. Evacuation. | |

Source: Compiled by the author.

## Number of Actions (MULTACT)

Given that the U.S. military is used more than once in an incident, the probability of a high level of activity is greater than if only a single action is taken. Aside from the obvious probabilistic argument (the more actions taken, the more likely, randomly, that one is to be at the high level), there are theoretical reasons for believing there should be an association between these two variables. If the U.S. government must repeatedly follow up its actions with additional uses of the military, then (1) the situation must be considered serious enough to call for repeated applications; and (2) the target of the influence attempt is not complying fully with the requests (or demands) of the U.S. government. For both reasons, I expect that the United States will be more inclined to initiate a high level of activity. For purposes of forecasting, this variable was coded dichotomously (one act or greater than one act). Most (almost two-thirds) of the incidents feature only a single action by the United States. Further, there is no increase in the probability of a high level of U.S. action when more than two actions were involved.

### Size of Forces Used (FORCESIZ)

This variable is a dichotomous coding of the composite size of military forces used. Blechman and Kaplan distinguish between what they call major and minor force components for each military service. I collapse their four-category coding into a simple major-minor coding.[2] There are several reasons to suspect that the size of the force components used is related to the level of activity. First, it is reasonable to believe that the U.S. government is more likely to undertake high levels of action if large, capable forces are available for use. For example, the imposition of a blockade requires many more naval vessels than a simple port visit. Second, large forces are used to convey great concern on the part of U.S. decision makers, and it is in these situations that it is more likely that the United States will use a high level of action in defense of an important U.S. position.

### Major Naval Units (NAVY)

As Blechman and Kaplan note, units of the U.S. Navy are most frequently called upon to function as a political instrument. Of the 215 cases in their book length study, 177 (82 percent) involve the use of U.S. naval forces (Blechman and Kaplan 1978, 38). Given the popularity of this service, it is useful to include a variable measuring the extent of naval commitment.

The specific variable coded measures the use of naval power projection forces. These power projection forces are of two types: capital ships (battleships and/or aircraft carriers), and amphibious forces (those containing major amphibious ships). This variable is coded as a trichotomy, with 0 indicating the absence of all power projection units, 1 indicating the presence of major capital ships or amphibious units, and 2 indicating the presence of both types of units. As with FORCESIZ, this variable taps both the ability of the United States to stage major military operations, and the communication of serious intent on the part of the U.S. government; both of these are related to the use of high levels of military activity by the United States.

### Nuclear Capable Forces (NUKE)

A final aspect of the forces used by the U.S. government is the use (or nonuse) of units that deliver strategic nuclear weapons. These forces are used very rarely: in only 19 of the 215 incidents in Blechman and Kaplan's book length study (1978, 47–49). The relative paucity of the use of these forces, as well as the extreme threat implicit in their use, argues for a separate variable indicting the use or nonuse of these types of forces. Situations in which these forces are used would be considered very serious by the U.S. government and likely to call for the use of high levels of activity by the U.S. military.

### Presidential Popularity (PRESPOP)

Notwithstanding the well-documented "rally 'round the flag" effect on U.S. public opinion of any decisive action taken by the president (Mueller 1973, 53–59), a low level of presidential popularity may constrain his ability to use military force as a political instrument. In their investigations, Blechman and Kaplan (1978, 26–29) find that presidential popularity is positively correlated with the number of U.S. involvements per year; this offers some support for the argument outlined above.

Use of this variable does cause a problem for analysis. If there were no Gallup Poll taken within two months of the initial use of the military by the United States, this variable was coded as missing. When these cases are dropped from analysis, I am left with only 168 incidents. This is a drop of 25 percent from the original number of cases; but this is still a large number of cases to work with. Furthermore, I have no reason to suspect that the excluded cases constitute any kind of special group. Finally, there appears to be no simple and valid way of generating alternative estimates for presidential popularity for the missing cases. Thus, the estimation of U.S. activity will be based on the 168 cases for which there is complete data.

### War Participation (WAR)

The two most extreme uses of military force by the United States during the post–World War II era were the Korean and Vietnam wars. Use of the military for combat during these wars is quite properly excluded from the Blechman and Kaplan data set. However, some incidents that occurred before the full-fledged U.S. involvement are included (for example, the Gulf of Tonkin incident). A key question is the effect of participation in these wars on concurrent uses of force by the United States. Accordingly, a dummy variable is coded for the years in which the United States is involved in either the Korean (1950–53) or Vietnam (1965–73) wars. Blechman and Kaplan (1978, 30) find that noninvolvement in war in the past three years is positively related to the number of incidents per year. But whether this same relationship should hold when predicting the level of force used is another question. At the very least, it is a wise precaution to control for these involvements when predicting the level of force.

## Type of Violence (VIOL)

One general characteristic of the situation confronting U.S. decision makers is whether violence has already occurred, and if so, what kind. Given Blechman and Kaplan's coding of the situation existing before the intervention of the U.S. military, I devised a four-point scale of level of violence. The four points are: 0 = no violence; 1 = violence within a nation; 2 = violence between nations; and 3 = violence directed at U.S. citizens and property.[3] This scale depicts succeedingly higher levels of serious threat to U.S. interests, and this, in turn, should be related to the propensity of the United States to use high levels of force in these incidents.

## USSR/PRC Use of Force (USRPRCUF)

The final substantive variable to be included in the model is the level of use of force by the other two superpowers, the Union of Soviet Socialist Republics (USSR) and the People's Republic of China (PRC). For most of this period, both of these nations were antagonists of the United States. A trichotomous coding was constructed, the following with values: 0 = no threat or use of force by USSR/PRC; 1 = threat of force by USSR/PRC; and 2 = use of force by USSR/PRC. High levels of involvement by these two nation-states are expected to call forth matching levels of involvement by the United States.

Regional/Situational Variables

A third set of variables is used to generate the forecasts of levels of U.S. force. It consists of a series of dummy variables for region (essentially) and for the general type of problem within the region.

Five regional type variables are coded, each representing a different region and/or type of nation:

- members of NATO (NATO),
- Communist states other than USSR/PRC (COMST),
- U.S. allies in East Asia and the Pacific (ASALY),
- U.S. allies or client states in the Middle East (MECLNT),
- nation-states in the Caribbean, Central or South America (LATAMR).

Each of these classes of nation-states are of concern to the government of the United States, but the level of this concern may vary from class to class. To control for this possibility, U.S. level of use of force, given involvement in an incident, will be forecast for each of these nation-state types. Each variable for nation-state type will also be included in the estimating equation so as not to bias the coefficients of the substantive variables.

Two general classes of problems are likely to be encountered by U.S. decision makers in these (and other) areas: internal and external conflicts. Internal conflicts (INTCON) are confined within the borders of a single nation-state, while external conflicts (EXTCON) involve at least two nation-states. A dummy variable is coded for each situation[4], and these two variable are also included in the forecasting equation.

Ideally, special nation-state dummy variables would have been substituted for the more general regional variables, and the interactions between these regional variables and type of situation would have been included. Perhaps the interacting variables would have been used to multiply through all the other variables in the equation to develop a more specific prediction. Unfortunately, such a research strategy would fall apart because so few cases would satisfy all the criteria for each interactive variable. As a result, I adopted the more general additive effects strategy outlined above.

To conclude, the forecasting model contains many elements that will aid in the prediction of the level of activity by the U.S. military in various incidents since World War II. Let me now turn to the descriptive statistics and bivariate correlations before building the multivariate model.

## UNIVARIATE AND BIVARIATE RELATIONSHIPS

Descriptive statistics and bivariate correlations for all variables are displayed in Tables 4-6–4-9 in the Appendix. Only a summary of the correlations is discussed here.

*Correlations with LEVEL:* Focusing first on the correlations of the predictor and regional/situational variables with LEVEL (Table 4-6), I am struck by the generally small values. Only the predictor variables of multiple actions (.27), level of violence (.27), and the situational variable for minor communist states (.33), and Latin America (.26) show even moderate values.

*Correlations among Predictor Variables:* The correlations among the substantive predictor variables (Table 4-7), though a bit higher, are still only moderate at best. The highest (between FORCESIZ and MULTACT, FORCESIZ and NUKE, and WAR and PRESPOP) still only account for about 12 percent of the variance.

It is perhaps worth noting that the highest of these moderate correlations (greater than or equal to .20) fall into meaningful groups. One group consists of the different measures of force size and amount of activity (MULTACT, FORCESIZ, NAVY, and, to a lesser extent, NUKE). Linked at a lower level is the level of involvement of USSR/PRC (USRPRCUF). These correlations indicate that the United States is involved in more activities and uses higher levels of force (though not naval involvement) when another superpower is involved at high levels. Finally, there is (unsurprisingly) a negative correlation between presidential popularity and U.S. involvement in the Korean and Vietnam wars.

*Correlations among Regional/Situational Variables:* Since the regional variables will only be used one at a time in the forecasts, I will not discuss the intercorrelations between them. But I do want to discuss the relationship between the measures of internal and external conflict, and the regional variables. The internal and external variables are not direct opposites; a variety of nonconflict situations are possible. The regional variable for NATO is associated (a bit) with external conflict. The presence of a small communist state is not associated with either form of conflict. Asian allies of the United States are more often associated with external conflict, while Latin American states are more often associated with internal conflict. Finally, there is a small negative correlation between the external and internal conflict variables.

*Correlations between Predictor and Regional/Situational Variables:* The most interesting set of associations is that between the substantive predictor variables and the individual regions and situations (Table 4-9). Incidents involving communist states are associated with large-sized U.S. forces. Incidents involving U.S. Asian allies are strongly associated with high levels of involvement by USSR/PRC. Incidents involving Latin American states are associated with small levels of U.S. forces, with presidential popularity, and do not usually involve the use of force by USSR/PRC. Finally, incidents involving external violence are usually associated with the use of force by USSR/PRC.

These univariate and bivariate analyses are the necessary first steps to any scientific investigation. They reveal little in the way of strong relationships among, or within, any set of variables. Since the primary purpose of the multivariate model is forecasting, the problem of multicolinearity is not as much of concern as it would be in "normal" research; it does not affect predictions, only the relative significance of coefficients. However, given the generally low correlation, it does not appear that this is much of a problem. At this point, let me turn to the technique for estimating the forecasting model and then present the estimated parameters.

ESTIMATING THE FORECASTING MODEL

Probit Analysis: Some Problems of Interpretation

The technique used to estimate the forecasting equation is probit analysis. Probit analysis predicts the probability of the level of U.S. activity being high in each incident, given the value of the predictor and regional/situational variables. Although the generation of these probabilities is a very appealing and useful feature, it does lead to some problems of interpretation.

The first problem is measuring the fit of the model. Usually, the overall fit of a multivariate statistical model is measured by the $R^2$. But unless the predicted probabilities from a probit equation are in the proper direction and are also extreme (close to 0 or 1), the $R^2$ from even a good probit model will be low. This happens because the statistic is computed by correlating the observed variable (the 0–1 outcome) and the predicted variables (the probability). Even a good prediction of .8 will produce some degree of error, since the observed value for that case will be 1.

To better evaluate the fit of the model, the predicted probabilities will be collapsed into four categories (.00–.25; .26–.50; .51–.75 .76–1.0), and then cross-tabulated against the actual low-high activity by the U.S. military in the incident.

The second problem with probit analysis is the interpretation of the individual effects of each variable in the equation. With a multiple regression equation, the interpretation of the coefficients is straightforward; for each unit change is the predictor variable, its regression coefficient indicates the amount of change in the outcome variable. For example, if the coefficient is 1.2, then a one-unit change in the predictor variable is associated with a 1.2-unit change in the outcome variable.

The situation with probit analysis is different. Given a unit change in a predictor variable, its coefficient measures the amount of change in an index, Z. This index can range from negative to positive infinity. It is converted to a probability with a 0–1 range through the use of the cumulative normal distribution. The relationship between the index, Z, and the probability is not constant. It varies with the values of all the other values. The effect is largest if the probability, net of the particular predictor variable, is close to .5, and the effect is smallest if the probability is close to the extreme values.

The only way to get a good picture of the impact of any predictor variable on the probability is to pick out several sets of values for all the other predictors, and then observe the effects of the final variable. Fortunately, generating several different forecasts for a particular region and situation involves just this procedure.

Coefficients and Fit of the Model

Table 4-2 displays the estimated coefficients from the probit analysis. The overall fit given by the $R^2$ (and bearing in mind the problems of this measure) is quite good (.37). A number of variables in the equation have little impact on the level of activity. Among the predictor variables, use of strategic nuclear forces (NUKE), presidential popularity before the outbreak of the incident (PRESPOP), and the simultaneous involvement of the United States in a shooting war (WAR) all have little effect on the probability of high level of activity by the United States. Among the regional/situational variables, involvement by a member of NATO (NATO) or of a Middle Eastern client state (MECLNT), as well as the presence of external violence (EXTCON), also have little effect on the chances of a high level of U.S. activity.

Two of the predictor variables with moderate to high t-ratios are negatively signed: use of significant naval forces (NAVY), and level of involvement by USSR/PRC

TABLE 4-2. Probit Equation Coefficients and T-Ratios for Forecasting Model

| Variable | Coefficient | T-Ratio |
|----------|-------------|---------|
| MULTACT | 1.38 | 4.03 |
| FORCESIZ | .40 | 1.28 |
| NAVY | -.79 | -3.37 |
| NUKE | .37 | .72 |
| PRESPOP | .009 | .83 |
| WAR | -.064 | -.21 |
| VIOL | .256 | 1.73 |
| USRPRCUF | -.37 | -1.57 |
| NATO | -.19 | -.51 |
| COMST | .98 | 2.98 |
| ASALY | 1.81 | 2.68 |
| MECLNT | .39 | .82 |
| LATAMR | 1.14 | 3.15 |
| INTCON | -.44 | -1.36 |
| EXTCON | -1.90 | -2.53 |

Source: Compiled by the author.

(USRPRCUF). Although I had hypothesized a positive relationship in both cases, several of the findings from Blechman and Kaplan's study foreshadowed these results. They find that both of these variables are associated with a lack of U.S. success in achieving its objectives.

To better evaluate the fit of the model to the data, Tables 4-3 and 4-4 are offered. Table 4-3 displays a test of the mean predicted probability of high level of activity, by actual level of activity. The t-value indicates that the probabilities assigned to actual high levels of activity are much higher than those assigned to actual low level of activity.

TABLE 4-3. T-Test of Predicted Probability of High Activity, by Actual Activity

| Activity | N | Mean. Prob. | Std. Dev. | T-Ratio | Prob. |
|----------|-----|-------------|-----------|---------|-------|
| Low | 110 | .21 | .22 | 9.90 | .0001 |
| High | 58 | .59 | .26 | | |

Source: Compiled by the author.

Table 4-4 breaks the predicted probabilities into quartiles and cross-tabulates them with actual low-high level of activity. As can be seen, the model predicts the actual level of activity very well at both extremes and less well in the middle range (.25–.75).

Overall, the fit of the model is quite encouraging, and leads me to believe that it can be a useful forecasting tool. In the next section of this chapter, I develop a group of forecasts of the change of a high level of U.S. activity in various regions of the world.

## FORECASTING THE LEVEL OF U.S. MILITARY ACTIVITY

Given the model, many combinations of variable levels are possible; only a small number of sets were actually tried. Several variables were held constant across all forecasts. Since strategic nuclear forces are rarely used (and their effect was so small), all forecasting assumed a zero value (nonuse) for this variable. I also assumed that the United

TABLE 4-4. Actual Level of Activity by Predicted Probability of High Level of Activity (Column Percentages in Parentheses)

| Actual Activity Level | Predicted Probability of High Level of Activity | | | | |
|---|---|---|---|---|---|
| | 0.0-.25 | .26-.50 | .51-.75 | .76-1.0 | Total |
| Low | 76 (96) | 20 (44) | 10 (48) | 4 (17) | 110 (65) |
| High | 3 (4) | 25 (56) | 11 (52) | 19 (83) | 58 (35) |
| Totals | 79 | 45 | 21 | 23 | 168 |

Note: Tau B = .58; Dyx = .47
Source: Compiled by the author.

States would not simultaneously be involved in a shooting war. Presidential popularity, another variable with little effect in the model, was set to 59—the mean value for the entire set of cases. Finally, since I am forecasting serious (that is, high level) activity by the United States, I assume that major forces are available for use in the area. The size of naval force available was determined by assessing the likelihood that such forces would be deployed close to the area of interest, and the usefulness of other forces for power projection inland.

The regional and situational variables are, of course, determined by the particular forecast being made. This leaves only a few combinations of the variables in the equation to be manipulated in order to arrive at some judgment about the prospects for a high level of U.S. activity. Specifically, the variables representing multiple actions by the U.S. military (MULTACT), the type of violence preceding U.S. action (VIOL), and the involvement by USSR/PRC (USRPRCUF) were the only variables manipulated within each forecast. The discussion of the forecasts assumes that the model is an accurate representation of the factors predicting level of U.S. involvement. (Note: the complete list of forecasts is contained in the Appendix, Table 4-10.)

Forecasts Involving NATO

The top defense priority of the United States in recent years (and, arguably, for most of the post–World War II era) has been Western Europe. The first set of forecasts concerns the level of activity by the U.S. military when dealing with incidents involving NATO states in external situations. As can be inferred from the sizes of the co-efficients in Table 4-2, the most crucial variable is MULTACT. If the United States is not involved in multiple actions, then even if violence is directed at U.S. personnel or property, and force is used by the Soviet Union, the chances of a high level response are small (the probabilities range from .07 to .16). The effect on the prediction of multiple actions is quite striking. With the same set of predictors, the range in probability of high level U.S. action given multiple involvements is .45 to .64. Given the importance of the NATO commitment to the United States, I would suspect that multiple involvements during an incident involving NATO are quite likely; therefore, the second range of probabilities is a more valid predictor of U.S. activity than the first set.

A second class of problem involving NATO states is internal. For example, consider Portugal, Turkey, and Greece, nation-states with a history of serious internal difficulties. Inherent in this situation is a lower level of Soviet involvement than the previous set of situations, since a Soviet use of force would externalize a previously internal situation. I also assume that such situations are not likely to involve violence directed at the United States. Without this level of violence, chances of a high level of U.S. action are small (.01 with no multiple actions; .13 to .22 with multiple actions). If, however, violence is directed at U.S. personnel or property, and multiple actions are taken by the U.S. government, the chance of a high level of U.S. response rises to .40.

## Forecasts Concerning Communist States

Another area of potential U.S. concern involves incidents that focus on a communist state other than the Soviet Union or China. One possibility would be an internal or external threat to Yugoslavia. Unfortunately, two problems prevent a direct forecast of U.S. actions during these situations. First, Yugoslavia itself is only involved in a few (10) incidents; any forecast based on previous U.S. involvement with Yugoslavia would be far too flimsy to stand up under much scrutiny. The alternative is to construct a surrogate for Yugoslavia, consisting of all communist states other than USSR/PRC. This was done, and entered into the fore-casting equation (COMST), but there is a second problem.

From Blechman and Kaplan's data set, there is no way to tell if the United States intervened with or against the communist state. Thus, the forecasting model cannot distinguish situations in which the United States is involved with Cuba (undoubtedly against the Castro government), and situations like the Hungarian Revolution in 1956, in which any U.S. involvement would be against the Soviet Union and perhaps on the side of the Hungarian government.

Internal situations (such as recent troubles in Poland) result in a moderate probability of a high level of action by the U.S. government if only a single action is undertaken (.23 to .31), and a high probability if multiple actions are undertaken (.74 to .81). External violence in the situation, when the Soviet Union is involved, results in a higher probability of drastic action by the United States; .45 if the United States undertakes no multiple actions, .89 if it does.

Forecasts Concerning U.S. Asian Allies

A third area of concern to U.S. policy makers is the Pacific, most specifically security issues involving Japan and South Korea. The forecasting model predicts a range of probabilities for external violence situations much like the previous cases. Without multiple actions by the United States, the range of probabilities for high levels of action is .43 to .58. With multiple actions by the United States, the range is from .89 to .94. Overall, the chances of a high level of action by the United States in this area are greater than any of the situations predicted by the model. While this may fly in the face of the post-Vietnam drawdown of U.S. forces in the area, and the additional effects of the Nixon Doctrine, it should not be forgotten that the United States has gone to war twice in this region since World War II and participated in a number of other serious confrontations (for example, the seizure of the Mayaguez in 1975).

A further possibility is that of internal violence leading to U.S. involvement. South Korea has a history of these difficulties. Given that one of our Asian allies is involved in such a situation, the model predicts a moderate to high chance of high level of U.S. action (.30 to .44 without multiple U.S. actions; .81 to .89 with multiple U.S. actions).

## Forecasts Involving the Middle East

Although the Middle East has been of concern to the U.S. government since the end of World War II, recent events have given this region an even higher priority. Observers have noted that the area is likely to be involved in a great turmoil that could involve either internal or external violence. The forecasting model is applied to those situations where a U.S. client state is involved.

Despite the increase in U.S. concern in the region, the forecasting model predicts only a small chance of U.S. involvement when the violence is internal, and the U.S. military is not used for multiple actions (.03 to .06). The use of the U.S. military in multiple actions raises the chances of high level of action by the United States significantly; the range is .29 to .42. External violence produces slightly higher predictions; a range of .04 to .11 with only a single action involving the United States and a range of .37 to .56 with multiple actions involving the United States.

## Forecasts Involving Latin America

The final region to be examined is the traditional sphere of U.S. influence, Latin America. There is, of course, a long history of direct U.S. involvement in the region under a variety of circumstances, and the Reagan administration is no exception. The forecasting model predicts a low level of U.S. action if the violence is internal, and only a single action is undertaken by the U.S. military (.12–.21). When multiple actions are initiated by the United States, the probability of a high level of action rises significantly (the range is .58 to .71). External violence leads to large predictions of probability of high level U.S. involvement (.20–.32 without multiple actions; .71–.81 when multiple actions are involved).

## Summary of Forecasts

Table 4-5 displays a summary of the forecasts from the model. Since I am interested in the "worse case," all the probabilities assume multiple actions by the United States. Based on the post–World War II behavior of the U.S. government, the area where the United States is most likely to become involved in high levels of activity is Asia. I believe that this is a reasonable forecast.

The next most likely "area" for high levels of U.S. involvement occurs when the incident features a communist state other than USSR/PRC. Because of the conglomeration of situations embedded in these cases, I have less confidence in this set of forecasts than those for Asia. The model should be refined to deal with situations of interest involving the smaller communist states in order to generate a better set of forecasts.

Latin America has historically involved high levels of activity by the U.S. military. I believe that this set of forecasts does have validity; little modification of the model is necessary here to accurately capture the changes of U.S. involvement in situations of potential combat.

The areas where high levels of U.S. action are least likely, according to the forecasting model, are the Middle East and Western Europe. Although these conclusions are surprising, given stated U.S. policy, several points should be borne in mind.

First, with regard to the Middle East, the current level of U.S. concern began no earlier than the 1973 oil embargo. The data set collected by Blechman and Kaplan ends in

TABLE 4-5. Ranges of Predicted Probabilities of High Level U.S. Activity by Region and Situation (Multiple Actions Only)

| Region | Situation | |
|---|---|---|
| | Internal | External |
| NATO | .15-.21 | .45-.64 |
| Communist State | .74-.81 | .89 |
| Asian Ally | .81-.89 | .89-.94 |
| Middle East Client | .29-.42 | .37-.56 |
| Latin America | .58-.71 | .71-.81 |

Source: Compiled by the author.

1976. Thus, any shift in U.S. priorities (and subsequent behavior) is barely reflected because of the time frame. An updating of the data set to the present might change the predictions of the model. But note that the only high level U.S. military activity in the area occurred only after extreme provocation: the seizure of the U.S. embassy by Iranian students. The United States did *not* involve itself (militarily) to any great extent during the Iranian revolution. Thus, the predictions of the model (and perhaps of other governments in the area) may not be at variance with U.S. behavior in the post-1973 situation.

Second, with regard to NATO, a high level of U.S. action in situations of internal and external threat may be less necessary than in other areas of the world. The credibility of U.S. interests in this area may be high enough that extreme actions are not necessary to send a convincing message to other governments.

Overall, I believe that the model shows promise as a device for predicting high levels of U.S. action during these situations.

SUMMARY

This chapter has demonstrated the pluses and minuses of the scientific approach to early warning indicators. A simple but rigorous model was developed to account for the historical patterns of U.S. behavior when using military force as a political instrument. This model was then used to make a set of conditional forecasts of U.S. actions in various areas and situations around the world. Overall, the forecasts appear reasonable.

Such models offer a more systematic basis for projecting a series of "what ifs" about U.S. government behavior. Only the future will tell if the model developed in this chapter is accurate; I would hope that my efforts would encourage others to use these techniques to create early warning indicators.

NOTES

1. The scaling procedure used was as follows: First, I assumed that activities of relatively equal level would be undertaken in the same situation. That is, if the United States was involved in a very serious situation, most of the activities undertaken would be at a high level; if the

situation was less serious, the activities undertaken by the U.S. government would be at a lower level. Given this assumption, I arbitrarily defined the use of firepower or other violent action as the highest point on the scale. I then computed the Kendall's tau B coefficient for each activity with the use of firepower. Tau B is a measure of strong monotonicity; a perfect relationship occurs if both activities are always either present or absent (Weisberg 1974, 1640–43). Given my assumption about what activities were likely to occur together, the activity with the highest positive tau B value represents the point on the scale next to the use of firepower; the activity with the second highest positive correlation with the use of firepower represents the third point on the scale, and so forth. This allowed me to rank order all 13 activities, from highest (use of firepower) to lowest (presence in or near area). Table 4-1 displays the activities in order from lowest to highest. The particular cutting point between low and high is arbitrary, but it does appear reasonable. It is quite close to that used by Blechman and Kaplan (1978, 57) in their distinction between manifest and latent activities. Their manifest activities are the same as my high level of conflict, except that the patrol, reconnaissance, and surveillance activity in my grouping is replaced by exercise right of transit in their grouping.

2. Blechman and Kaplan define a major force component as one of the following: (1) a ground combat force larger than one battalion; (2) a naval force at least as large as two aircraft carrier (or battleship) task groups; or (3) a land-based combat air force unit at least as large as one wing.

3. The categorization was as follows: (1) violence directed against the U.S. government—government-supported threat or attack, or nongovernment-supported threat or attack on U.S. citizens or property, and threat or attack against U.S. armed forces or bases; (2) external violence—continuing or sporadic violence between nations other than the United States, externally supported insurgency; (3) internal violence—major violence within a nation, strife within a nation, or a recent overthrow or attempt to overthrow the government; (4) no violence—all other categories of situation in the Blechman and Kaplan coding scheme.

4. External conflict is coded when there is continuing or sporadic interstate violence or unfriendly relations between other nations. Internal conflict is coded if there is an insurgency, major violence within a nation, civil strife, or a coup attempt within the nation.

APPENDIX

TABLE 4-6. Descriptive Statistics and Bivariate Correlations
with LEVEL (N = 168)

| Variable | Mean | Std. Dev. | Minimum | Maximum | Corr.w. LEVEL |
|----------|------|-----------|---------|---------|---------------|
| LEVEL | .345 | .447 | 0 | 1 | -- |
| MULTACT | .375 | .486 | 0 | 1 | .27 |
| FORCESIZ | .381 | .487 | 0 | 1 | .13 |
| NAVY | .750 | .663 | 0 | 2 | -.18 |
| NUKE | .071 | .258 | 0 | 1 | .09 |
| PRESPOP | 58.5 | 14.2 | 23 | 80 | .19 |
| WAR | .304 | .461 | 0 | 1 | .04 |
| VIOL | 1.17 | .985 | 0 | 3 | .27 |
| USRPRCUF | .345 | .784 | 0 | 2 | .03 |
| NATO | .202 | .403 | 0 | 1 | -.15 |
| COMST | .238 | .427 | 0 | 1 | .33 |
| ASALY | .060 | .237 | 0 | 1 | .13 |
| MECLNT | .125 | .332 | 0 | 1 | -.16 |
| LATAMR | .285 | .453 | 0 | 1 | .26 |
| INTCON | .399 | .491 | 0 | 1 | -.08 |
| EXTCON | .274 | .447 | 0 | 1 | .01 |

Source: Compiled by the author.

TABLE 4-7. Bivariate Correlations between Predictor Variables (N = 168)

| | MULTACT | FORCESIZ | NAVY | NUKE | PRESPOP | WAR | VIOL | USRPRCUF |
|---|---|---|---|---|---|---|---|---|
| MULTACT | -- | | | | | | | |
| FORCESIZ | .33 | -- | | | | | | |
| NAVY | .22 | .23 | -- | | | | | |
| NUKE | .17 | .35 | .07 | -- | | | | |
| PRESPOP | .00 | .13 | -.15 | -.05 | -- | | | |
| WAR | .05 | -.01 | -.10 | .02 | -.34 | -- | | |
| VIOL | .08 | .05 | .13 | -.12 | .18 | -.02 | -- | |
| USRPRCUF | .26 | .23 | .15 | .28 | -.14 | .11 | .10 | -- |

Source: Compiled by the author.

TABLE 4-8. Bivariate Correlations between Regional/Situational Variables

| | NATO | COMST | ASALY | MECLNT | LATAMR | INTCON | EXTCON |
|---|---|---|---|---|---|---|---|
| NATO | -- | | | | | | |
| COMST | -.25 | -- | | | | | |
| ASALY | -.13 | .10 | -- | | | | |
| MECLNT | -.10 | -.21 | -.10 | -- | | | |
| LATAMR | -.25 | -.08 | -.16 | -.24 | -- | | |
| INTCON | -.14 | .06 | -.15 | .02 | .18 | -- | |
| EXTCON | .12 | -.03 | .24 | .17 | -.27 | -.27 | -- |

Source: Compiled by the author.

TABLE 4-9.  Bivariate Correlations between Predictor and Regional/
Situational Variables (N = 168)

|          | NATO | COMST | ASALY | MECLNT | LATAMR | INTCON | EXTCON |
|----------|------|-------|-------|--------|--------|--------|--------|
| MULTACT  | .13  | .17   | -.09  | -.11   | -.08   | -.10   | .13    |
| FORCESIZ | .15  | .25   | .06   | .00    | -.22   | -.06   | .15    |
| NAVY     | -.01 | .02   | .06   | .06    | -.18   | .09    | .09    |
| NUKE     | .09  | .01   | .13   | -.03   | -.02   | -.18   | .04    |
| PRESPOP  | .07  | .08   | .07   | -.16   | .25    | .21    | -.09   |
| VIOL     | -.13 | .14   | .19   | .03    | .18    | .04    | .14    |
| WAR      | -.01 | .02   | .06   | .06    | -.16   | .09    | .09    |
| USRPRCUF | .03  | .02   | .43   | .07    | -.21   | -.36   | .42    |

Source: Compiled by the author.

TABLE 4-10.  Forecasts of High Level Action by U.S. Military

| REGION | SITUATION | MULTACT | VIOL | NAVY | USRPRCUF | PR (Hi Level Act) |
|--------|-----------|---------|------|------|----------|-------------------|
| NATO   | EXT       | 0       | 0    | 0    | 1        | .07               |
| NATO   | EXT       | 0       | 2    | 0    | 1        | .16               |
| NATO   | EXT       | 0       | 3    | 0    | 2        | .13               |
| NATO   | EXT       | 1       | 0    | 0    | 1        | .45               |
| NATO   | EXT       | 1       | 2    | 0    | 1        | .64               |
| NATO   | EXT       | 1       | 3    | 0    | 2        | .60               |
| NATO   | INT       | 0       | 0    | 1    | 0        | .01               |
| NATO   | INT       | 0       | 1    | 1    | 0        | .02               |
| NATO   | INT       | 0       | 1    | 1    | 1        | .01               |

TABLE 4-10. Continued

| REGION | SITUATION | MULTACT | VIOL | NAVY | USRPRCUF | PR (Hi Level Act) |
|--------|-----------|---------|------|------|----------|-------------------|
| NATO   | INT | 1 | 0 | 1 | 0 | .15 |
| NATO   | INT | 1 | 1 | 1 | 0 | .22 |
| NATO   | INT | 1 | 1 | 1 | 1 | .13 |
| COMST  | EXT | 0 | 2 | 0 | 2 | .45 |
| COMST  | EXT | 1 | 2 | 0 | 2 | .89 |
| COMST  | INT | 0 | 0 | 0 | 1 | .23 |
| COMST  | INT | 0 | 1 | 0 | 1 | .31 |
| COMST  | INT | 1 | 0 | 0 | 1 | .74 |
| COMST  | INT | 1 | 1 | 0 | 1 | .81 |
| ASALY  | EXT | 0 | 2 | 1 | 1 | .58 |
| ASALY  | EXT | 0 | 2 | 1 | 2 | .43 |
| ASALY  | EXT | 0 | 3 | 1 | 2 | .53 |
| ASALY  | EXT | 1 | 2 | 1 | 1 | .94 |
| ASALY  | EXT | 1 | 2 | 1 | 2 | .89 |
| ASALY  | EXT | 1 | 3 | 1 | 2 | .93 |
| ASALY  | INT | 0 | 0 | 1 | 0 | .85 |
| ASALY  | INT | 0 | 1 | 1 | 0 | .44 |
| ASALY  | INT | 0 | 1 | 1 | 1 | .30 |
| ASALY  | INT | 1 | 0 | 1 | 0 | .84 |
| ASALY  | INT | 1 | 1 | 1 | 0 | .89 |
| ASALY  | INT | 1 | 1 | 1 | 1 | .81 |
| MECLNT | EXT | 0 | 0 | 1 | 1 | .04 |
| MECLNT | EXT | 0 | 2 | 1 | 1 | .11 |
| MECLNT | EXT | 0 | 2 | 1 | 2 | .06 |
| MECLNT | EXT | 1 | 0 | 1 | 1 | .87 |
| MECLNT | EXT | 1 | 2 | 1 | 1 | .56 |
| MECLNT | EXT | 1 | 2 | 1 | 2 | .42 |

TABLE 4-10. Continued

| REGION | SITUATION | MULTACT | VIOL | NAVY | USRPRCUF | PR (Hi Level Act) |
|--------|-----------|---------|------|------|----------|-------------------|
| MECLNT | INT | 0 | 1 | 1 | 0 | .06 |
| MECLNT | INT | 0 | 1 | 1 | 1 | .03 |
| MECLNT | INT | 1 | 1 | 1 | 0 | .42 |
| MECLNT | INT | 1 | 1 | 1 | 1 | .29 |
| LATAMR | EXT | 0 | 2 | 1 | 1 | .32 |
| LATAMR | EXT | 0 | 2 | 1 | 2 | .20 |
| LATAMR | EXT | 1 | 2 | 1 | 1 | .81 |
| LATAMR | EXT | 1 | 2 | 1 | 2 | .71 |
| LATAMR | INT | 0 | 1 | 1 | 0 | .21 |
| LATAMR | INT | 0 | 1 | 1 | 1 | .12 |
| LATAMR | INT | 1 | 1 | 1 | 0 | .71 |
| LATAMR | INT | 1 | 1 | 1 | 1 | .58 |

Source: Compiled by the author.

# REFERENCES

Allen, Charles D., Jr. 1980. *The Use of Navies in Peacetime.* Washington: American Enterprise Institute.

Blechman, Barry, and Stephen Kaplan. 1978. *Force Without War: U.S. Armed Forces as a Political Instrument.* Washington, D.C.: Brookings Institution.

Brown, Harold. 1980. *Department of Defense Annual Report Fiscal Year 1981.* Washington, D.C.: U.S. Government Printing Office.

Kaplan, Stephen. 1977. *Force Without War: The United States' Use of the Armed Forces as a Political Instrument: Manual.* Washington, D.C.: Brookings Institution.

Mueller, John. 1973. *War, Presidents, and Public Opinion.* New York: John Wiley.

Singer, J. David, and Michael Wallace. 1979. *To Augur*

*Well: Early Warning Indicators in World Politics.* Beverly Hills: Sage.

Weisberg, Herbert. 1974. "Models of Statistical Relationship." *American Political Science Review* 68(December 1974):1638–55.

*Part III*

**Predicting
Serious Disputes and Conflict Resolution**

# 5

# Voices Prophesying War: Events and Perceptions as Indicators of Conflict Potential in the Middle East

## Frank Whelon Wayman

The Middle East has been called the Balkans of our time, and, whatever the merits of that analogy, the record of warfare, preemptive strikes, and great power confrontations does command the attention of those concerned with peaceful resolution of conflict. The present chapter describes and analyzes the patterns of Middle Eastern friendship and hostility, and examines their relationship to the outbreak of violence in the region. The chapter is based on the hope that clear, reliable, and comparable observations, compiled insofar as possible into a predictive model, will increase our understanding of the region and hence our capacity to

The author would like to acknowledge the support of this study by several groups and organizations. Event data were made available by the Inter-University Consortium for Political and Social Research. The Correlates of War Project at the University of Michigan provided its dispute data, as well as some valuable computing assistance from its programmer, Mary Macknick. The University of Michigan-Dearborn campus grants committee funded the interviews at the United Nations. The academic and officials who completed the questionnaires contributed their valuable time and opinions. The Statistical Research Laboratory of the University of Michigan provided assistance in data management. Any errors in analysis or interpretation are, of course, the responsibility of the author.

manage regional tensions. In the chapter, two distinct sets of problems are addressed: (1) Can the judgments of specialists about the degree of friendship or hostility in the region be used to predict future armed conflict? If so, how good are these predictions? (2) What sorts of prior events are associated with these specialists' judgments of friendship/hostility? Are there particular event (or other) data sets, and variables within those data sets, that are strongly associated with the regional specialists' own judgments?

## INDICATORS OF CONFLICT IN THE MIDDLE EAST

This chapter, then, focuses on the judgments of Middle Eastern specialists as to the degree of friendship or hostility between key actors in the Middle East. It examines the genesis of these judgments, their reliability, and their utility in predicting conflict in the region.[1] The judgments were made in a 1975 survey of U.S. State Department and Defense Department officials and of U.S. academic specialists on the Middle East; these judgments were updated with a 1981 survey of U.S. State Department officials. The actors being analyzed are the United States, Soviet Union, France, China, Israel, Egypt, Syria, Jordan, Saudi Arabia, Kuwait, Iran, Iraq, the People's Democratic Republic of Yemen (PDRY, formerly Aden), Algeria, and the Palestine Liberation Organization (PLO).

These assignments of friendship and hostility can be viewed, in the framework of Mansbach and Vasquez (1981, 236), as an indicator of one aspect of overall cooperation/conflict between nations. Mansbach and Vasquez suggest that global cooperation/conflict has three basic aspects:

- agreement versus disagreement on issues (for example, different national policies on the status of the West Bank)
- positive versus negative acts (for example, Israeli or PLO uses of force); and
- friendship versus hostility (for example, an alignment of Israel against the PLO).

They argue that the development of event data sets, while it has had the beneficial effect of operationalizing one of these three aspects of cooperation/conflict, has had the negative side effect of diverting attention away from the other two aspects (Mansbach and Vasquez 1981, 237).

They contend that the different aspects of cooperation and conflict interact with each other, and hence cannot be fully understood in isolation from each other.  For example:

> Of the three cooperation/conflict variables, friendship/hostility is probably the most important in producing generalized expectations concerning the *intentions* or *motivations* of other actors.  Actors that are generally friendly will tend to explain away one another's misdeeds (if not persistent) in terms of misunderstanding, accident, or impulse, whereas hostile actors are prone to explain one another's positive deeds as misleading and even treacherous. (Mansbach and Vasquez 1981, 238)

Such a hypothesis could be tested by comparing event data sets to a friendship/hostility data set.  The friendship/hostility data set would have a second use as well if its existence would reduce any exaggerated attention to positive/negative acts that have developed during the event data sets' virtual monopoly of operationalization.

In order to measure the friendship/hostility between global actors, it is necessary to tap a state of mind, since friendship/hostility is an "attitude reflecting emotional reactions and psychological tendencies" (Mansbach and Vasquez 1981, 236).  Measuring this directly would be difficult, given the reluctance of many actors to speak frankly in public about other important actors.  The approach taken in the present chapter is to measure friendship/hostility indirectly, by interviews with regional specialists, both in the academic community and in the U.S. foreign policy bureaucracy.

Assuming for the moment (but to be discussed later) that these estimates are reliable, one can proceed to consider their potential usefulness.  In the present chapter, this will be done by attempting to predict future use of force in the region on the basis of the friendship/hostility indicator.  This approach is compatible with the initial goals of the early warning indicator movement (Singer and Wallace, 1979, 13):

1. "Identify a . . . condition . . . whose social undesirability . . . can be reasonably demonstrated." The reliance on force as a major means of interaction in the Middle East is surely such an undesirable condition, and it is the dependent variable in the present study.
2. "Measure with high reliability . . . that condition."

This is done by utilizing World Event/Interaction Study (WEIS) data on the Middle East (as well as some Correlates of War [COW] serious dispute data on the Middle East).

3. "Identify and measure one or more predictor conditions or events that might be expected . . . to regularly precede the outcome condition or event." This predictor condition, whose reliability and validity as a predictor are assessed in the current paper, is of course the specialists' judgments of friendship/hostility in the Middle East.

4. "Demonstrate the extent to which such an association has obtained . . . in the international system of the past." This is done by documenting how the judgments of friendship/hostility enhance one's ability to predict future predominant use of force between pairs of nations, while controlling for the predictive power of past uses of force between the same dyads.

The predictive model that merges from the analysis in the present chapter is summarized in Figure 5-1. In that model, the balance between conflictual and cooperative events, as measured in the WEIS data set, and militarized disputes, as measured in the COW data set, help shape specialists' judgments of friendship and hostility patterns. These friendship/hostility patterns interact with prior conflict/cooperation patterns in the region to help shape future patterns of force/cooperation.

Figure 5-1.    An Hypothesized Causal Model of Middle East Conflict

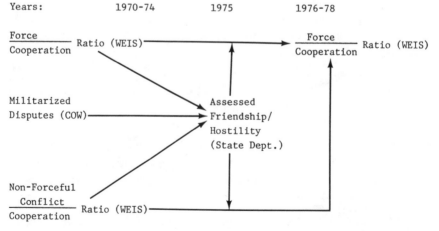

APPLICATIONS: DISSEMINATION AND UTILIZATION OF
THE FRIENDSHIP/HOSTILITY INDICATOR IN THE POLICY
COMMUNITY

Singer and Wallace, in their original call for a study of
early warning indicators (1979, 13) specified six objectives
that seemed appropriate for early warning indicator studies.
The first four have already been discussed above. The
remaining two dealt with the transmission of information
from the academic community to the policy community:

5. "Clearly articulate the ways in which some or all
   policy makers could, if they chose, utilize such
   predictive indicators to reduce the incidence of
   inter-state war."
6. "Clearly articulate the normative and pragmatic considerations that might, at the same time, make the
   utilization of such indicators detrimental to the interests or needs of any affected parties."

The fifth of these goals deals with benefits, the sixth with
costs. Let us consider them in turn.

## Benefits

The benefits to be derived from the indicator of friend-
ship/hostility are its descriptive value and its predictive
value. The predictive value is developed by patient validation studies such as the one presented in this chapter,
and, since the predictions remain probabilistic even after
years of testing, no one would claim that they will be of
direct and immediate policy relevance; for example, no one
would suggest that a regression analysis will pinpoint the
next war in the Middle East. But, assuming that these
academic analyses have lent some validity to an indicator of
early warning, the indicator may be of immediate value in a
relatively nonquantitative, descriptive way within the policy
community.

In the case of the friendship/hostility indicator, its
descriptive value can best be understood in relation to the
current transformations of our international system and its
regional subsystems. There is wide agreement that the
international system has been moving over the past 20 years
from a bipolar to a multipolar condition (Kegley and
Wittkopf 1981, 394; Rapkin, Thompson, and Christopherson
1979). There has been a debate over whether this change
will enhance prospects for peace or will increase the levels

of world conflict (Deutsch and Singer 1964; Waltz 1964; Waltz 1967; Wayman 1981). Two of the major arguments in that debate are relevant here. Deutsch and Singer contend that a basic advantage of multipolarity is that, as the number of poles increases, each actor is forced to divide his attention among more and more poles. This divided attention makes escalating arms races of the type Richardson describes less likely (Deutsch and Singer 1964, 399). Waltz also addresses the matter of divided attention, but argues that as the number of poles increases, divided attention breeds miscalculation and thereby increases the probability of war (Waltz 1964, 882–84).

The friendship/hostility indicator, when aggregated to the system level through the use of multidimensional scaling (see Figure 5-2),[2] indicates that, in the view of U.S. specialists, alignments in the Middle East are far from purely bipolar: smaller nations are distributed loosely throughout the space, rather than being clustered around either the United States or the Soviet Union. Yet, such regional specialists as Quandt have complained that U.S. decision makers inappropriately treat the Middle East as dominated by East-West conflict, and underemphasize the intraregional sources of tension (Quandt 1977, 298-99).[3] This misunderstanding seems to have intensified since the advent of the Reagan administration, which has proposed providing AWACs to Saudi Arabia and billions of aid to Pakistan on the bipolar view that these weapons will be used to deter the Soviet Union and will not exacerbate intraregional conflicts and arms races. Thus, there is evidence that the foreign policy decision makers of one superpower have clung to a bipolar view of the Middle East long after its own specialists have come to describe the region's alignments as multipolar. Explicit indicators of hostility/friendship (such as Figure 5-2), utilized descriptively in briefing papers, might enhance the reality principle in attentive U.S. foreign policy decision makers. Accurate perception that the regional alignments are multipolar might have the beneficial effect suggested by the Deutsch and Singer argument: a reduction in the super-power component of the region's arms race.

Second, the argument of Waltz also indicates the need for accurate indicators in the new multipolar world. He contends that multipolarity is dangerous because its complexity is confusing. This suggests that as the world shifts towards multipolarity, the descriptive task grows more difficult. If the tradition that inspires conventional statecraft remains closed to methodological innovation and growth, the analyses will be increasingly less sufficient to

Figure 5-2. State Department and Academic Spaces Compared. (T=State Department Location; R=Academic Location.)

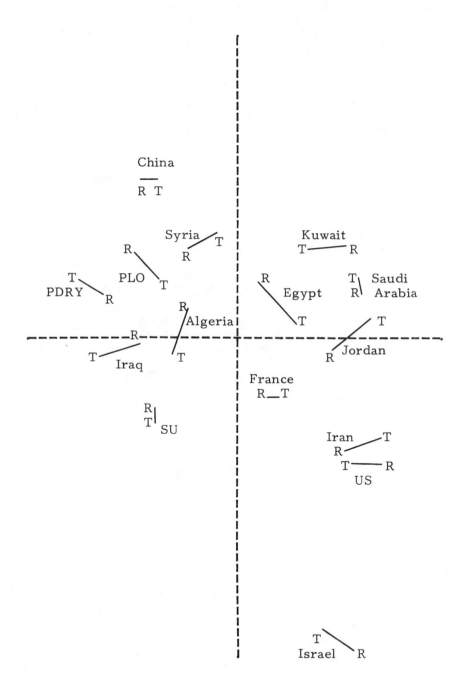

the task. In order to prevent growing confusion, there is a need to develop accurate and readily assimilated indicators of this new complexity of the international system. To illustrate (with the State Department judgments), consider the following precise analyses based solely on the friendship/hostility indicator:

- in 1975, when the Sino-Soviet-U.S. triangle was a puzzle to many, the Soviet-U.S. dyad was the warmest (that is, friendliest) of the three (33 degrees), followed by the Sino-U.S. (29 degrees), and then the Sino-Soviet (23 degrees);
- in 1981, the Sino-U.S. relationship had blossomed (62 degrees), while the Soviet-American (24 degrees) and the Sino-Soviet (18 degrees) had worsened; indeed, in 1981, former ally China had become Russia's worst enemy on the list;
- Saudi Arabia's worst enemy, in 1981, was Israel (13 degrees), not the Soviet Union (21 degrees);
- should the United States desire to make an approach to Syria, with which it has cool relations, it could seek the help of France, which has predominantly friendly relations with Syria as well as with the United States;
- the ten most hostile pairs of actors (as of May 1981) were, in order of decreasing hostility, Israel-PLO (1 degree), Iran-Iraq (2 degrees), Israel-Syria (4 degrees), Israel-PDRY (5 degrees), Israel-Iraq (6 degrees), U.S.-PLO (10 degrees), Israel-Algeria (11 degrees), Israel-Saudi Arabia (13 degrees), Israel-Kuwait (13 degrees), and U.S.-Iran (14 degrees).

In such ways, the friendship/hostility indicator may be useful in making comparable measures available across time and across dyads, in a system that can no longer be described by simple reference to a U.S. or Soviet center of gravity.

Obstacles

Academics should be aware by now, however, that quantitative indicators of variables in world politics are likely to be rejected in wide circles of government. (Caplan, Morrison, and Sambaugh 1975, discuss factors affecting the government's utilization of scientific knowledge.) Kringen (1981) has suggested four reasons for this problem:

- Academics focus intently on developing general models, while foreign policy officials see a need to focus on particular cases, problems, and issues.
- Academics tend to emphasize complexity, while foreign policy officials are forced toward brevity and concise judgment.
- Academics operate under less time pressure, since they can engage in retrospective explanation, while foreign policy officials must operate quickly, in order to make timely predictions.
- Academics tend to address an academic audience, while foreign policy officials often do not have the luxury of communicating in that language or for that audience.

The present study attempts to breach these four barriers in the following ways:

- The theory barrier. Consistent with the spirit of the early warning indicators movement (Singer and Wallace 1979, 10-13), the study avoids elaborate theory construction by focusing on the development of an indicator. While not explicitly related to a theory, the present indicator does tap (at both the dyadic and systemic levels) one of the core concerns of realist theories: who aligns with whom? The realist model, while limited (Mansbach and Vasquez 1981; Keohane and Nye 1977; Allison 1971), has long appealed to many policy makers and academics. Because of this traditional appeal, the current project need not invoke a novel theory, or delve into theoretical controversies, in order to win adherents in the academic and policy communities.

- The complexity barrier. The results can be presented in simple, even nonquantitative form. Rank orderings of a nation's friends and enemies (see Table 5-1) summarize the patterns clearly at the dyadic level. Graphs of the basic dimensions of conflict in the region (Figure 5-2) provide a simplified picture of the overall pattern at the systemic level.

- The time barrier. Because it focuses on the measurement of a small number of elite judgments, the indicator can—in principle—be in the hands of the policy maker within days, or even hours, of the initiation of a study. On the other hand, the indicator remains intact for subsequent academic analysis (reliability and validity studies) at the analyst's leisure.

• The audience barrier. This barrier, insofar as it is not subsumed in the above three, may be primarily a function of the style, empathy, and interests of the data analyst, and how these are perceived by the official audience. In the present study, the utilization of official judgments may enhance the elements of rapport between the two communities.

TABLE 5-1. State Department Friendship/Hostility Ratings for Two Illustrative Countries, 1975 and 1981 (Thermometer Scores above Fifty Degrees Indicate Friendly Relationships)

| 1975 Ratings | | | | 1981 Ratings | | | |
|---|---|---|---|---|---|---|---|
| U.S. and | | Egypt and | | U.S. and | | Egypt and | |
| Israel | 88 | Saudi Arabia | 78 | Israel | 85 | U.S. | 80 |
| Iran | 83 | France | 69 | Egypt | 80 | France | 65 |
| Jordan | 80 | Kuwait | 64 | France | 76 | Israel | 59 |
| Saudi Arabia | 78 | Algeria | 62 | Saudi Arabia | 75 | China | 56 |
| France | 62 | U.S. | 61 | Jordan | 71 | Jordan | 45 |
| Egypt | 61 | Iran | 60 | China | 62 | Saudi Arabia | 44 |
| Kuwait | 61 | Syria | 60 | Kuwait | 61 | Kuwait | 41 |
| Algeria | 46 | Jordan | 58 | Algeria | 52 | Algeria | 35 |
| Syria | 44 | PLO | 58 | Iraq | 34 | Iraq | 35 |
| USSR | 33 | USSR | 54 | USSR | 24 | PLO | 33 |
| China | 29 | China | 51 | Syria | 23 | Syria | 30 |
| Iraq | 22 | Iraq | 46 | PDR Yemen | 15 | USSR | 25 |
| PLO | 13 | PDR Yemen | 39 | Iran | 14 | Iran | 22 |
| PDR Yemen | 8 | Israel | 17 | PLO | 10 | PDR Yemen | 14 |

Source: Compiled by the author.

In short, the present indicator has qualities that enhance its applicability: it can present a succinct portrait of how area specialists view friendship/hostility patterns in an explosive, multipolar region, and it is simple and easily transmissible.

## THE SURVEY DESIGN, QUESTIONNAIRE,
## AND RESPONDENTS

In order to measure the friendship/hostility patterns, a questionnaire was designed for administration to regional specialists. The key item in the survey, designed to measure the hostility or friendship between pairs of actors, was worded as follows:

> For each pair of states or organizations below, rank the relationships between the two governments or organizations from zero for complete hostility (extremely cold, hostile relations) to 100 for complete friendship (extremely warm, friendly relations), with the mid-point of 50 indicating neutral feelings (neither predominantly friendly nor predominantly hostile). Please do not allow formal diplomatic non-recognition to determine your answer.

This set of questions, referred to as "thermometer items" in survey research, yielded 105 answers from each respondent.

The initial survey was conducted during February, March, and early April 1975. State Department responses were collected in February. The bulk of the academic responses were returned in the first week of March. A follow-up letter produced 17 additional responses in early April.

Only U.S. respondents were used in the survey because of concern that Arabs, Israelis, and Soviets, when interviewed by a U.S. professor, would be inclined to give biased responses. The Arabs, for example, would tend to close ranks and report that pan-Arab sentiments were high. (See Schuman and Hatchett for a discussion of interviewer bias when the interviewer and respondent are of different ethnic backgrounds.) To assess the cross-national similarity of perceptions in a way that could bypass these contamination problems, a dozen Arab and Israeli United Nations ambassadors and counsellors were asked to evaluate the U.S. response patterns. Thus, any tendencies to bias responses may be tempered by the fact that they are not being asked their own opinions, but rather are being asked whether U.S. opinions seem accurate.

The survey was initially sent to academic specialists and State Department officials. The academic specialists selected for the study were the 153 members of the American Political Science Association who listed themselves as Middle Eastern specialists in the 1973 *Biographical Directory* of the association. They appear to represent a broad spectrum of opinions and backgrounds. Eighteen of the questionnaires were returned undelivered by the Post Office. Of the 135 remaining, 71 responded. The 53 percent response rate is well above that usually expected for a mail survey.

In the U.S. State Department, eleven officers from the Bureau of Near Eastern and South Asian Affairs, the Policy Planning and Coordinating Staff, the Bureau of Intelligence and Research, and the Bureau of Politico-Military Affairs were included in the study. They do not constitute a random sample, but they do represent 53 percent of the study population of 21 targeted specialists in the above bureaus.

In the Department of Defense, five officers in the Office of Net Assessment, Office of the Secretary of Defense, participated in the study. These individuals were, by their own self-report, not Middle Eastern specialists, but they were attentive observers of the Middle East, and their office was included in the study as a third group for comparison.

Major diplomatic changes in the Middle East during the time of the survey could easily have produced changes in the responses. During February and early March, the major news out of the Middle East involved the ongoing U.S. efforts to arrange a "piece of land for a piece of peace" formula between Egypt and Israel. On the 22nd of March, the talks broke down and Secretary Kissinger admitted that his strategy had not succeeded. The Israelis and the Egyptians blamed each other for the breakdown of the talks. The United States seemed to side with the Egyptians when it announced a reassessment of its policy of support of Israel. Plans were made to reconvene the Geneva Conference, which might offer a last chance for a peace settlement. Almost simultaneously, and coincidentally, King Faisal of Saudi Arabia, a close friend of the United States, was assassinated. Those academic respondents who mailed their surveys after these events have been analyzed separately to check for any shifts in academics' perceptions of the system following the dramatic events of late March 1975. No significant differences were found between the early and late respondents, and this insures a consistency in perceptions throughout the weeks of interviewing.

To update the study, and to explore the rate of medium term change in the assessments, a follow-up survey was conducted at the U.S. Department of State in May 1981. As in the first survey, a statistical sampling procedure was not employed, but an attempt was made to get a cross-section of views. Thirteen respondents from the Bureau of Near Eastern and South Asian Affairs and the Bureau of Politico-Military Affairs participated in the survey. Respondents were selected so that desk officers from as many national desks as possible would be included. None of the 1975 respondents was included in the new survey. The 1981 response rate was 100 percent.

The 1981 survey came at a time of mounting tensions in the region. Although the Israeli attack on the Iraqi nuclear plant had not yet occurred, the Israeli elections were approaching, and Prime Minister Begin was campaigning hard for reelection. The Syrian seige of the Christian Lebanese town of Zahle had led to an Israeli-Syrian dispute over the presence of Syrian SAM missiles in Lebanon, and the U.S. envoy, Philip Habib was trying to mediate that dispute and prevent an escalation of the violence in Lebanon.

In the next section of this chapter, these 1981 State Department responses, the 1975 State Department responses, the Defense Department responses, and the academic responses will be compared to each other as well as to the evaluations of them that were made by the Arab and Israeli diplomats at the United Nations.

## RELIABILITY AND CROSS-CULTURAL VALIDITY OF THE FRIENDSHIP/HOSTILITY INDICATOR

The reliability of the judgments can be initially approached by considering the variation of opinion on a few dyads, such as the U.S.-Soviet dyad portrayed in Table 5-2. As may be seen in that table, the Soviet-U.S. relationship was rated more warmly by academic than by governmental respondents. The range of opinion (standard deviation) is about the same for all three groups. This is slightly atypical. On most of the 105 dyads, the State Department seems to have had slightly greater levels of agreement than the academics. For example, for the U.S.-Israeli dyad, the State Department standard deviation is six degrees, whereas the academic one is eleven degrees.

Assuming for the moment that the groups selected were random samples from a population, one can examine the generalizability of the sample results to the populations. In the Soviet-U.S. case, the standard error of the mean suggests that 95 percent of State Department random samples of 11 people will have a mean within approximately eight degrees of the true State Department mean. The confidence interval for the academics is twice as small

TABLE 5-2. Academic, State, and Defense Assessments of the United States-Soviet Dyad

| Group | Mean | Standard Deviation | N | Standard Error of the Mean |
|-------|------|--------------------|---|----------------------------|
| Academic | 45° | 16° | 70 | 1.9° |
| Defense | 37° | 14° | 5 | 6.3° |
| State | 33° | 14° | 11 | 4.2° |

Source: Compiled by the author.

(+ 4°). One may infer that the underlying academic population had a more confident view of *detente* than the State Department, because the 12 point disagreement between the two samples is bigger than would be expected by chance (one standard error of the difference being 4.6°). Across all 105 dyads, the average difference between the State Department and academic means was 6.4°. Between academia and the Pentagon, it was 9.7°. Between the State Department and the Pentagon, it was 10.4°.

Another way to consider the reliability of the three sets of opinions is to examine the correlations between opinions.[4] If the intercorrelations are very high, we can have confidence that the three sets of respondents have a similar view of the world. The correlations between the three groups are displayed in Table 5-3. The State Department and academia have an extraordinarily high level of agreement, especially when one considers the major differences in their sources of information (Jensen 1972, 22-23). The Pentagon group, which consists of people who are not Middle East specialists, has a lower pair of correlations than the State Department or academic groups, and the Pentagon is especially divergent from the State Department views ($r^2 = .72$).

In the 1981 follow-up study, the agreement within the State Department remained high. For example, splitting a dozen respondents arbitrarily into odd and even numbered respondents, one obtains two groups of a half-dozen officials, and the correlation between the assessments of these groups is .97; this suggests that groups of a half-dozen could have been used almost as effectively for predictive purposes as the larger group, since the opinions in this

TABLE 5-3.  Correlations between Group Friendship/Hostility Ratings

| Group | State | Academic |
|---|---|---|
| Academic | .96 | -- |
| Defense | .85 | .90 |

Note: Pearson product-moment correlation coefficients; N = 105.
Source: Compiled by the author.

instance were so convergent.  Of course, any one individual's views will correlate at a much lower level with the
group average.  In the 1981 survey, the correlations between an individual's judgments and the group's ranged
from .85 to .93.  For one thing, there are true differences
of opinion from person to person about the Middle East, and
also, since the scale is only defined for the respondents at
three points (0°, 50°, and 100°), there will be idiosyncratic
differences in how people interpret the remaining 98 degree
markings.  When group averages are computed, however,
even for groups of a dozen or so, these individual differences seem to have largely washed out.

The academics and State Department officials have such a
high level of agreement as to be interchangeable with each
other for some purposes; the correlation between their
views (r = .96) is about the same, for example, as that
between the two halves of the State Department sample in
1981 (r = .97).  The Pentagon group has somewhat lower
correlations, both with the State Department (r = .85) and
with the academics (r = .90); these lower correlations may
partly be due to a higher error rate (especially when
nonspecialists guess at obscure dyads) and partly to the
small sample size at Defense, which is even smaller than at
State, and has an even greater tendency to magnify any
idiosyncratic respondent.

Cross-Cultural Validation at the United Nations

The Arab and Israeli delegates at the United Nations (UN)
were asked to evaluate the U.S. State Department opinions.
The U.N. Missions representing all Middle Eastern nations
in the questionnaire were contacted, and the PLO's UN

Observer Mission was included. All the missions except that of People's Yemen participated in the analysis. The interviews were conducted in the first three months of 1976.

The U.S. judgments were largely shared by the Arab and Israeli delegates at the U.N. Missions. In particular, the Arab and Israeli respondents were unanimous in saying that the two-dimensional clustering diagram (Figure 5-2) made sense. Some of the respondents, however, had reservations about some of the dyadic relations. The typical evaluator disagreed with 15 percent of the dyadic ratings he examined, but 6 percent—two out of five of the disagreements—were adjustments of one to five thermometer points, leaving only 9 percent with more serious disagreements. As for particular dyads, half or more of the Arab and Israeli evaluators had serious objections to the warmth U.S. respondents assigned to relations between Iran and Israel, Jordan and Israel, and Egypt and Israel. A number of the Arab delegates insisted that the relations between any Arab country and Israel could not be higher than zero. Several evaluators also questioned the Iran-Iraqi assessment, which they viewed as warmer than it had been rated by the State Department. They uniformly withdrew this objection, however, when it was clarified that the U.S. judgments had been made in the period just before the Iran-Iraqi rapprochement in 1975. Some individual Arabs and Israelis differed from State Department opinions on the other dyads, but on these, no consensus was evident. In general, the level of cross-cultural agreement seems to have been high.

Stability of Assessed Friendship/Hostility

While novel events could cause rapid changes in the assessments, during the 1975–81 period the ratings seem to have remained unchanged for many dyads. Indeed, over the six year period, about half (55 out of 105) of the assessments changed less than ten points. Among those that did experience double-digit change, the major shifts are ranked as follows:

| FRIENDLIER RELATIONS | MORE HOSTILE RELATIONS |
|---|---|
| 1. Israel-Egypt (+42°) | 1. U.S.-Iran (-69°) |
| 2. Iraq-Kuwait (+40°) | 2. Jordan-Iran (-60°) |
| 3. Iran-PDRY (+40°) | 3. Saudi Arabia-Iran (-40°) |
| 4. Jordan-Iraq (+39°) | 4. Egypt-Iran (-38°) |
| 5. Jordan-PL0 (+35°) | 5. Israel-Iran (-37°) |

6. U.S.-China (+33°)        6. Egypt-Saudi Arabia (-34°)
7. Iran-PL0 (+33°)          7. Iraq-PDRY (-30°)
8. China-Jordan (+32°)      8. Iran-Kuwait (-30°)
9. China-Saudi Arabia (+24°) 9. Egypt-Syria (-30°)
10. Iraq-Saudi Arabia (+23°) 10. USSR-Egypt (-28°)

These large shifts, plus smaller adjustments, produced enough change so that the correlation between the State Department assessment in 1975 and their assessment in 1981 is only .62 ($r^2$ = .38). With 38 percent of the variance in 1981 scores accounted for by 1975 scores, it seems that over half of the variance in 1981 scores could be the result of novel events occurring in the six years between surveys. Certainly two major developments account for most of the big negative shifts. The overthrow of the Shah of Iran and the had such great impact that all but one of the worst instances of decay involve Iran or Egypt. The pattern of improved relations, on the other hand, seems much more complex in that it involves many more nations.

In general, the changes do indicate how the assessments are sensitive to novel events. But the assessments do not seem to undergo total transformation either in the short run (comparing the early and late survey responses in 1975) or what might be called the medium run (that is, the six years from 1975 to 1981).

Having considered the reliability, cross-cultural validity, and stability of the judgments of friendship/hostility, let us turn to the remaining two questions: what sorts of events shape these opinions; and of what value are the judgments in predicting future patterns of force and cooperation in the region?

PREDICTING THE FRIENDSHIP/HOSTILITY JUDGMENTS

The causes of the State Department friendship/hostility judgments are interesting for a number of reasons. First, at the theoretical level, it would be useful to know more about what process generates such judgments: does the impact of events fade with the passage of time, or are at least some memories periodically reinforced and stabilized? Do belligerent actions have a stronger impact on perceptions than peaceful actions have? Second—almost hopelessly intertwined with the first level of questions in this study, because we have only one event data set to work with are questions about event indicators: do certain WEIS event categories (for example, "seize," or "force") have greater impact on perceptions than other event categories (for example, "yield," or "consult")?

These issues will be explored in the present chapter by examining which international events are the best predictors of the friendship/hostility judgments. Such an examination will do for the study of conflict and cooperation what has already been done for the study of power in world politics.

Measuring the capability, or power, of a country has been approached in three ways. One method has been to look for concrete power attributes, or capabilities, which can be used as measures of countries' power (Knorr 1955; Ray and Singer 1973). A second approach to power is to look for measures of *perceived* national power. This assumes that statesmen and other observers of the international system make judgments about the power of states, and that these judgments may affect how nations act. A third approach in the study of national power has been to look for objective attributes that predict perceived power. Alcock and Newcombe (1970, 339-42), studying the perceptions of students and citizens in Canada and Latin America, concluded that GNP and military expenditures are both excellent predictors of perceived national power, with military expenditures being a better predictor if warring nations are included in the ratings. Their approach integrates the first two by demonstrating that attributes, such as GNP, are highly correlated with perceived power.

The degree of conflict or cooperation between nations can be approached in each of the same three ways. First, the actual actions or interactions of nations can be measured, through such indicators as alliance data (Singer and Small 1966) or event data (McClelland and Hoggard 1969). Second, the degree of friendship or hostility between pairs of nations can also be measured with perceptual—or "judgmental"—data. Klingberg (1941) pioneered this approach with his analysis of the beliefs of nonelite respondents, who were administered a questionnaire. More recent studies of perceptions of hostility, threat, and friendship have focused on content analysis of diplomatic documents from major international crises, as in the studies of the outbreak of World War I (Zinnes 1968). These studies are provocative in suggesting that perceived threat, if not perceived hostility, is a key determinant of the decision to go to war.

This chapter returns to Klingberg's original approach in that it uses a questionnaire to measure the perceptions of hostility and friendship between pairs of states that are not immediately in an acute international crisis. The present questionnaire is addressed to attentive foreign policy elites, however, rather than, as Klingberg's was, to mass publics. Conducting such a survey opens up the possibility of a third approach to the study of cooperation and conflict among nations—a comparison of the perceptual with the event or alliance data. Such a study would parallel the work of Alcock and Newcombe, noted above, on the relation of perceived to actual power capabilities. This can be done, and is done in the present study, by comparing an event data set to the questionnaire responses.

## Event Data Sets

Of the three major event data sets in world politics Conflict and Peace Data Bank (COPDAB), Comparative Research on the Events of Nations (CREON), and the World Event on Interaction Survey (WEIS), only the WEIS data set could be utilized in this study. The CREON data set does not cover the relevant time span. The COPDAB data are currently being assembled for incorporation in the next iteration of this study.[5] The WEIS data set, available for analysis over the 1970–78 time span, has been thoroughly documented elsewhere and will not be discussed in detail here. (For an introduction to the data set, see McClelland and Hoggard 1969.) The WEIS data set is based on events as described in *The New York Times,* and classifies these events into 22 categories:

|     |           |     |             |
| --- | --------- | --- | ----------- |
| 1.  | Yield     | 12. | Accuse      |
| 2.  | Comment   | 13. | Protest     |
| 3.  | Consult   | 14. | Deny        |
| 4.  | Approve   | 15. | Demand      |
| 5.  | Promise   | 16. | Warn        |
| 6.  | Grant     | 17. | Threat      |
| 7.  | Reward    | 18. | Demonstrate |
| 8.  | Agree     | 19. | Reduce      |
| 9.  | Request   | 21. | Expel       |
| 10. | Propose   | 21. | Seize       |
| 11. | Reject    | 22. | Force       |

Attempts to typologize these categories, using factor analysis, have yielded a variety of results, depending on the time period and the set of countries being analyzed (McClelland and Hoggard 1969; Wilkenfeld, Hopple, and Rossa 1979). Initially, in the present study, each of the 22 categories was enumerated and analyzed separately.

The WEIS event data contain two scores for each dyad over each unit of time: the number of events in which actor A was the activist and actor B was the target, and the number of events in which actor B was the activist and actor A was the target. The judgmental data in the present study provide only one summary measure of friendship/hostility for each dyad. In order to make the two data sets compatible for analysis, the 210 WEIS dyads (all the permutations of the pairs) were collapsed into the 105 friendship/hostility dyads (all the combinations of the pairs); this was done, for each class of events (for example, force), by adding the number of cases in which A acted on B to the number of cases in which B acted on A.

In the present study, the 22 categories of WEIS event data were aggregated over a five year period (1970–1974) for each dyad, to see which categories were most associated with, and best predicted, the judgments of the specialists in 1975. The patterns are summarized in Table 5-4.[6] Not only the conflictual events, but also a potentially surprising array of cooperative and neutral events (for example, grant, comment, propose, agree), correlate positively with the hostility/friendship scale. This association between conflict and cooperation would occur if *The New York Times* were giving extra coverage to relations between unfriendly countries, so that most of the granting, commenting, proposing and agreeing as reported in *The New York Times* is done between enemies. In short, "no news is good news" seems to be the source bias unveiled in Table 5-4.

The WEIS events that seem best able to predict the State Department judgments are the abrasive, "newsworthy" items (underlined at the top of the table: accusations, demands, threats, denials, uses of force, and seizures. Even these associations are relatively modest. The raw event data do not seem to have much relationship to subsequent judgments about the hostility/friendship between pairs of nations.

It seemed likely, however, that stronger associations could be detected if the event and judgmental measures were made more comparable. Since the judgmental data measure the relative balance between friendship and hostility, the event data should be converted into relative indices, too. This could be done by forming a conflict/cooperation event ratio to correlate to the hostility/friendship scores. This approach would have the second advantage of controlling for a possible bias in event coverage: if *The New York Times* tends to overreport conflict between certain dyads simply because it has reporters assigned to them, then dividing the reported conflict by a baseline of reported cooperation might be a way of holding

TABLE 5-4. Correlations of WEIS Event Categories (1970-74) with Subsequent
State Department Assessments (1975)

| WEIS Category | Correlation | WEIS Category | Correlation |
|---|---|---|---|
| (#21) Seize | .37 | (#2) Comment | .09 |
| (#22) Force | .34 | (#13) Protest | .08 |
| (#14) Deny | .30 | (#10) Propose | .05 |
| (#17) Threat | .29 | (#20) Expel | .04 |
| (#15) Demand | .28 | (#8) Agree | .04 |
| (#12) Accuse | .27 | (#19) Reduce | .02 |
| (#1) Yield | .25 | (#9) Request | .02 |
| (#6) Grant | .24 | (#4) Approve | -.10 |
| (#16) Warn | .23 | (#5) Promise | -.12 |
| (#11) Reject | .20 | (#3) Consult | -.13 |
| (#18) Demonstrate | .20 | (#7) Reward | -.18 |

Note: WEIS event categories are ranked from strongest positive to
strongest negative correlation with subsequent State Department hostility/
friendship judgments. All correlations are Pearson product-moment correlation coefficients. N = 105. Relationships significant at the .01 level
are underlined. The numbers in parentheses are the WEIS code number for
the particular event type.
Source: Compiled by the author.

such bias constant. For these two reasons, the WEIS event
data were transformed into ratios. The denominator was in
every case the sum of the "Cooperative/Collaborative
Behavior Types" defined by McClelland and Hoggard (1969,
714–15). These types are the first ten event categories
(Yield to Propose) in the list of 22 categories given previously. Their sum was incremented by one, to avoid dividing by zero if a case had no cooperative interaction recorded. Three event ratios were computed, corresponding
to three different numerators:

- the total use of force (event category #22);
- the sum of nine relatively nonviolent conflict items
  (#11-#19), the nine chosen were all the "Conflict
  Behavior Types" (McClelland and Hoggard 1969,
  714–15) except expel, seize, and force; and
- the sum of the conflictual, nonforceful event categories (#11-21) (McClelland and Hoggard. 1969,
  714–15).

A crucial set of questions about these ratios involves the time span over which events affect specialists' judgments: are only recent events important? Does the impact of more distant events fade uniformly, or do some past events seem to become etched in memory? These questions can be partially addressed by considering the data in Table 5-5. The table shows the correlations between the yearly force/cooperation ratios and the hostility/friendship judgments of the three respondent groups. (In every year up to the year of the survey, the Defense Department opinions are most highly correlated with the WEIS event data, and the State Department opinions are least highly correlated with the WEIS data. Given what has been said above about the three respondent groups, it may be that the less the expertise, the higher the correlation with *The New York Times* record of events.) It is striking that in all three groups, the 1973 events are most highly correlated with the assessments, and the 1970 correlations tend to be second. These were years of severe crisis in the Middle East (Quandt 1977). The dramatic events of these years may have had a major, lasting impact on perceptions (Jervis 1976). In any case, the early events are as correlated with the judgments as are the later events. Since there was no sign of decay over time, each year's events were weighted equally when constructing the five and three year aggregations used in this chapter. A five-year sum of events, from 1970 through 1974, was used to predict State Department judgments in 1975. A three-year sum, from 1976 through 1978, was used as the criterion variable in the validity tests to see if perceptions could help in the prediction of future events.

TABLE 5-5. Hostility/Friendship Judgments (1975)
Correlated with Force/Cooperation Event Ratios (1970-78)

| | 1970 | 1971 | 1972 | 1973 | 1974 | 1975 | 1976 | 1977 | 1978 |
|---|---|---|---|---|---|---|---|---|---|
| State | .33 | .26 | .34 | .38 | .32 | .21 | .23 | .17 | .05 |
| Defense | .45 | .35 | .39 | .46 | .36 | .30 | .19 | .27 | .09 |
| Academic | .40 | .29 | .36 | .44 | .33 | .26 | .17 | .21 | .06 |

Note: Pearson product-moment correlation coefficients. N = 105. All correlations significant at the .05 level except those in 1978.

Source: Compiled by the author.

The three conflict/cooperation ratios, summed over those years, were correlated with the judgmental data (see Table 5-6). These correlations are, as predicted, higher than the correlations for the 22 raw event categories (Table 5-4). The nine-item conflict/cooperation ratio in the center of Table 5-6 will be heavily used below; it will henceforth be called the: quarrel/cooperation" ratio. It has the advantage that, while it is as highly correlated with the State Department judgments as the nonforceful conflict/cooperation ratio, it is less collinear with the force/cooperation ratio (as seen in Table 5-7).

TABLE 5-6. Correlation of Hostility/Friendship Judgments (1975) with WEIS Event Indices (1970-74)

| Event Ratios: | Judgments | | |
| --- | --- | --- | --- |
| | State | Defense | Academic |
| Force to Cooperation | .45 | .54 | .51 |
| Nine-Item Conflict to Cooperation | .67 | .64 | .69 |
| Nonforceful Conflict to Cooperation | .64 | .67 | .69 |

Note: All correlations are Pearson product-moment correlation coefficients. N = 105. All relationships are significant at the .01 level.
Source: Compiled by the author.

TABLE 5-7. Correlations between WEIS Event Indices (1970-74)

| | Force to Cooperation | Quarrel to Cooperation | Nonforceful Conflict to Cooperation |
| --- | --- | --- | --- |
| Force to Cooperation | 1.0 | | |
| Quarrel to Cooperation | .49 | 1.0 | |
| Nonforceful Conflict to Cooperation | .88 | .84 | 1.0 |

Note: All correlations are Pearson product-moment correlation coefficients. N = 105. All relationships are significant at the .01 level.
Source: Compiled by the author.

COW Dispute Data

The Correlates of War (COW) project at the University of Michigan has constructed a list of all militarized disputes between nation-states, 1816–1976. Disputes are classified according to whether they involve the threat, display, or use of force. The use of force is itself subdivided into war (conflict involving more than 1,000 battle-connected deaths) and conflict short of war. This COW list has the advantage that it is not shaped by coverage in *The New York Times*. It will therefore be used in the present chapter as a predictor of State Department judgments, to indicate the extent to which they are shaped by militarized events outside the scope of *The New York Times*/WEIS coverage.

The COW data set has two disadvantages from the point of view of the present study. First, it excludes nonstate actors, such as the PLO, and thus omits 14 cases from the data set. Second, it currently only extends to 1976, and cannot be used as a dependent variable in the present study because there are not enough post-1975 disputes for meaningful analysis.

For the present chapter, dyads were classified dichotomously as (1) having had a COW dispute in the five-year period, 1970–74, or (2) not having had such a dispute. The timing of the dispute (close to the time of the State Department assessments, or more remote), the level of the dispute (threat of force, display of force, use of force short of war. or war), and the number of disputes are all ignored in this dichotomy. A more complicated COW dispute variable was also employed. This variable was created by giving a score to each dyad depending on its type of involvement in each dispute. The scores were based on the COW dispute codes:

1 = threat of force;
2 = display of force;
3 = use of force short of war; and
4 = war.

A pair of nations on opposite sides in a dispute was given a positive score, which was the lower of the two levels each had reached in the dispute. A pair of nations on the same side in a dispute was scored in the same fashion, except for a change of sign from positive to negative to reflect cooperation in the dispute rather than conflict. Since only sixteen dyads opposed each other in disputes, and only nine dyads were on the same side in a dispute, one should not expect this COW variable to account for variance in the hostility/friendship scores of most of the dyads; but it may well account for many of the extreme cases of variance in hostility/friendship.

## EXPLAINING THE HOSTILITY/FRIENDSHIP JUDGMENTS

Only about half of the variance in hostility/friendship judgments can be accounted for by event and dispute data. A basic reason for this has been suggested by Mansbach and Vasquez's typology of conflict/cooperation: hostility/friendship patterns are shaped by agreement/disagreement on issues, as well as by acts. A second reason is that many acts do not get recorded as media "events" (and some do not leave any trace). To illustrate these problems (for the year 1974):

- the WEIS data set records 51 non-U.S. dyads that had no cooperation; the COPDAB data set shows that 24 of them did not cooperate; indeed, some of those 24 cases—such as France and Algeria, Egypt and Iran, and Syria and Iraq—had very high cooperation scores in the COPDAB data set;[7]
- even the COPDAB data, which appears to be relatively complete in documenting "events," reports no conflictual events between such known enemies as Israel and Iraq, Saudi Arabia and the Soviet Union, or Israel and Saudi Arabia;
- the crucial oil shipments by the Shah to Israel do not show up in either event data set as cooperation between Israel and Iran.

These remarks are not intended as indictments, since in fact the event data sets have been carefully collected by responsible scientists following explicit coding rules. The point is that one should not expect the event data to determine the judgments, for the same reason that one should not expect the dispute data to determine the judgments: many important activities and policies are purposely excluded from the event data.

As for the dispute data, the relationship of the State Department judgments to prior militarized disputes can be seen in Table 5-8. Sixteen of the 90 dyads had a serious dispute, and all of those 16 are rated hostile. The other dyads did not have a serious dispute, and most of them are rated friendly. So the occurrence of a serious dispute allows one to predict, in all but 22 of the cases, the dichotomized State Department judgments. Since none of the friendly pairs had a serious dispute, however, the variations in friendship (51° to 100°) are clearly not going to be explained by whether or not the pair had a serious dispute. With that portion of the variance due to other factors (for example, arms transfers, trade, or diplomatic support), it is still true that serious disputes account for a significant amount of the overall variance in hostility/friendship.

TABLE 5-8. State Department Judgments of Hostility/Friendship (1975) and Serious Dispute History (1970-74)

| | | Militarized Disputes, 1970-74 | |
| | | At Least One | None |
| --- | --- | --- | --- |
| State Department Judgment in 1975 | Hostile(0°-49°) | N = 16 | N = 22 |
| | Neutral (50°) or Friendly (51°-100°) | N = 0 | N = 52 |

Source: Compiled by the author.

The efforts to predict the State Department judgments can be summarized in a series of regression equations. Combining the COW dispute and WEIS event data, one obtains the following results:

| Independent Variable | Beta |
| --- | --- |
| Quarrel/Cooperation Ration (WEIS) | .52 |
| Number and Level of Disputes (COW) | .18 |
| Force/Cooperation Ratio (WEIS) | .09 $R^2$=.46 (N=91) |

The quarrel/cooperation ratio, which encompasses so many types of activity, accounts for the bulk of the variance that can be accounted for. The dispute score has about one-third as much impact, and the WEIS force/cooperation ratio is about half as influential as the COW index.[8] This suggests that the COW dispute data are capturing something that has been missed by *The New York Times*/WEIS indices, and that this element explains a significant amount of variation even though only about a quarter of the cases in this data set were engaged in militarized disputes.

Somewhat similar patterns emerge from attempts to predict the academic and Defense Department judgments:

| Independent Variable | Beta for Pentagon | Beta for Academics |
|---|---|---|
| Quarrel/Cooperation Ration (WEIS) | .39 | .49 |
| Number and Level of Disputes (COW) | .38 | .26 |
| Force/Cooperation Ratio (WEIS) | .10 | .12 |
| | $R^2 = .52$ (N=91) | $R^2 = .52$ (N=91) |

Since the force/cooperation ratio is not statistically significant, one might want to eliminate it from the analysis. The result slightly enhances the contribution of the other two variables. For example, in the State Department case:

| Independent Variable | Beta | |
|---|---|---|
| Quarrel/Cooperation Ration (WEIS) | .54 | |
| Number and Level of Disputes (COW) | .22 | $R^2 = .45$ (N=91) |

The persistent ratio of about two or three to one between the influence of the quarrel variable and the dispute variable is similar to the bivariate $r^2$ ratio of the same variables:

| Variables | $r^2$ (N = 91) |
|---|---|
| State Department Judgments and Quarrel/Cooperation | .41 |
| State Department Judgments and Dispute Index | .21 |

It would appear that the judgments about hostility and friendship between nation-states are primarily affected by tie quarrel/cooperation ratio, as recorded in *The New York Times,* secondarily affected by the number and level of militarized disputes, and less significantly affected by the force/cooperation ratio from the WEIS event data set. The only exception to this generalization occurs in the case of the Pentagon judgments, which are influenced as much by the militarized disputes as by the quarrel/cooperation balance—as one might expect from officials who focus primarily on military issues.


## PREDICTING RELIANCE ON FORCE

The most important issue remaining to be considered is whether (and how) the hostility/friendship indicators, which are intended to be descriptions of the present, can be used to predict future reliance on force in the Middle East. Jensen (1972) took a more direct approach to this prediction problem by asking State, Defense, academic, and journalistic respondents to forecast future international events. He found several important differences among the groups, and determined that the State Department personnel were on the average better than the other groups at making the sorts of prediction examined in his study. In the present analysis, the State Department judgments (from February 1975) will be used to attempt to predict events from ten to fifty-eight months in the future (1976–78).

Predicting future conflict is difficult in the tumult of the Middle East. For example, the correlation between the 1970–74 force/cooperation ratio and the 1976 force/cooperation ratio is only $r = .53$ for the 105 cases (and is lower if the PLO dyads are excluded). Future patterns can better be predicted by transforming the data from ratios to differences. To do this, two new variables were created: force minus cooperation and nonforceful conflict minus cooperation. (They have the same components as the earlier ratios; the second term is now subtracted from the first term, rather than being the denominator in a fraction of which the first term is a numerator. These two variables, as measured in 1970–74, can predict 76 percent of the variance in force-cooperation in 1976–78.[9] Adding the State Department judgments as a third predictor in a linear, additive regression only increases the percentage of variance explained to 77 percent. A multiplicative model, which operationalizes the interaction hypothesis of Mansbach and Vasquez (1981, 238), is more successful. If one multiplies the prior cooperation-conflict scores to the friendship/hostility ratings, this has the effect of reducing the impact of conflict if the countries are friendly, and reducing the impact of cooperation if they are hostile. When the State Department judgments are thus multiplied by the prior cooperation-force and cooperation-nonforceful conflict scores, the two variables created can explain 88 percent in future force-cooperation.[10]

As in Jensen's study, the State Department judgments are the most useful in predicting the future. When used to adjust prior event scores, as we have just seen, they cut in half the percentage of variance unexplained (the $R^2$ increases to .88). The academic hostility/friendship judgments are slightly less effective ($R^2$ = .84). The Pentagon judgments, when used in the same way, are the least effective of all ($R^2$ = .82).

An examination of the scatter plot between prior, State-adjusted force-cooperation and future force-cooperation revealed the only large outlier to be the Egyptian-Israeli dyad, which of course had undergone true and revolutionary change by 1976–78 because of the U.S. mediating efforts culminating in Camp David. This suggests that the model has a realistic fit in its gross features at least.

## CONCLUSIONS

Two major issues in the analysis of world politics have been identifying the dimensions of international conflict and cooperation; and determining the relationship of perception to reality. The present chapter has examined these two themes by measuring the association between two aspects of conflict/cooperation, and by measuring the strength of the linkage between perceptual, event (WEIS), and historical (COW) records of international interactions.

The general model that has been documented in this paper has already been schematically summarized in Figure 5-1. To summarize the basic relationships: (1) event data explain somewhat less than half of the variance in hostility/friendship judgments of specialists; (2) future "events"—not surprisingly, given the first point—are better predicted by past events than by the hostility/friendship judgments of specialists; (3) despite the first point, there is some evidence for the interactive (Mansbach and Vasquez) hypothesis, in which the impact of past events on future events is modified by the level of hostility/ friendship between the pair of actors.

The influence of the friendship/hostility variable is especially significant in that the dependent variable (WEIS force-cooperation) was also being predicted by an earlier version of itself. This procedure would be expected to overstate the importance of the lagged predictor, since the 1970–74 and 1976–78 WEIS data share a common set of biases. That overstatement, in turn, reduces the percentage of variance that other variables might be able to explain. For this reason, it would be useful to conduct a follow-up study at such time as COW dispute and/or COPDAB event data may be analyzed, for at least the 1976–78 period, as dependent variables.

This chapter has reported the reliability of an indicator of one aspect of cooperation/conflict between nations. It has examined the predictive validity of that instrument as an early warning indicator of reliance on force in the Middle East. It has integrated that indicator into a model of cooperation/conflict developed by Mansbach and Vasquez, and has found some support for that model. The hostility/friendship measured by the new indicator seems to interact with previous international events to affect future international tensions. The indicator has also shown some promise as a criterion for a validation study of event data Event data sets can only be as accurate as their source, and it is useful to have a set of specialists' judgments against which to examine the patterns of events. The analysis in the present chapter indicates that event data are measuring only one fraction of the conflict and cooperation between nations, and that the event data indicators can only explain about one-half of the variation in friendship/hostility scores. In the view of this author, the event indicators are useful but would benefit from incremental improvements.

All of this validation and predictive work is, one hopes, a step along the road to a more complete, empirically based model of international conflict. In the meantime, it is important to have indicators available for their purely descriptive value. As discussed near the beginning of the present chapter, the judgmental indicator of friendship/hostility has a number of advantages in that context: it describes the increasingly complex array of international alignments in a succinct, timely, economical, and potentially nonquantitative way for the policy community. Increasingly multipolar alignment patterns (both of our global system and its regional subsystems) may enhance the prospects for international peace (Deutsch and Singer 1964; Wayman 1981). But this will be true only, it is argued above, if decision makers develop improved sensitivities to the subtleties of multipolar international alignments. This improved sensitivity is the potential descriptive value of the friendship/hostility indicator.

NOTES

1. For stylistic variety, the "judgments" are occasionally referred to as opinions, perceptions, or assessments.

2. Figure 5-2 represents a Goodman-Kruskal multidimensional scaling analysis of the friendship/hostility data from the State Department and the academic respondents. The two groups have been compared using the Schonemann-Carroll technique of fitting one matrix to another with rigid rotation. The lines in the graph indicate the distance between the State Department and academic locations of a country. The shortness of the lines indicates a high level of agreement between the two groups. Nations close to each other in the graph have similar sets of friends and enemies. The vertical dimension in the graph seems to represent conflict between Israel and her enemies, and the horizontal dimension seems to represent conflict between radical and conservative states.

3. The distinction being drawn here between foreign policy decision makers and regional specialists is emphasized by Kringen (1981, 10), who argues that academics need to be more sensitive to divisions within the government: "How many times have you read 'policy' papers offering advice to members of the foreign policy community as though they did not differ by type (analysts vs. decision makers), areas of responsibility (political, economic, military), or organizational function (intelligence vs. policy implementation)?"

4. This has an advantage over the standard error of the mean, since the correlations are not based on an assumption that the groups are a representative sample of an underlying population.

5. Plans to include the COPDAB data have been delayed by problems with the version of the COPDAB monthly aggregation data currently available at the University of Michigan.

6. In that table, and in all subsequent analyses in this paper, the variables have been reversed in direction where necessary so that conflict is on the high end of the scale and cooperation on the low end. (Hence, the State Department friendship/hostility judgments have been recoded and relabeled as "hostility/friendship" scores.) This insures that all directional hypotheses later in the paper will be confirmed by positive coefficients and disconfirmed by negative coefficients.

7. Non-U.S. dyads are used because the monthly aggregations for the United States appear to be missing in the COPDAB data at the University of Michigan.

8. The correlations between these independent variables

are as follows: $r_{12}$ = .45, $r_{13}$ = .46, and $r_{23}$ = .56, where one is the quarrel/cooperation ratio, two is the COW dispute variable, and three is the force/cooperation ratio.

9. The hyphen is intended to denote a difference, just as the slash indicated a ratio.

10. Although the percentage of "explained" variance was lower, the same patterns recurred when the conflictual cooperative event ratios were divided by the State Department friendship/hostility scores: the new variable, consistent with the Mansbach-Vasquez hypothesis, explained more variance than any linear, additive set of its parts.

## REFERENCES

Alcock, N., and A. Newcombe. 1970. "The Perception of National Power." *Journal of Conflict Resolution* 14:335–3.

Allison, G. 1971. *Essence of Decision*. Boston: Little, Brown.

Caplan, N., A. Morrison, and R. Stambaugh. 1975. *The Use of Social Science Knowledge in Policy Decisions at the National Level*. Ann Arbor: Institute for Social Research, University of Michigan.

Deutsch, K., and J. D. Singer. 1964. "Multipolar Systems and International Stability." *World Politics* 16:390–406.

Jensen, L. 1972. "Predicting International Events." *Peace Research Reviews* 4(6). Oakville, Ontario: Canadian Peace Research Institute.

Jervis, R. 1976. *Perception and Misperception in International Politics*. Princeton, N.J.: Princeton University Press.

Kegley, C., and E. Wittkopf. 1981. *World Politics*. New York: St. Martin's.

Keohane, R., and J. Nye. 1977. *Power and Interdependence*. Boston: Little, Brown.

Klingberg, F. 1941. "Studies in the Measurement of the Relations among Sovereign States." *Psychometrica* 6:335–52.

Knorr, K. 1955. *The War Potential of Nations*. Princeton, N.J.: Princeton University Press.

Kringen, J. 1981. "Institutional Constraints on the Transfer of Technology for International Policy Analysis." Paper presented to the Annual Meeting of the International Studies Association, Philadelphia, March 18–21.

Mansbach, R., and J. Vasquez. 1981. *In Search of Theory: A New Paradigm for Global Politics*. New York: Columbia University Press.

McClelland, C., and G. Hoggard. 1969. "Conflict Patterns in Interactions among Nations." In J. Rosenau, ed. *International Politics and Foreign Policy.* New York: Free Press.

Quandt, W. 1977. *Decade of Decisions: American Policy toward the Arab-Israeli Conflict, 1967–1976.* Berkeley: University of California Press.

Rapkin, David P., William R. Thompson, and Jon A. Christopherson. 1979. "Bipolarity and Bipolarization in the Cold War Era." *Journal of Conflict Resolution* 23,2:261–95.

Ray, J., and J. D. Singer. 1973. "Measuring the Concentration of Power in the International System." *Sociological Methods and Research* 1(4):403–37.

Schuman, H., and S. Hatchett. 1974. *Black Racial Attitudes.* Ann Arbor: Institute for Social Research, University of Michigan.

Singer, J. D., and M. Small. 1966. "Formal Alliances, 1815–1939: A Quantitative Description." *Journal of Peace Research* 3:1–32.

Singer, J. D., and M. Wallace. 1979. *To Augur Well: Early Warning Indicators in World Politics.* Beverly Hills: Sage.

Waltz, K. 1964. "The Stability of a Bipolar World." *Daedalus* 93:882–84.

Waltz, K. 1967. "International Structure, National Force, and the Balance of World Power." *Journal of International Affairs* 21:215–231.

Wayman, F. 1981. "Bipolarity, Multipolarity, and the Threat of War." Paper presented at the Annual Meeting of the International Studies Association, Philadelphia, Pa.

Wilkenfeld, J., G. Hopple, and P. Rossa. 1979. "Sociopolitical Indicators of Conflict and Cooperation," in J. D. Singer and M. Wallace, eds. *To Augur Well.* Beverly Hills: Sage.

Zinnes, D. 1968. "The Expression and Perception of Hostility in Prewar Crisis: 1914," in J. D. Singer, ed. *Quantitative International Politics.* New York: Free Press.

# 6

# Profiles of Conflict: *A* Methodological Note

## *I. William Zartman*

The notion of "escalation" implies both a quantitative and a qualitative dimension—an increase in intensity of inter-actions and a change in nature as relations pass from one level of intensity to another. Some important insights into the optimal practice of conflict resolution are also related to levels and intensities of conflict. But measures of levels and intensities remain elusive. They have their ups and downs and have long been portrayed in the jagged moun-tain-climbing presentations of event data, but without providing the texture that is needed to portray the com-plexities of escalation and resolution. This brief discussion arises from an attempt to grapple with that problem. Unfortunately, it is not a success, in that it does not produce the sought after portrayal. But it does throw light on the difficulties of doing so, leaving the basic problem as a clearer challenge to be surmounted.

CONFLICT AND ESCALATION

This is not the place to review the entire literature on conflict and escalation. Suffice it to note that significant writings, from Schelling (1960, 170 and passim) to Smoke (1979), have identified escalation with changes in nature rather than degree of intensification, crossing saliencies, and moving from one level to another. In poker terms, escalation is not just a raise but a significant raise past some sort of limit or threshold that the other party had set for himself; the other party has the alternatives of dropping, calling, or raising. Calling means that the parties have to show their hands, and that communication toward an outcome begins.

Raising can either be routine intensification or another round of escalation if it is significant in nature. The most important thing about such escalations is that they are decision points, moments at which parties take a conscious decision to raise the means in order to get out of an impasse that prevents them from achieving their chosen ends; and then other parties decide whether such a raise has taken the determination of the ends out of their hands or whether they should commit enough additional means to annul the raise and thus reimpose the impasse, or add on enough additional means of their own to end the conflict once and for all in their favor (hoping the other parties in turn will not meet or raise further). Hence, the image of levels as stalemates and escalation to break out of stalemates is realistic, reinforcing the notion of decision points.

The general conceptualization of conflict as a series of levels of testing and stalemate separated by specific escalatory decision steps also relates to new concepts of conflict resolution. A focus on the texture of conflict produces the notion that there are ripe moments when third party attempts at conciliation are likely to be more effective than at other times (Zartman 1983; Zartman forthcoming). One definition of that ripe moment is couched in terms of two vertical characteristics of intensity—the plateau and the precipice. Plateau is a mutually perceived and intolerable stalemate, a flat terrain stretching into the future, providing no later possibilities for decisive escalation. Precipice is the conceptual opposite, an impending catastrophe when things get worse for both sides in the conflict, possibly as a result of one side's desperate attempt to escalate its way out of the stalemate. One interesting question (that goes beyond the metaphores) is whether an impending precipice, with its perceived deadline, is effective (as it was in Zimbabwe or in the Cuban Missile Crisis), or whether the obstinacy and cloudy perceptions of human nature require a precipice experienced from the recent past to shock the parties into reconciliation more effectively, but less efficiently since there is no longer a deadline (as was the case between Arabs and Israel in the past decade, or between Capulets and Montagues).

To examine these hypothetical notions and real questions, a study has been undertaken of four African conflict areas—Shaba, Odagen, Western Sahara, and Namibia—in search of both patterns of conflict and escalation, and moments and practices of conflict resolution (Zartman forthcoming). A convenient way of summarizing the cases is to identify their crucial decision points. In Shaba, there were two decisions by the Congolese National Liberation Front (FLNC) to escalate the conflict with Zaire, in early 1977 and early 1978; their implementation in March and May immediately triggered two Zairois decisions to counter-escalate with foreign assistance, and the successful counterattack finally prepared the way for a mutual decision by Zaire and Angola in June to reconcile differences.

In the Horn, a Somali decision to prepare guerrilla warfare, in early 1975, was followed by a decision to commit regular army units to the attack in mid-1977 and was met by the counter-escalating Ethiopian decisions to invite foreign assistance in November and to counterattack in February 1978, and then to stop at the border in March. This time the successful counterattack led neither side to a decision to reconcile. In the Sahara, the Moroccan-Mauritanian decision to appeal to the World Court in 1974 was followed by the Moroccan decision to escalate the conflict with Spain through a civilian invasion in October 1975 and then to de-escalate by settling out of court and off the battlefield in November. The Polisario decision to oppose the subsequent military takeover of the area was defeated, leading to a decision in mid-1976 to focus on Mauritania, and then the decision in July 1978 to concentrate on Morocco through attacks on both sides of its pre-1975 borders. Morocco then changed its military tactics in the fall of 1979, and thereafter decided to accept an Organization for African Unity (OAU) referendum, in July 1981. The Polisario's decision to go for a diplomatic "quick fix" in early 1982 returned the conflict to mutually blocking stalemate, and a roughly simultaneous Moroccan and Algerian decision to look for a means of accommodation in early 1983.

In Namibia, the South African decision to elaborate confederal independence in 1975 was followed by the decision in April 1977 to prepare internal conditions for acceptable sovereign independence, taken under Western pressure, and then implemented as an electoral decision in December 1978, without decisive outcome or effective counteraction. The history of the conflict and the negotiations since 1978 has above all been characterized by the inability of either opponents—the Frontline States and the South West African Peoples Organization (SWAPO)—or mediators—the Western Five—to make South Africa make a decision at all, instead of simply continuing the conflict inconclusively. The methodological challenge in this type of conflict is to devise a way of portraying intensities and levels of conflict so that escalations and ripe moments become apparent. If such historical profiles can be presented and analyzed, then the possibility of identifying the same characteristics and foreseeing moments of escalation and conciliation may come closer to realization.

## ADDITIONAL INDICATORS OF CONFLICT

In the search for an appropriate means of constructing a profile of conflict, two indicators have been used and both have proven unsuccessful. But there are lessons in failure. The value of the exercise lies in two types of lessons, one as a side effect of one measure and the other as a weakness of the other measure itself. The two measures are military expenditures as an indicator of the means of conflict, and events interaction data as an indicator of the state of relations between the conflicting parties. Unfortunately, from the start, military expenditures are a rather gross indicator. The data are only available—and meaningful—on a yearly basis when a much finer focus is required. Events interaction data provide this finer focus, since they are easily available on a monthly basis, and if need be could be available on a weekly basis with equal realism. Lag time is little. Furthermore, events data indicate other dimensions beyond simply the means of conflict. They can be divided into indicators of conflict and cooperation at the same time, showing if there are last minute attempts to reach accommodation at the same time as conflict is being prepared or last minute attempts at positioning through renewed conflict at the same time as accommodation is being arranged. They can also combine inherent and cognitive values, showing both what happened and the way it was viewed. Conceptually, therefore, events interaction data seems admirably suited to the needs, but military expenditures do act as an important indicator as well. The two can be examined in detail, using data from the cases in question.

### Arms Expenditures

An additional problem with arms expenditures is that they are multi-determined. Unless armaments are part of a clear bilateral rivalry, causal relationships are so diffuse as to be uncertain. Only two of the cases lend themselves to any interpretation as arms races—Morocco-Algeria and Ethiopia-Somalia (see Figures 6-1 and 6-2). As expected, since they are meaningful and available only as annual figures, they are too insensitive to serve as an indicator of levels of conflict and escalation. They do however indicate something of the relationship between wars and arms races, since both pairs of countries had wars with each other in 1963, and again in 1977–78 for Somalia-Ethiopia and 1975–82 for Morocco-Algeria (by proxy).

Figures from the 1960s show arms races that are caused by war and not the reverse; having not clearly won their 1963 wars, all four parties set about to arm for the next round, Algeria leading Morocco and Ethiopia leading Somalia. Algeria continued to lead Morocco in the 1970s, giving no conclusive evidence of Moroccan preplanning for the 1975 conflict. Somalia outstripped Ethiopia in military spending in the mid-1970s, but again there is no proof whether this was a result of the military coup or a prelude to the irredentist conflict. Only diplomatic history, not arms charts, can provide the conclusive evidence. What the charts do suggest quite solidly—in confirmation of diplomatic analysis—is that conflicts have a self-escalating power of their own, dragging arms expenditure along or behind them.

## Events Interaction Data

It might be expected that events interaction data could provide a more sensitive indicator of conflict escalation, including plateaus and precipices. Such data are available monthly and are even broken down into different kinds of cooperation and conflict. They portray a continuous flow of events so they can show peaks and troughs in the dynamics of conflict. Because of these advantages, the Conflict and Peace Data Bank (COPDAB) data produced at the University of North Carolina were used to map the conflicts.*

The data show some interesting effects. In the area of early warnings, all three conflicts were mixed with elements of cooperation, and indeed the outbreak of the crisis itself was preceded by several months dominated by cooperation. It is not apparent whether this was a smokescreen for hostile preparations or a last attempt at working out things that could be helped along by positive intervention. Then

---

*I am grateful to Edward Azar, now of the University of Maryland, for making the COPDAB data available.

Figure 6-1. Millions of Dollars in Expenditures on Arms Imports, 1956–80

MOROCCO–ALGERIA

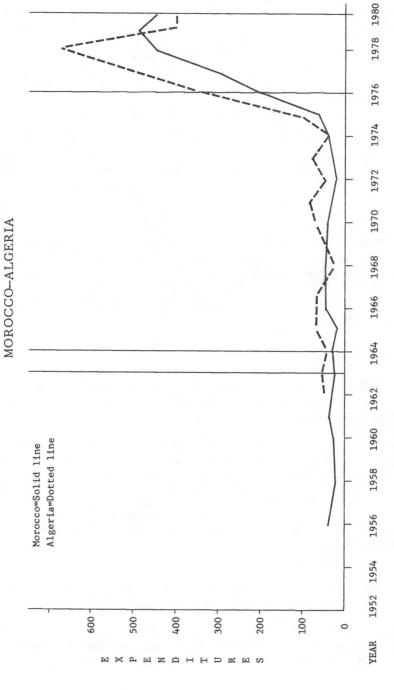

Morocco=Solid line
Algeria=Dotted line

*Note:* Vertical lines indicate wars
*Note:* 1956–68=1968 constant $, 1969–80=1977 constant $

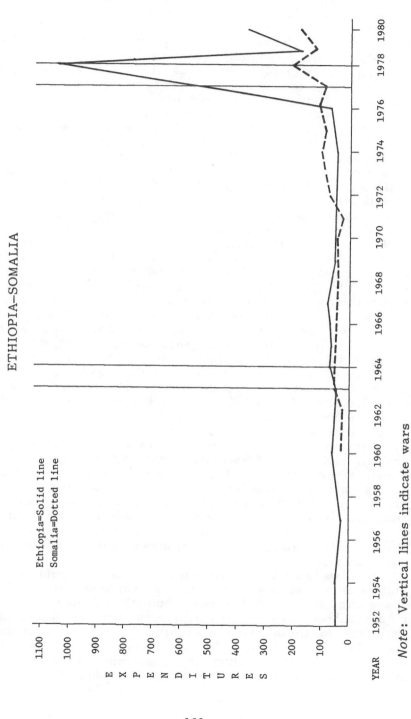

Figure 6-2. Millions of Dollars in Expenditures on Arms Imports, 1952–80

ETHIOPIA–SOMALIA

Ethiopia=Solid line
Somalia=Dotted line

Note: Vertical lines indicate wars
Note: 1956–68 constant $, 1969–80=1977 constant $

193

again, all conflict areas appear to show attempts at cooperation in the midst of crises—and in fact in most cases at the height of crisis—suggesting that even when conflict takes over, the two-track policy is still in operation, providing an opportunity to be seized by helpful conciliators, external appearances of conflict notwithstanding. Such inferences are supportive of the preceding analysis. They could be considered clinching, if there were not doubts about the quality of the data.

Instead, a closer look at the "map" of the events raises some questions. In the Angola/Zaire conflict one of the months of Shaba I and all of Shaba II do not appear in the data from one party. In the Moroccan-Algerian conflict, nothing records any change of behavior on the part of Algeria—the very element that an analysis seeks to locate—until apparently unprovoked hostility broke out against Morocco in November 1975. The crucial year of 1974 has no recorded events of either a hostile or a cooperative nature. In the conflict in the Horn of Africa, the picture given is one of repeated Somali attempts at cooperation through 1974–75, meeting first a positive response from Ethiopia during the moderate year of the revolution and then repeated provocations under General Tefari Bante in 1975–76, which brought forth a Somali response on occasion until Tefari's successor, General Mengistu, responded to a Somali conflict move in May 1977 after an exchange of cooperation and started the Ogaden war. The diplomatic record is quite different, for it shows a Somali irregular effort planned from January 1976 on and gradually rising in intensity until the end of 1977.

There is a difference between counter-intuitive effects brought out by a new method of data portrayal or generation, and a data presentation that has such gaps in the known record as to call its entire value into question. Events data portrayals have been used to show the rise and fall, escalation and de-escalation, of conflicts, and they are admirably suited for this purpose—in concept. But if there is no way of distinguishing missing data troughs from absent event troughs, then troughs—and peaks—become meaningless.

The data analyzed here make use of no sophisticated statistical techniques. But if this informal analysis is misleading, then even the most sophisticated analysis techniques cannot provide insightful results. The interesting questions in these cases of conflict concern the gradual escalation of the conflict in its precrisis stage—the early warnings that the conflict itself provides—so that conciliators can defuse the bomb before it explodes. COPDAB data on these cases provide no way of answering these questions, and the inadequacies in the data that prevent such answers also throw doubts on the usefulness of the data for any other purpose than to indicate that there was a war in the Horn in 1977 or a battle in the Sahara in 1976. Until better aggregate data are available, only diplomatic analysis can provide even tentative answers to the questions.

## REFERENCES

An exhaustive bibliography about the four African conflicts discussed in this chapter is found in Zartman forthcoming.

Azar, Edward, et al. 1972. Special Issue on Arab-Israeli Conflict. *Journal of Conflict Resolution* 16,2.

Barringer, Richard E., with Robert Ramers. 1977. *War: Patterns of Conflict.* New York: Oxford.

Doran, Charles F. 1980. "Leading Indicators of the June War." *International Journal of Middle East Studies* 11,1:23–58.

Schelling, Thomas C. 1960. *The Strategy of Conflict.* Cambridge: Harvard University Press.

Smoke, Richard. 1979. *Wars: Controlling Escalation.* Cambridge: Harvard University Press.

Wright, Quincy. 1965. "The Escalation of International Conflict." *Journal of Conflict Resolution* 9,4:439–49.

Zartman, I. William. 1983. "The Strategy of Preventive Diplomacy in Third World Conflicts." In Alexander George, ed., *Managing U.S.-Soviet Rivalry.* Boulder: Westview.

Zartman, I. William. Forthcoming. *Ripe for Resolution: Conflict and Intervention in Africa.* New Haven: Yale University Press.

# Part IV

## Predicting
## Conflict in the International System

# 7

# Alliance Norms and the Management of Interstate Disputes

*Charles W. Kegley, Jr., and Gregory A. Raymond*

> . . . a prudent ruler ought not to keep faith when by so doing it would be against his interest, and when the reasons which made him bind himself no longer exist.
>
> —*Machiavelli*

> . . . the universality of a law that everyone believing himself to be in need can make any promise he pleases with the intention of breaking it would make promising, and the very purpose of promising, itself impossible, since no one would believe he was promised anything, but would laugh at utterances of this kind as empty shams.
>
> —*Kant*

Researchers engaged in developing macro quantitative indicators that can warn policy makers about the probable advent of global instability have generally concentrated their efforts on the *structural* attributes of the international system. In particular, considerable attention has been given to measuring the *magnitude of alliance commitments*, under the assumption that alliance aggregation affects the degree to which the international system is violence prone. Recently, however, Sullivan and Siverson (1981, 18) have pointed out that in order to predict the consequences of those structural configurations generated by alliance bonds, the *reliability of alliance commitments* should be considered. The same alliance levels, for example, could be associated with different international outcomes if at one point in time system members held a Machiavellian attitude toward their obligation to abide by treaty commitments, while at another point in time they maintained a Kantian view. Therefore, if we can determine which principles of conduct are accepted by system members, we should be able to improve our ability to predict their behavior.

In order to investigate this proposition, a series of tests will be conducted on the 1820–1914 time period to ascertain whether changes in those normative principles that bear upon the reliability of alliance commitments have been associated with changes in the frequency, scope, or intensity of serious major power disputes. The premise of this study is that by measuring the degree to which international norms support binding obligations, we can devise a macro quantitative indicator of treaty commitment that is grounded in the *cultural* attributes of the international system and can be used in conjunction with indicators based on structural attributes to warn policy makers whenever conditions arise that increase the probability of global conflict.

## THE RESEARCH PROBLEM

The tendency of many interstate disagreements to escalate into military confrontations suggests that if the danger of war is to be reduced, policy makers must find ways to manage more successfully the disputes their states seem to experience so often. Toward this end, they must necessarily confront two interrelated questions: (1) What position should they take on the irrevocability of the commitments that they make? (2) What attitudes regarding the irrevocability of commitments do they wish to see held by other members of the international system? For all policy makers, these questions are important, a decision is unavoidable, and the results that flow from their actions are profound. Regardless if they decide to honor their commitments, or renege on them in order to acquire some immediate gain, they must live with the consequences of their choice—a choice that potentially could determine whether others are willing to trust their word in future encounters. Thus those normative principles that define the extent of one's obligation to fulfill a commitment have a direct impact on the prospects for peacefully resolving disputes.

The relationship between the reliability of alliance commitments and the occurrence of serious disputes has had a prominent place in theoretical discussions of international affairs since the time of Kautilya (Bozeman 1960, 122). In particular, this relationship has received special attention in the *realpolitik* literature that continues to be popular today within the policy-making community. When the decentralized, anarchical character of the international political system is so acknowledged, the role of norms takes on added significance (Masters 1969). The system's grand norm—sovereignty—grants states the right to ignore rules that are not in their national interest. Hence under conditions where conflict is believed to be endemic, the struggle for power insatiable, and reliance on self-help the only recourse available to injured parties, whether commitments adopted voluntarily are accepted as binding assumes an extraordinary causal importance. Because such a system breeds bad faith, mistrust, and suspicion, the degree to which international norms sanction the opportunistic disavowal of commitments will be crucial in determining if an alliance treaty actually binds its signatory parties and thereby makes a given pact meaningful.

Brought into focus by the nature of the global environment, therefore, are some empirical research questions that contain very pragmatic implications: As the norms governing the sanctity of alliance commitments have slowly evolved with changing international realities, have they been associated with fluctuations in the frequency, scope, or intensity of serious disputes among great powers? If so, what is the nature of these associations? What do they inform us about the norms policy makers could embrace, if they chose, in order to more often succeed in reconciling their differences without threatening to use force? It is these questions which the present study seeks to address.

Before proposing a strategy of inquiry to investigate these questions, it should be noted that conflict theory is divided on the answers. The prescriptions it advances point to an embarrassingly divergent set of conclusions about alliance norms. On the one hand, a substantial portion of the literature operates from the inviting assumption that the willingness of states to honor treaty commitments adds stability to the international system. Both national and global interests are served because, among other things, compliance with agreements:

- clarifies national priorities;
- encourages amity between states by fostering a climate of trust;

- strengthens the resolve of allies;
- diminishes the need of others to monitor adherence to treaty provisions;
- cuts communication costs;
- reduces systemic uncertainty;
- promotes international security by reducing the fear of external attack;
- enhances credibility in bargaining;
- avoids the stigma associated with erratic behavior; and
- contributes to consensus about the criteria for differentiating between right and wrong.

Thus from this point of view, norms that support compliance with treaty commitments limit conflict and increase cooperation by adding greater predictability, order, and mutual confidence to the relations among nations. These benefits are compelling; and with considerable justification there is reason to believe that the prospects for the peaceful resolution of disputes can be improved when policy makers stand by their commitments (Kaplan and Katzenbach 1961, 341–55; Andrews 1975; Cantor 1976, 264–71; Janis and Mann 1977; Suganami 1979).[1]

On the other hand, however, conflict theory is also equally cogent in suggesting that there are many problems associated with binding commitments. According to some theorists, the steadfast maintenance of alliance commitments may be undesirable globally and counterproductive nationally because it would tend to:

- foreclose options;
- reduce the capacity of states to adapt to changing circumstances (Katz and Kahn 1978);
- weaken a state's influence capability by decreasing the number of additional partners with which it can align (Morgenthau 1966);
- eliminate the advantages in bargaining that can be derived from deliberately fostering ambiguity about one's intentions (Schelling 1960);
- provoke the fears of a state's adversaries;
- entrap states in disputes with their ally's enemies (Beilenson 1969);
- interfere with the negotiation of disputes involving an ally's enemy by precluding certain issues from being placed on the agenda for debate;
- preserve existing rivalries;
- stimulate envy and resentment on the part of friends who are outside the alliance and therefore are not beneficiaries of its advantages; and

• increase tensions by requiring states to adhere to agreements whose costs over time may have come to exceed their benefits.

Most of these problems center on the loss of flexibility that a binding conception of alliance commitments entails. During periods when such conceptions are dominant, it is more difficult for national leaders to preserve room for maneuver: in essence, they find it hard to maximize alternatives, exploit emergent opportunities, and gain advantage by surprise. Within an arena where there can be no permanent friends or enemies, leaders who treat their commitments as binding cannot shift their allegiances easily, with the result that the effective operation of a balance of power is virtually eliminated. To put it another way, systemic uncertainty may not be altogether destabilizing insofar as it may breed caution, inhibit risk taking, and, in turn, reduce the frequency of disputes between states (Waltz 1964). Conversely, as commitments come to be regarded as more binding, the number of parties to disputes may actually increase and antagonisms may grow more, not less, intense. The prescription that follows from this line of reasoning is that leaders should not take a fixed position on things that are not fixed. The international system would be less prone to serious disputes in the absence of norms that insist alliance commitments be religiously respected.

Conflict theory thus points to contradictory conclusions: "Flexibility and commitment in statecraft offer juxtaposed advantages and drawbacks, and the relative merits of these alternative stances [remain] an issue for several theorists of international politics" (Lockhart 1978, 545). To evaluate the relative merits of these arguments and thereby help resolve this theoretical controversy, a systematic analysis of the consequences of these logically opposed norms is required.[2] Empirical evidence can enable us to ascertain which theoretical perspective has the most to recommend it, and assist us in better predicting the effects that will result when either of these norms is embraced by policy makers. Therefore, let us now present the methodological procedures we have used in order to make the data that will permit us to pursue this kind of inquiry.


INDICATOR CONSTRUCTION

Although the importance of norms as a determinant of international outcomes is universally recognized, psychocultural variables have largely resisted measurement. A multitude of methodological obstacles have discouraged researchers from seeking to analyze norms in a rigorous, empirical fashion. For the purposes to which we have assigned ourselves, undoubtedly the most troublesome of these obstacles stems from the fact that the decision calculuses of those leaders choosing to fulfill their commitments is not open to public inspection; nor, for that matter, are the motives of those who have chosen to disregard their treaty obligations. While we can make inferences about their intentions from biographical material and from the promises they voice in announcing the agreements they make, we are largely precluded from observing how sincerely they hold these expressions of loyalty, honor, and the like. If we cannot directly observe the preference schedules of decision makers, how can we measure the degree of commitment they attach to the agreements they make?

Perhaps the most advantageous approach to transcending this methodological obstacle is to shift from the national to a systemic level of analysis. This prevents us from ascertaining the extent to which individual decision makers feel bound by the alliance agreements they make. But it facilitates the study of change in the psycho-cultural environment of nations, a perspective that has long been advocated but seldom pursued (Singer 1968, 1980).

Norms are an expression of those opinions that are generally held throughout a system about specific kinds of behavior (Thibaut and Kelly 1959). That is to say, they define the "cultural climate" within which political interaction takes place.[3] At any given point in time, this rudimentary global political culture places greater or less stress on flexibility (as opposed to commitment) in its definition of what constitutes an appropriate conception of alliance obligations. In emphasizing one norm rather than the other, the cultural climate will either facilitate rapid alliance formation and swift realignments, or, instead, foster permanence by prescribing faithful adherence to treaty guarantees.

If the cultural attributes of the international system can serve as a key point of reference for analyzing the behavioral processes that occur within it, how might change in these attributes be detected? The approach taken here involves monitoring changes in the content of the international legal order, since international law is a medium through which prevailing opinions about acceptable forms of behavior are communicated to members of the state system (Coplin 1966, 170). Furthermore, because alliance "tends to sustain international law . . . and in turn derives support from it," and because "treaties are employed for formal expression of alliance" (Freidman 1970, 28), an examination of changes in treaty law over time should provide reproducible evidence about changes in those international norms pertaining to the sanctity of alliance agreements. Thus, in order to measure the climate of opinion produced by the cultural attributes of the international system, we shall construct an index that is anchored in the evolving international law of alliances.

Alliance treaties are contractual agreements that create legal rights and obligations between the signatory parties. Perhaps the most controversial of these rights and obligations are the grounds accepted by international law for unilaterally terminating an agreement prior to its expiration. According to the norm *pacta sunt servanda,* a valid treaty is binding upon the signatories and must be performed by them in good faith. In contrast, the *clausa rebus sic stantibus* justifies unilateral termination under certain conditions. Based on its most narrow interpretation, the *clausa* authorizes termination only if a fundamental and unforeseen change of circumstances occurs that radically transforms the obligations of the signatories. However, a more broad interpretation holds that termination is warranted if performance of the obligations entails an unreasonable sacrifice, an excessive burden, or is injurious to such so-called "fundamental rights of state" as self-preservation, development, and independence (Woolsey 1926; Gardner 1927; Briggs 1949; Lissitzyn 1967). While these two norms need not be considered mutually exclusive (Kunz 1945, 190), in historical practice they frequently have been treated as opposites, especially during periods when the broader interpretation of the *clausa* prevailed. Consequently, international law has at times drawn a sharp distinction: "Treaties either were binding or not binding at all" (Gould 1957, 57).

Knowing whether treaties were considered binding at a particular point in time is central to any analysis of the reliability of alliance commitments. In effect, the relative importance attributed by the international legal order to *pacta sunt servanda* and *rebus sic stantibus* establishes the psycho-cultural foundations for alliance dynamics. During periods when international norms stress the sanctity of treaties and a faithful adherence to contractual guarantees, we would expect to find that systemic uncertainty was reduced. Conversely, whenever norms depict treaties in conditional terms and allow signatory parties to repudiate them in order to free themselves from their obligations, we would expect to find a period of high uncertainty (David

1975, 12–19). In short, the greater the flexibility accorded to the interpretation of one's obligations in an alliance commitment, the more likely national leaders will be concerned that their allies might desert them.

In order to identify empirically the consequences that result from the degree to which norms promoting alliance commitments are embraced, a macro quantitative indicator that measures changes in the relative importance of *pacta sunt servanda* and *rebus sic stantibus* needs to be constructed. The indicator we developed for this purpose comes from a content analysis that the Transnational Rules Indicators Project conducted on 244 authoritative legal treaties written since the Congress of Vienna.[4] The objective of the content analysis was to identify the kind of alliance behavior that the authors of these treatises perceived as legally permissible when they were writing. Each treatise was coded according to whether existing legal norms were seen as supporting or rejecting a binding interpretation of treaty obligations. Once every treatise in a particular half-decade was coded, a disposition score was calculated for that five-year interval that ranged from +1.00 (alliance commitments are binding) to -1.00 (alliance commitments may be terminated unilaterally), with intermediate positions arrayed in between and a perfect balance (0.00) indicating neither norm was dominant in the period in question.[5] By treating these authors as expert observers who attempted to describe and communicate to others those norms that held sway when they wrote their treatises, it becomes possible to measure indirectly changes in the relative importance of specific norms over time. Moreover, since the writings of publicists have traditionally been accepted by judicial tribunals as a subsidiary means of determining the rules of law, it would appear that this approach to constructing our macro indicator of alliance commitment was reasonable.

Let us now turn our attention to the procedures used to measure the occurrence of major power disputes. Briefly, serious disputes are defined here as incidents involving explicit threats, displays, or uses of military force by one state against another. That is, they involve threatening or actually committing such acts as blockades, occupations, seizures, and so on. Raw data on these acts have been collected by the Correlates of War Project (Wallace 1979, 9–11), and these data have been used to create three outcome variables: *frequency* (the number of serious disputes normalized by major power sub-system size), *scope* (the percentage of major powers involved in serious disputes), and *intensity* (the percentage of major power disputes that escalated to war).[6] Since our indicator of alliance commitment gives a composite score for each half-decade we observe, we have aggregated these variables at five-year intervals.

## DATA ANALYSIS

Having presented the operational measures of our predictor and outcome variables, we can now take up the question of whether binding conceptions of alliance commitments increase or decrease the extent to which serious disputes occur among the major powers. We shall begin with a bivariate analysis of the 1820–1914 time period, and conclude with a multivariate analysis. The rationale for selecting this period can be summarized as follows. First, studies by McGowan and Rood (1975), Job (1976), Siverson and Duncan (1976), Li and Thompson (1978), and Duncan and Siverson (1982) have demonstrated that this was a multipolar balance of power period where the temporal and spatial distribution of alliance initiations was random. Second, various researchers (for example, Chi 1968, 424; Franke 1968, 454–56) have pointed to the scarcity of reliable alliance commitments as a key factor in producing the serious disputes that led to the breakdown of other balance of power systems. Third, legal theory postulates that authoritative international law flourishes during balance of power periods (Oppenheim, cited in Hoffmann 1969, 138). In sum, the 1820–1914 time period constitutes a crucial historical test: not only do we expect that changes in the reliability of alliance commitments will be related to the incidence of serious disputes, but changes in the extent to which alliance commitments were considered inviolable should be clearly reflected in the content of legal norms.

Table 7-1 presents the results from a simple bivariate analysis of the relationship between our macro indicator of alliance treaty commitment and the frequency, scope, and intensity of serious major power disputes. Insofar as the existence of auto-correlated disturbances in our time series data would make least-squares estimators inefficient, we used a form of regression analysis known as generalize least squares (GLS). Our use of this procedure involved employing ordinary least squares to estimate the parameters of each regression equation, estimating the serial correlation coefficient $\rho$ with the Cochrane-Orcutt iterative technique, transforming the data based on $\rho$, and then running a regression on the transformed data (Intriligator 1978, 165–73; Pindyck and Rubinfeld 1976, 111–12). Although the magnitude of the correlations is modest at best, their negative direction supports the contention that serious major power disputes decrease as alliance commitments come to be seen as binding. Obviously a bivariate analysis of this kind is merely a preliminary investigation into the relationship between international norms and serious major power disputes. Hence we need to find additional ways to acquire reproducible evidence that will strengthen the grounds for our inferences.

TABLE 7-1. Bivariate Relationships between Norms Regarding the Extent of Treaty Commitments and Serious Major Power Disputes

| Outcome Variable | Extent to Which Commitments are Considered Binding | | | |
|---|---|---|---|---|
| | $r$ | $b$ | $\rho$ | DW |
| Frequency | -.42 | -.71 | -.43 | 1.49 |
| Scope | -.37 | -.98 | -.34 | 2.01 |
| Intensity | -.20 | -.12 | .21 | 1.94 |

Source: Compiled by the author.

One possibility would be to examine the relationship between alliance commitment and serious disputes while controlling for what we shall henceforth call structural flexibility. Traditionally, studies of alliance dynamics have conceptualized flexibility in a structural sense; that is, in terms of the degree to which alliances are equiprobable and time-independent. It is conceivable that the relationships reported in Table 7-1 are spurious, with the correlations between commitment norms and serious disputes being due to the fact structural flexibility is mutually related to both variables. In an effort to discover whether this actually occurred, we have relied on the Poisson-based measurement technique that Rood and McGowan (1974, 6, 11) used in their study of alliance flexibility. Simply stated, they calculated the average rate of alliance formation by five-year intervals ($m$), and then determined the cumulative probability that the observed number of alliances formed in each period ($x$) was less than $m$. These probabilities were a measure of changes in the rate of alliance formation: the higher the probability score, the greater the flexibility during the half-decade under study. Upon incorporating these data into our analysis, we found that the first-order partial correlations between alliance commitment and serious disputes, controlling for structural flexibility, indicated that the relationships involving frequency (-.39), scope (-.34), and intensity (-.16) remained negative in direction, though they were slightly weaker than the zero-order correlations displayed in Table 7-1.

Another way to strengthen the grounds for our inferences would be to introduce time lags into our analysis. Rather than assuming a contemporaneous relationship between serious disputes and those norms governing the sanctity of alliance commitments, we can take precedent into account by distributing the impact of legal norms over time. In so doing, we assume that our outcome variables at time point $t$ are affected by the content of legal norms from several preceding points in time. However, to avoid multicollinearity between the measures of alliance commitment at $t$, $t-1$, $t-2$, . . . , $t-i$, we must specify a priori some conditions about the form of the distributed lags. In accordance with the Almon method, we have posited that the lag weights can be approximated by a polynomial function (Dhrymes 1971; Ostrom and Hoole 1978, 228).[7]

Table 7-2 shows the results from a multivariate analysis of the combined impact of structural flexibility and commitment norms upon the frequency, scope, and intensity of serious major power disputes. Although as we would expect, structural flexibility is inversely related to the extent to which alliance obligations are considered binding ($r = -.18$), legal theory suggests that each variable exerts an independent influence on the occurrence of serious disputes. It is one thing, according to this line of reasoning, to be able to switch alliance partners regardless of ideology, cultural affinities, or personal ties; it is quite another to do so prior to the expiration of one's current alliance agreements. The possibility of either action would increase systemic uncertainty. Thus, for example, despite signing a 25-year defensive alliance at Venice in 1454, the acceptability of repudiating commitments made the leaders of those Italian city-states that joined the Most Holy League uncertain about the future behavior of their new allies. As Mattingly (1971, 90) has described their concerns: "Most of them believed that if the lamb had to lie down with the lion, or even if one wolf lay down with another, a wise animal kept one eye open." Given the argument that alliance flexibility and treaty commitment are independently related to the occurrence of serious disputes, we have included both predictor variables in our multivariate GLS equations.

Each equation portrays the best fit that could be made to the data. A comparison of the multiple coefficients of determination for the three equations reveals that we can account fairly well for the frequency and scope of serious major power disputes, but we cannot account very well for their intensity. In other words, our indicators permit us to predict the incipience of interstate disputes and the number of parties to them better than they allow us to predict the escalation of serious disputes into war.

According to the regression coefficients in the frequency equation, there is a curvilinear relationship between structural flexibility and the number of serious disputes between major powers. The sequence of a negative followed by a positive coefficient indicates that the curve is a parabola with the shape an inverted U. Hence we can infer that the number of serious major power disputes that occurred between 1820 and 1914 was high whenever alliance structures were either extremely rigid or extremely fluid. Combining this inference with the negative lag coefficients that appear in the equation for our treaty commitment index, we conclude that dangerous disputes occur less often when there is a moderate degree of structural flexibility and treaty obligations are interpreted as binding.

The negative coefficients in the scope equation reveal that the number of major powers engaged in serious disputes decreases as alliance configurations become more fluid and treaty obligations become more binding. As in the frequency equation, the relationship between structural flexibility and disputes was curvilinear, although an examination of the scatterplot for this relationship showed that the shape of the curve was not parabolic, and thus could be modeled by transforming each flexibility score into its natural logarithm.[8] The implication of this model is that the scope of dangerous disputes declines at a decreasing (rather than constant) rate as structural flexibility increases. In summary, then, the parameters of the first two GLS equations indicate that serious disputes happen less frequently and tend to involve fewer great powers when system members perceive all other states as equally eligible as potential allies, but also perceive that once an alliance treaty is signed, it will not be unilaterally terminated prior to its expiration.

Turning finally to the intensity equation, it is clear from the multiple coefficient of determination that we lack the predictive power of the first two equations. While the coefficients for both of our independent variables are once

TABLE 7-2. Multivariate Relationships between Structural Flexibility, Treaty Commitments, and Serious Major Power Disputes

---

$\text{FREQUENCY}_t$ = .76 - 2.57 $\text{FLEXIBILITY}_t$ + 2.49 $\text{FLEXIBILITY}_t^2$ - $\sum_{i=0}^{4} a_i \text{ COMMITMENT}_{t-1}$

Almon lag coefficients:

$a_o$ = -.27          $a_3$ = -.04

$a_1$ = -.10          $a_4$ = -.07

$a_2$ = -.03          $a_i$ = -.51

Mean lag = 1.11

R = .71    $R^2$ = .51    SER = .31    DW = 2.10 (-.22)

$\text{SCOPE}_t$ = 1.17 - 1.16 $(\log_e \text{ FLEXIBILITY})_t$ - $\sum_{i=0}^{4} a_i \text{ COMMITMENT}_{t-1}$

Almon lag coefficients:

$a_o$ = -.16          $a_3$ = -.04

$a_1$ = -.10          $a_4$ = -.14

$a_2$ = -.04          $a_i$ = -.48

Mean lag = 1.79

R = .79    $R^2$ = .63    SER = .22    DW = 2.40 (-.82)

$\text{INTENSITY}_t$ = .27 - .26 $\text{FLEXIBILITY}_t$ - $\sum_{i=0}^{4} a_i \text{ COMMITMENT}_{t-1}$

Almon lag coefficients:

$a_o$ = .01          $a_3$ = -.05

$a_1$ = -.21          $a_4$ = -.05

$a_2$ - -.16          $a_i$ = -.46

Mean lag = 1.94

R = .42    $R^2$ = .18    SER = .39    DW = 2.00 (.02)

---

Note: The value of $\rho$ is given in parentheses following the Durbin-Watson statistic.

Source: Compiled by the authors.

again negative, we should be cautious not to infer too much from this finding since the model is so weak. Similarly, we should exercise caution when making inferences based on the frequency and scope equations insofar as they are grounded in a limited temporal domain. Nevertheless, we believe that the results from these equations suggest that it would be fruitful to develop macro quantitative indicators that *combine* separately derived measures of the international system's structural and cultural attributes.

## POLICY IMPLICATIONS

The purpose of this chapter has been to demonstrate that by measuring the content of international norms we can devise macro indicators that will enhance our ability to make system level predictions. Toward this end, we have sought to extend our previous research (Kegley and Raymond 1982) on the relationship between war and those norms that pertain to the extent of one's alliance commitments by attempting to determine whether such norms are also related to the frequency, scope, or intensity of serious major power disputes.

Historically speaking, the notion that every treaty or alliance has an unwritten clause to the effect that changes in those conditions that existed at its signing free the parties from their obligations can be traced to Roman law. Over the years, support for a loose interpretation of the binding force of treaties has come from a variety of sources, including such philosophers as Aquinas, Machiavelli, Spinoza, Hobbes, and Hegel. But though the *clausa rebus six stantibus* has been recognized by publicists and referred to in court decisions (for example, *Free Zones of Upper Savoy and the District of Gex*, Permanent Court of International Justice [1932] Ser. A/B, No. 46), it has been attacked by those who see it as a source of uncertainty that can provoke national fear and, in turn, international conflict. For instance, the Declaration of London (1871), which opposed Russia's denunciation of the demilitarization of the Black Sea under the 1856 Treaty of Paris, and the Declaration of Stresa (1935), which opposed Germany's repudiation of the military clauses of the Versailles Treaty, both implied that uncertainties about the behavior of states are reduced if they cannot unilaterally modify or terminate a valid treaty. Whether allies can be counted on to comply with the treaty obligations they swear to execute is thus critical in estimating the potential impact of alliances. Binding oneself to an alliance agreement means revealing important information to friend and foe alike (Bueno de Mesquita 1981). As Collett (1977, 18) has put it: Our assessments of others are "irrevocably bound up with attributions of intentions," and these judgments hinge upon "inferences concerning their knowledge of the rules and with inferences concerning their perceptions of the conditions that call forth the actions required by the rules."

Two regularities have been uncovered in this preliminary analysis of the relationship between serious major power disputes and those normative rules that define the nature of alliance commitments. First, the evidence suggests that the number of serious disputes decreases when international norms support a binding conception of treaty commitments. Second, it indicates that the percentage of major powers involved in serious disputes also decreases when norms of this type prevail. These findings warn us that in periods when the opportunistic renunciation of commitments to allies is widely condoned, both the number of great power disputes and the number of parties to them can be expected to increase. In short, adherence to commitments augers well for harmony among states; the inclination to disregard commitments does not.

At the national level of analysis, our results imply a policy relevant conclusion. In revealing that the international system is likely to experience fewer serious disputes when commitments to allies are generally regarded as binding, they suggest that one's long term interest would be best served by faithful adherence to the international agreements: to avoid serious disputes, honor commitments. This prescription thus would support one school of thought in the literature, even while it makes another conventional wisdom appear more conventional than wise.

But correlation is not causation, and cross-level generalization is dangerous. It is important to differentiate carefully between what our indicators permit us to predict, and what they do not, so as to avoid committing a serious ecological fallacy.

Our macro indicators of global norms *do not* allow us to predict micro phenomena. We cannot forecast the outbreak of each discrete dispute between major powers. Nor do they allow us to predict that the premature severance of a state's commitments to an ally will be invariably followed by a serious dispute or war, or, for that matter, that the ally of an unreliable actor will be the recipient of external threats (even though these are the general historical tendencies). The likely consequence of treaty violations for each individual state is beyond our reach. For these kinds of time point forecasts, micro indicators and micro models are needed that look at the contextual contingencies that surround each formal alliance commitment between states.

Nonetheless, macro indicators *can* serve as reliable predictors of aggregate trends in the general international pattern of great power disputes, as well as of fluctuations around that and other macro trend lines. They do enable us to anticipate how frequently major power disputes are likely to occur, and how many parties to them there will be. This, in itself, is no small service, for every actor must seek to monitor changes in the global condition if it hopes to improve its national circumstances. It is not reckless to argue that macro developments such as changes in the climate of international normative opinion, the level of global tension, or the incidence of disputes between great powers will exert a powerful impact upon the behavior of states within the global system. Nor is it unreasonable to suspect that this impact will increase as the world becomes more interdependent. The global environment provides the context for micro decisions. It presents a plethora of constraints, opportunities, and challenges that policy makers must confront because the nature of the system as a whole shapes substantially the national destinies of states.

In conclusion, we would do well to keep in mind that just as macro attributes have micro consequences, so too, micro behaviors affect macro conditions (see Schelling 1978; Kegley, Raymond, and Skinner 1980, 250–51; and Kegley and Wittkopf 1981, 461–93). Inasmuch as the behavior of statesmen can either facilitate the maintenance of existing norms or stimulate the development of new ones, it is hoped that policy makers will realize the contribution their decisions make to norm formation and norm decay, and, ultimately, to the kind of international political culture that their successors will inherit. It will make a difference whether policy makers promote the creation of a world in which norms advocating the sanctity of commitments to allies are accepted and those rationalizing disregard for commitments are correspondingly rejected. For as Cohen (1981, 163) observes, "If rules of the game . . . are neglected or mismanaged, others less advantageous will simply take their place." Thus, in seeking to discover ways in which the human condition might be improved, the evidence assembled here provides an important clue as to how states might better cope and behave. When weighed, on balance it suggests that the prospects for the successful management of disputes among states will be enhanced when countries feel themselves obligated to adhere to the commitments that they pledge.

## NOTES

1. An example is provided by the advent of the Korean War, an episode generally regarded as having been precipitated by the uncertainty created by Secretary of State Dean Acheson's ambiguous signals about the willingness of the United States to abide by its commitment to come to the aid of South Korea in the event of an external attack upon it.

2. Although both publicists and social scientists have theorized at length about the systemic effects of alliance reliability, very few data based studies have been done on this subject. See Sabrosky (1980), Kegley and Raymond (1982), and Berkowitz (1983).

3. For a more detailed presentation of our conceptualization of international legal norms, see Kegley and Raymond (1981).

4. Given that the Transnational Rules Indicators Project (TRIP) has compiled its first longitudinal data base to permit "the search for systematic connections between *cultural* conditions and the incidence of war" (Singer 1980, 357), our index of alliance commitment will be derived from this source. The criteria used by TRIP to select the treatises centered on whether a work had gone through multiple revised editions, or had been identified as authoritative by either independent scholarship (for example, listed in the Association of Law School's bibliography of international law texts) or by a recognized legal body such as the World Court. Because descriptions of the TRIP data-making procedures are readily available in published form (see Kegley 1975, 1982; and Raymond 1977, 1980), we refer the reader to these works for further discussion of the data collection procedures.

5. The disposition index was derived by coding each author's conception of treaty commitment in terms of whether he saw *pacta sunt servanda* or a broad interpretation of *rebus sic stantibus* as the dominant norm within the international system. A summary index of commitment was then calculated for each half-decade in our temporal domain by means of the following formula: (the percentage of authors who saw legal norms supporting a binding interpretation of treaty obligations) - (the percentage of authors who saw norms supporting a flexible interpretation of treaty obligation) / 100.

6. See Singer and Small (1972, 23) for a discussion of the membership criteria used by the Correlates of War Project to define the major power subsystem. Our analysis will focus on the European major powers.

7. More specifically, in the analysis that follows we have utilized a four-period lag structure where:

$$w_i = c_0 + c_1 i + c_2 i^2 + c_3 i^3$$

for $i = 0, 1, 2, 3, 4$ and $w_i = 0$ for $i$ less than 0 and greater than 4. This specifies that the lag weights will follow a third-degree polynomial for the first four lagged values and 0 otherwise.

8. Because the natural logarithm of zero does not exist, we added one to each flexibility score prior to transformation.

## REFERENCES

Andrews, Bruce. 1975. "Social Rules and the State as a Social Actor." *World Politics* 27:521–40.

Beilenson, Laurence. 1969. *The Treaty Trap.* Washington, D.C.: Public Affairs Press.

Berkowitz, Bruce D. 1983. "Realignment in International Treaty Organizations." *International Studies Quarterly* 27:77–96.

Bozeman, Adda B. 1960. *Politics and Culture in International History.* Princeton: Princeton University Press.

Briggs, Herbert W. 1949. "Rebus Sic Stantibus Before the Security Council." *American Journal of International Law* 43:762–69.

Bueno de Mesquita, Bruce. 1981. *The War Trap.* New Haven: Yale University Press.

Cantor, Robert D. 1976. *Introduction to International Politics.* Itasca: F. E. Peacock.

Chi, Hsi-sheng. 1968. "The Chinese Warlord System as an International System." In *New Approaches to International Relations,* edited by Morton A. Kaplan, pp. 405–25. New York: St. Martin's.

Cohen, Raymond. 1981. *International Politics: The Rules of the Game.* London and New York: Longman.

Collett, Peter. 1977. "The Rules of Conduct." In *Social Rules and Social Behavior,* edited by Peter Collett, pp. 1–27. Totowa: Rowman and Littlefield.

Coplin, William D. 1966. *The Functions of International Law.* Chicago: Rand McNally.

David, Arie E. 1975. *The Strategy of Treaty Termination: Lawful Breaches and Retaliations.* New Haven: Yale University Press.

Dhrymes, P. J. 1971. *Distributed Lags: Problems of Estimation and Formulation.* San Francisco: Holden-Day.

Duncan, George T., and Randolph M. Siverson. 1982. "Flexibility of Alliance Partner Choice in a Multipolar System: Models and Tests." *International Studies Quarterly* 26:511–38.

Franke, Winfried. 1968. "The Italian City-State System as an International System." In *New Approaches to International Relations,* edited by Morton A. Kaplan, pp. 426–58. New York: St. Martin's.

Friedman, Julian R. 1970. "Alliance in International Politics." In *Alliance in International Politics,* edited by Julian R. Friedman, Christopher Bladen, and Steven Rosen, pp. 3–32. Boston: Allyn and Bacon.

Gardner, J. W. 1927. "The Doctrine of Rebus Sic Stantibus and the Termination of Treaties." *American Journal of International Law* 21:509–16.

Gould, Wesley L. 1957. *An Introduction to International Law.* New York: Harper.

Hoffmann, Stanley. 1969. "International Systems and International Law." In *International Security Systems,* edited by Richard B. Gray, pp. 127–62. Itasca: F. E. Peacock.

Intriligator, Michael D. 1978. *Econometric Models, Techniques and Applications.* Englewood Cliffs: Prentice-Hall.

Janis, Irving L., and Leon Mann. 1977. *Decision Making: A Psychological Analysis of Conflict, Choice and Commitment.* New York: Free Press.

Job, Brian. 1976. "Membership in Inter-Nation Alliances, 1815–1965: An Exploration Utilizing Mathematical Probability Models." In *Mathematical Models in International Relations,* edited by Dina Zinnes and John Gillespie, pp. 74–109. New York: Praeger.

Kaplan, Morton A., and Nicholas deB. Katzenbach. 1961. *The Political Foundations of International Law.* New York: John Wiley.

Katz, Daniel, and Robert L. Kahn. 1978. *The Social Psychology of Organizations.* New York: John Wiley.

Kegley, Charles W., Jr. 1982. "Measuring Transformations in the Global Legal System." In *Law-Making in the Global Community,* edited by Nicholas G. Onuf, pp. 173–209. Durham: Carolina Academic Press.

————. 1975. "Measuring the Growth and Decay of

Transnational Norms Relevant to the Control of Violence: A Prospectus for Research." *Denver Journal of International Law and Policy* 5:425–39.

Kegley, Charles W., Jr., and Gregory A. Raymond. 1982. "Alliance Norms and War: A New Piece in an Old Puzzle." *International Studies Quarterly* 26:572–95.

──────. 1981. "International Legal Norms and the Preservation of Peace, 1820–1964: Some Evidence and Bivariate Relationships." *International Interactions* 8:171–87.

Kegley, Charles W., Jr., and Eugene R. Wittkopf. 1981. *World Politics: Trend and Transformation.* New York: St. Martin's.

Kegley, Charles W., Jr., Gregory A. Raymond, and Richard A. Skinner. 1980. "A Comparative Analysis of Nuclear Armament." In *Threats, Weapons, and Foreign Policy,* edited by Patrick McGowan and Charles W. Kegley, Jr., pp. 231–55. Beverly Hills: Sage.

Kunz, Josef L. 1945. "The Meaning and the Range of Norm Pacta Sunt Servanda." *American Journal of International Law* 39:180–97.

Li, Richard, and William R. Thompson. 1978. "The Stochastic Process of Alliance Formation Behavior." *American Political Science Review* 72:1288–303.

Lissitzyn, Oliver J. 1967. "Treaties and Changed Circumstances (Rebus Sic Stantibus)." *American Journal of International Law* 61:895–922.

Lockhart, Charles. 1978. "Flexibility and Commitment in International Conflicts." *International Studies Quarterly* 22:545–68.

Masters, Roger D. 1969. "World Politics as a Primitive Political System." In *International Politics and Foreign Policy,* edited by James N. Rosenau, pp. 104–18. New York: Free Press.

Mattingly, Garrett. 1971. *Renaissance Diplomacy.* Boston: Houghton Mifflin.

McGowan, Patrick, and Robert M. Rood. 1975. "Alliance Behavior in Balance of Power Systems: Applying a Poisson Model to Nineteenth Century Europe." *American Political Science Review* 69:859–70.

Morgenthau, Hans J. 1966. *Politics Among Nations.* 3rd ed. New York: Alfred A. Knopf.

Ostrom, Charles W., and Francis W. Hoole. 1978. "Alliances and War Revisited: A Research Note." *International Studies Quarterly* 22:215–36.

Pindyck, Robert S., and Daniel L. Rubinfeld. 1976. *Econometric Models and Economic Forecasts.* New York:

McGraw Hill.

Raymond, Gregory A. 1980. *Conflict Resolution and the Structure of the State System: An Analysis of Arbitrative Settlements*. Montclair: Allanheld and Osmun.

——. 1977. "The Transnational Rules Indicators Project: An Interim Report." *International Studies Notes* 4:12–16.

Rood, Robert M., and Patrick McGowan. 1974. "Flexibility in Balance of Power Systems and International War." Paper presented at the annual meeting of the Peace Science Society (International)/South, Durham, N.C., April 4–5.

Sabrosky, Alan Ned. 1980. "Interstate Alliances: Their Reliability and the Expansion of War." In *The Correlates of War: II, Testing Some Realpolitik Models,* edited by J. David Singer, pp. 161–98. New York: Free Press.

Schelling, Thomas C. 1978. *Micromotives and Macrobehavior.* New York: Norton.

——. 1960. *The Strategy of Conflict.* New York: Oxford University Press.

Singer, J. David. 1980. "Accounting for International War: The State of the Discipline." *Annual Review of Sociology* 6:349–67.

——. 1968. "Man and World Politics: The Psycho-Cultural Interface." *Journal of Social Issues* 24:127–56.

Singer, J. David, and Melvin Small. 1972. *The Wages of War: A Statistical Handbook.* New York: John Wiley.

Siverson, Randolph M., and George T. Duncan. 1976. "Stochastic Models of International Alliance Initiation." In *Mathematical Models in International Relations,* edited by Dina Zinnes and John Gillespie, pp. 110–31. New York: Praeger.

Suganami, Hidemi. 1979. "Why Ought Treaties To Be Kept?" In *The Year Book of World Affairs,* edited by George W. Keeton and Georg Schwarzenberger, pp. 243–56. London: Stevens & Sons.

Sullivan, Michael P., and Randolph M. Siverson. 1981. "Theories of War: Problems and Prospects." In *Cumulation in International Relations Research,* pp. 9–37. Denver: University of Denver School of International Studies.

Thibaut, John W., and Harold H. Kelley. 1959. *The Social Psychology of Groups.* New York: John Wiley.

Wallace, Michael D. 1979. "Arms Races and Escalation: Some New Evidence." *Journal of Conflict Resolution* 23:3–16.

Waltz, Kenneth N.   1964.   "The Stability of a Bipolar
    World."  *Daedalus* 93:892–927.
Wehberg, Hans.   1959.   "Pacta Sunt Servanda."  *American
    Journal of International Law* 53:775–86.
Woolsey, L. H.   1926.   "The Unilateral Termination of
    Treaties."  *American Journal of International Law*
    20:346–53.

# About the Editors

*J. David Singer* received his B.A. from Duke University, and his doctorate from New York University. He is currently professor in the Political Science Department at the University of Michigan, having been coordinator of the World Politics Program from 1969–75. He has previously held teaching positions at New York University, Vassar College, and Harvard University, and has been a visiting faculty member at the University of Oslo and Institute for Social Research, Norway; the Carnegie Endowment for International Peace and Graduate Institute of International Studies, Geneva, Switzerland; and ZUMA and the University of Mannheim, West Germany.

His most recent books are *Resort to Arms; Correlates of War I: Research Origins and Rationale,* a Free Press anthology of his papers on the science-policy relationship; and *Correlates of War II: Testing Some Realpolitik Models.* Others are *To Augur Well: Early Warning Indicators in World Politics* (with Michael Wallace, 1979); *Explaining War* (1979); *The Study of International Politics: A Guide to Sources for the Student, Teacher, and Researcher* (with Dorothy LaBarr, 1976); *Beyond Conjecture in International Politics: Abstracts of Data-Based Research* (with Susan Jones, 1972); *The Wages of War, 1816–1965: A Statistical Handbook* (with Melvin Small, 1972); *Deterrence, Arms Control, and Disarmament: Toward a Synthesis in National Security Policy* (1962); *Financing International-Organization: The United Nations Budget Process* (1961); as well as numerous articles in such journals as *American Political Science Review, International Security, British Journal of International Studies,* and *Journal of Conflict Resolution.*

*Richard J. Stoll* is an Assistant Professor of Political Science at Rice University. He received his B.A. in Political Science from the University of Rochester in 1974, and his Ph.D. in Political Science from the University of Michigan in 1979. His current research interests involve the use of statistical analysis and computer simulation to predict the escalation of serious disputes to war, the maneuverings of the major powers in a balance of power system, and the study of American national security policy.